THEORY AND INTERPRETATION OF NARRATIVE

James Phelan and Peter J. Rabinowitz, Series Editors

WHY WE READ FICTION

THEORY OF MIND AND THE NOVEL

Lisa Zunshine

THE OHIO STATE UNIVERSITY PRESS
COLUMBUS

Library of Congress Cataloging-in-Publication Data

Zunshine, Lisa.
Why we read fiction : theory of mind and the novel / Lisa Zunshine.
  p. cm.—(Theory and interpretation of narrative series)
Includes bibliographical references and index.
ISBN 0–8142–1028–7 (cloth : alk. paper)—ISBN 0–8142–5151-X (pbk. : alk. paper)
1. Fiction. 2. Fiction—Psychological aspects. 3. Books and reading. 4. Cognitive science. I. Title. II. Series.
PN3331.Z86 2006
809.3—dc22
                    2005028358

Cover design by Laurence Nozik.
Text design and typesetting by Jennifer Forsythe.
Type set in Adobe Garamond.
Printed by Thomson-Shore, Inc.

The paper used in this publication meets the minimum requirements of the American
National Standard for Information Sciences—Permanence of Paper for Printed Library
Materials. ANSI Z39.48-1992.

9 8 7 6

~ *Contents* ~

Illustrations

Acknowledgments

I had a great time working on this book because of the people whom I have met in the process. First, in the late 1990s, I had the privilege to sit in for several semesters on the graduate seminars taught by Leda Cosmides and John Tooby at the University of California, Santa Barbara, an experience that I immediately recognized back then and continue to consider now a once-in-a-lifetime learning opportunity. Second, over the last seven years, I have been fortunate to get to know a distinguished cohort of scholars working with cognitive approaches to literature. I am simply listing them here in alphabetical order to resist the temptation to fill pages with the expression of my admiration for their work and my gratitude for their friendship: Porter Abbott, Frederick Louis Aldama, Mary Crane, Nancy Easterlin, Elizabeth Hart, David Herman, Patrick Colm Hogan, Alan Palmer, Alan Richardson, Ellen Spolsky, and Blakey Vermeule. I could similarly talk forever about James Phelan—who has been encouraging my work since the time of publication, in his journal *Narrative,* of my essay on Theory of Mind and *Mrs. Dalloway*—but let me just say that one could not wish for a better editor or mentor. Peter Rabinowitz, Phelan's co-editor of The Ohio State University Press's book series "Theory and Interpretation of Narrative," and Uri Margolin, a reader for the series, offered the most thorough and thoughtful responses to my manuscript. If the final product does not live up to their excellent suggestions, the fault is all mine. The Ohio State University Press continues to impress me as an exemplary press, a privilege for any scholar to publish with: I am grateful to Laurie Avery, Sandy Crooms, Maggie Diehl, Malcolm Litchfield, and Heather Lee Miller for their hard work and support. The participants of the Lexington IdeaFestival (2004); of the annual meeting of the International Society for the Study of Narrative (2003, 2004, 2005); and of the "Cognitive Theory and the Arts" seminar at the Humanities Center at Harvard University (2004) asked great questions and made excellent suggestions. Jason E. Flahardy and Christian Trombetta from the Special Collections and Archives at the University of Kentucky's King Library have been most helpful with illustrations, and so has been the College of Arts and Sciences at the University of Kentucky, which once more came through in the most timely and generous manner to pay for the reproduction of these illustrations. Last but not least, I am indebted to Chris Hair and Anna Laura Bennett, who were invaluable for editing various drafts of my manuscript; to my students at the University of Kentucky, Lexington, whose smart and creative responses to *Clarissa* and *Lolita* have made teaching those challenging novels a pleasure; and to Etel Sverdlov, who reads and jokes with the best.

PART 1

ATTRIBUTING MINDS

~ 1 ~

WHY DID PETER WALSH TREMBLE?

L et me begin with a seemingly nonsensical question. When Peter Walsh, a protagonist of Virginia Woolf's *Mrs. Dalloway,* unexpectedly visits Clarissa Dalloway "at eleven o'clock on the morning of the day she [is] giving a party," and, "positively trembling" and "kissing both her hands" (40), asks her how she is, how do we know that his "trembling" is to be accounted for by his excitement at seeing his old love again after all these years and not, for instance, by his progressing Parkinson's disease?

Assuming that you are a particularly good-natured reader of *Mrs. Dalloway,* you could patiently explain to me that had Walsh's trembling been occasioned by an illness, Woolf would have told us so. She wouldn't have left us long under the impression that Walsh's body language betrays his agitation, his joy, and his embarrassment and that the meeting has instantaneously and miraculously brought back the old days when Clarissa and Peter had "this queer power of communicating without words" because, reflecting Walsh's own "trembling," Clarissa herself is "so surprised, . . . so glad, so shy, so utterly taken aback to have [him] come to her unexpectedly in the morning!" (40). Too much, you would point out, hinges on our getting the emotional undertones of the scene right for Woolf to withhold from us a crucial piece of information about Walsh's health.

I then would ask you why is it that had Walsh's trembling been caused by an illness, Woolf would have had to explicitly tell us so, but as it is not, she simply takes for granted that we will interpret it as having been caused by his emotions. In other words, what allows Woolf to assume that we will automatically read a character's body language as indicative of his thoughts and feelings?

She assumes this because of our collective past history as readers, you perhaps would say. Writers have been using descriptions of their characters' behaviors to inform us about their feelings since time immemorial, and we expect them to do so when we open the book. We all learn, whether consciously or not, that the default interpretation of behavior reflects a character's state of mind, and every fictional story that we read reinforces our tendency to make that kind of interpretation first.[1]

Had this imaginary conversation about the automatic assumptions made by readers taken place twenty years ago, it would have ended here. Or it never would have happened—not even in this hypothetical form—because the answers to my naïve questions would have seemed so obvious. Today, however, this conversation has to continue on because recent research in cognitive psychology and anthropology has shown that not *every* reader can learn that the default meaning of a character's behavior lies with the character's mental state. To understand what enables most of us to constrain the range of possible interpretations, we may have to go beyond the explanation that evokes our personal reading histories and admit some evidence from our evolutionary history.

This is what my book does. It makes a case for admitting the recent findings of cognitive psychologists into literary studies by showing how their research into the ability to explain behavior in terms of the underlying states of mind—or *mind-reading* ability—can furnish us with a series of surprising insights into our interaction with literary texts. Using as my case studies novels ranging from Woolf's *Mrs. Dalloway* to Dashiel Hammett's *Maltese Falcon,* I advance and explore a series of hypotheses about cognitive cravings that are satisfied—and created!—when we read fiction.

I divide my argument into three parts. The present part, "Attributing Minds," introduces the first key theoretical concept of this book: mind-reading, also known as Theory of Mind. Drawing on the work of Simon Baron-Cohen (*Mindblindness: An Essay on Autism and Theory of Mind*), I suggest that fiction engages, teases, and pushes to its tentative limits our mind-reading capacity. Building on the recent research of Robin Dunbar and his colleagues, I then consider one particular aspect of Woolf's prose as an example of spectacular literary experimentation with our Theory of Mind (hence, ToM). Finally, I turn to Steven Pinker's controversial analysis of Woolf in *The Blank Slate* to discuss the possibilities of a more profitable dialogue between cognitive science and literary studies.

The second part, "Tracking Minds," introduces my second theoretical mainstay: metarepresentationality. I base it on Leda Cosmides and John Tooby's exploration of our evolved cognitive ability to keep track of sources of our representations (i.e., to metarepresent them). I begin by returning to the point made in the first part—which is that our ToM makes literature as we know it possible—to argue that the attribution of mental states to literary characters is crucially mediated by the workings of our metarepresentational ability. Fictional narratives, from *Beowulf* to *Pride and Prejudice,* rely on, manipulate, and titillate our tendency to keep track of *who* thought, wanted, and felt what and *when.* I further suggest that research on metarepresentationality sheds light on readers' enduring preoccupation with the thorny issue of the "truth" of literary narrative and the distinction between "history" and "fiction." I conclude with the case studies of two novels (Richardson's *Clarissa* and Nabokov's *Lolita*), showing how several overlapping and yet distinct literary traditions are built around the narratives' exaggerated engagement of our metarepresentational capacity.

The third part, "Concealing Minds," continues to explore the exaggerated literary engagement with our source-monitoring capacity by focusing on the detective novel. Following the history of the detective narrative over one hundred and fifty years, I show that the recurrent features of this genre, including its attention to material clues, its credo of "suspecting everybody," and its vexed relationship with the romantic plot, are grounded in its commitment to "working out" in a particularly focused way our ToM and metarepresentational ability. I conclude by arguing that the kind of cognitive analysis of the detective novel advocated by my study (and, indeed, the analysis of *any* novel with respect to its engagement of our Theory of Mind) requires close attention to specific historical circumstances attending the development of the genre.[2]

This emphasis on historicizing is in keeping with my broader view on the relationship between the "cognitive" and other, currently more familiar, approaches to literature. I do not share the feelings (be they hopes or fears[3]) of those literary critics who believe that cognitive approaches necessarily invalidate insights of more traditional schools of thought.[4] I think that it is a sign of *strength* in a cognitive approach when it turns out to be highly compatible with well-thought-through literary criticism, and I eagerly seize on the instances of such compatibility.[5] Given that the human mind in its numerous complex environments has been the object of study of literary critics for longer than it has been the object of study of cognitive scientists, I would, in fact, be suspicious of any cognitive reading so truly "original" that it can find no support in any of the existing literary critical paradigms.[6]

But, compatible with existing paradigms or not, any literary study that grounds itself in a discipline as new and dynamic as cognitive science is today takes serious chances. In the words of cognitive evolutionary anthropologist Dan Sperber, "[O]ur understanding of cognitive architecture is [still] way too poor, and the best we can do is try and speculate intelligently (which is great fun anyhow)."[7] I proceed, then, both sobered by Sperber's warning and inspired by his parenthetical remark. Every single one of my speculations resulting from applying research in cognitive psychology to our appetite for fiction could be wrong, but the questions that prompted those speculations are emphatically worth asking.

~ 2 ~

WHAT IS MIND-READING
(ALSO KNOWN AS THEORY OF MIND)?

*I*n spite of the way it sounds, mind-reading has nothing to do with plain old telepathy. Instead, it is a term used by cognitive psychologists, interchangeably with "Theory of Mind," to describe our ability to explain people's behavior in terms of their thoughts, feelings, beliefs, and desires.[1] Thus we engage in mind-reading when we ascribe to a person a certain mental state on the basis of her observable action (e.g., we see her reaching for a glass of water and assume that she is thirsty); when we interpret our own feelings based on our proprioceptive awareness (e.g., our heart skips a beat when a certain person enters the room and we realize that we might have been attracted to him or her all along); when we intuit a complex state of mind based on a limited verbal description (e.g., a friend tells us that she feels sad and happy at the same time, and we believe that we know what she means); when we compose an essay, a lecture, a movie, a song, a novel, or an instruction for an electrical appliance and try to imagine how this or that segment of our target audience will respond to it; when we negotiate a multilayered social situation (e.g., a friend tells us in front of his boss that he would love to work on the new project, but we have our own reasons to believe that he is lying and hence try to turn the conversation so that the boss, who, we think, may suspect that he is lying, would not make him work on that project and yet would not think that he didn't really want to); and so forth. Attributing states of mind is the default way by which we construct and navigate our social environment, incorrect though our attributions frequently are. (For example, the person

6

who reached for the glass of water might not have been thirsty at all but rather might have wanted us to think that she was thirsty, so that she could later excuse herself and go out of the room, presumably to get more water, but really to make the phone call that she didn't want us to know of.)

But why do we need this newfangled concept of mind-reading, or ToM, to explain what appears so obvious? Our ability to interpret the behavior of people in terms of their underlying states of mind seems to be such an integral part of what we are as human beings that we could be understandably reluctant to dignify it with fancy terms and elevate it into a separate object of study. One reason that ToM has received the sustained attention of cognitive psychologists over the last twenty years is that they have come across people whose ability to "see bodies as animated by minds"[2] is drastically impaired—people with autism. By studying autism and a related constellation of cognitive deficits (such as Asperger syndrome), cognitive scientists began to appreciate our mind-reading ability as a special cognitive endowment, structuring our everyday communication and cultural representations.

Cognitive evolutionary psychologists working with ToM think that this adaptation must have developed during the "massive neurocognitive evolution" which took place during the Pleistocene (1.8 million to 10,000 years ago). The emergence of a Theory of Mind "module" was evolution's answer to the "staggeringly complex" challenge faced by our ancestors,[3] who needed to make sense of the behavior of other people in their group, which could include up to 200 individuals. In his influential 1995 study, *Mindblindness: An Essay on Autism and a Theory of Mind,* Simon Baron-Cohen points out that "attributing mental states to a complex system (such as a human being) is by far the easiest way of understanding it," that is, of "coming up with an explanation of the complex system's behavior and predicting what it will do next."[4] Thus our tendency to interpret observed behavior in terms of underlying mental states (e.g., "Peter Walsh was *trembling* because he was *excited* to see Clarissa again") seems to be so effortless and automatic (in a sense that we are not even conscious of engaging in any particular act of "interpretation"[5]) because our evolved cognitive architecture "prods" us toward learning and practicing mind-reading daily, from the beginning of awareness.

Baron-Cohen describes autism as the "most severe of all childhood psychiatric conditions," one that affects between approximately four to fifteen children per 10,000 and "occurs in every country in which it has been looked for and across social classes."[6] Although, as Gloria Origgi and Dan Sperber have pointed out, "mind-reading is not an all-or-none affair

. . . [p]eople with autism lack [this] ability to a greater or lesser degree,"[7] and although the condition may be somewhat alleviated if the child receives a range of "educational and therapeutic interventions," autism remains, at present, "a lifelong disorder."[8] Autism is highly heritable,[9] and its key symptoms, which manifest themselves in the first years of life, include the profound impairment of social and communicative development and the "lack of the usual flexibility, imagination, and pretence."[10] It is also characterized—crucially for our present discussion—by a reduced interest in fiction and storytelling (although one should keep in mind here, and I will address shortly, the important issue of *degree* to which people within the autistic range are indifferent to storytelling).

One immediate, practical implication of the last two decades of research in ToM is that developmental psychologists are now able to diagnose autism much earlier (e.g., the standard age for diagnosis used to be three or four years, whereas now it is sometimes possible to diagnose a child at eighteen months[11]) and to design more aggressive therapeutic techniques for dealing with it. Moreover, cognitive anthropologists are increasingly aware that our ability to attribute states of mind to ourselves and other people is intensely context dependent. That is, it is supported not by one uniform cognitive adaptation but by a large cluster of specialized adaptations geared toward a variety of social contexts.[12] Given this new emphasis on context-sensitive specialization and the fact that Theory of Mind appears to be our key cognitive endowment as a *social* species, it is difficult to imagine a field of study within the social sciences and the humanities that would not be affected by this research in the coming decades.

What criteria do psychologists use to decide whether a given individual has an impaired Theory of Mind? In 1978, Daniel Dennett suggested that one effective way to test for the presence of normally developing ToM is to see whether a child can understand that someone else might hold a false belief, that is, a belief about the world that the child knows is manifestly untrue. The first false-belief test was designed in 1983 and has since been replicated many times by scientists around the world. In one of the more widespread versions of the test, children see that "Sally" puts a marble in one place and then exits the room. In her absence, "Anne" comes in, puts the marble in a different place, and leaves. Children are then asked, "Where will Sally look for her marble when she returns?" The majority of neurotypical children (after the age of four[13]) pass the test, responding that Sally will look for the marble in the original place, thus showing their understanding that someone might hold a false belief. By contrast, only a small minority of children with autism do so, indicating instead where the marble really is. According to Baron-Cohen, the results of the test support the notion that "in autism the mental state of belief is poorly understood."[14]

But, apart from the carefully designed lab test, how do people with autism see the world around them? In his book *An Anthropologist on Mars*, Oliver Sacks introduces Temple Grandin, who built a brilliant career on strengths associated with autism, such as heightened viual memory and attention to details. She has a doctorate in agricultural science, teaches at the University of Arizona, and can speak about her perceptions, thus giving us a unique insight into what it means to be unable to read other people's minds. Sacks reports Grandin's school experience: "Something was going on between the other kids, something swift, subtle, constantly changing—an exchange of meanings, a negotiation, a swiftness of understanding so remarkable that sometimes she wondered if they were all telepathic. She is now aware of the existence of those social signals. She can infer them, she says, but she herself cannot perceive them, cannot participate in this magical communication directly, or conceive of the many-leveled, kaleidoscopic states of mind behind it."[15]

To compensate for her inability to interpret facial expressions, which at first left her a "target of tricks and exploitation," Grandin has built up over the years something resembling a "library of videotapes, which she could play in her mind and inspect at any time—'videos' of how people behaved in different circumstances. She would play these over and over again, and learn, by degrees, to correlate what she saw, so that she could then predict how people in similar circumstances might act."[16] What the account of such a "library" suggests is that we do not just "learn" how to communicate with people and read their emotions (or how to read the minds of fictional characters based on their behavior)—Grandin, after all, has had as many opportunities to "learn" these things as you and I—but that we also have evolved cognitive architecture that makes this particular kind of learning possible, and if this architecture functions differently, as may be with autism, a wealth of experience can't erase that difference.

Predictably, Grandin comments on having a difficult time understanding fictional narratives. She remembers being "bewildered by *Romeo and Juliet:* 'I never knew what they were up to.'"[17] Perhaps fiction presents a challenge to people with autism because in many ways it calls for the same kind of mind-reading—that is, the inference of the mental state from the behavior—that is necessary in regular human communication.[18]

Whereas the correlation between the autistic ToM and a reduced interest in fiction and storytelling is highly suggestive, the jury is still out on the exact nature of the connection between the two. It could be argued, for example, that the cognitive mechanisms[19] that evolved to process information about thoughts and feelings of human beings are constantly on the alert, checking out their environment for cues that fit their input conditions. On some level, then, works of fiction manage to "cheat" these mechanisms into "believing" that they are in the presence of material that they were "designed" to process, that is, that they are in the presence of agents endowed with a potential for a rich array of intentional stances.

Thus one preliminary implication of applying what we know about ToM to our study of fiction is that it makes literature as we know it possible. The very process of making sense of what we read appears to be grounded in our ability to invest the flimsy verbal constructions that we generously call "characters" with a potential for a variety of thoughts, feelings, and desires and then to look for the "cues" that would allow us to guess at their feelings and thus predict their actions.[20] Literature pervasively capitalizes on and stimulates Theory of Mind mechanisms[21] that had evolved to deal with real people, even as on some level readers do remain aware that fictive characters are not real people at all.[22] The novel, in particular, is implicated with our mind-reading ability to such a degree that I do not think myself in danger of overstating anything when I say that in its currently familiar shape it exists because we are creatures with ToM.[23] As a sustained representation of numerous interacting minds, the novel feeds the powerful, representation-hungry[24] complex of cognitive adaptations whose very condition of being is a constant social stimulation delivered either by direct interactions with other people or by imaginary approximation of such interactions.

~ 3 ~

THEORY OF MIND, AUTISM, AND FICTION:
THREE CAVEATS

*I*n theorizing the relationship between our evolved cognitive capacity for mind-reading and our interest in fictional narratives, one has to be careful in spelling out the extent to which one builds on what is currently known about autism. Three issues are at stake here. First, though the studies of autism were crucial for initially alerting cognitive scientists to the possibility that we have an evolved cognitive adaptation for mind-reading, those studies do not define or delimit the rapidly expanding field of ToM research. For example, later in this section I discuss the work of cognitive evolutionary psychologist Robin Dunbar, who deals with autism only tangentially and who grounds his study of cognitive regularities underlying our mind-reading processes in a different kind of compelling empirical evidence. Similarly, Alan Palmer's recent groundbreaking study of cognitive construction of fictional consciousness, *Fictional Minds,* mentions autism only briefly. I use research on autism mainly to provide a vivid hypothetical example of what it means not to be able to attribute minds (just as in Part II I use research on schizophrenia to show what it means not to be able to keep track of the sources of one's representations); the bulk of my argument does not rely on it.

Which brings me to the closely related second point. Increasingly probing and sophisticated as research on autism is becoming, it still is—and will remain for the foreseen future—a research-in-progress. Given the broad range of autistic cases—indeed it is often said that no two autistic individuals are alike—it seems that the more cognitive scientists learn about the condition, the more complex it appears. Again, the complexity of the issues involved should be a warning to cultural critics casually pronouncing some texts, individuals, or groups somehow deficient in their mind-reading ability—an increasingly popular practice, as autism becomes what one researcher has called a "fashionable"[1] cognitive impairment. I remember giving a talk once on ToM and fiction, after which one of my listeners suggested that adolescents today must all be "slightly autistic" because they are not interested in reading books anymore and want to watch television instead; as if—to point out just one of many problems with this suggestion—making sense of an episode of *Friends* or *Saved by the Bell* somehow did not require the full exercise of the viewer's Theory of Mind. Consequently, my present inquiry into Woolf's, Richardson's, James's, and Nabokov's experimentation with our mind-reading capacity should not be taken as a speculation about what so-called neurotypical versus so-called borderline autistic readers can or cannot do.

My final point sounds a similar note of caution about applying our still-limited knowledge of autism to the literary-critical analysis of reading and writing practices. Although I used the now-iconic story of Temple

Grandin to illustrate the challenge faced by autistic individuals in understanding fictional narratives, we have to remember that this challenge varies across the wide spectrum of autism cases. For example, if we include within that spectrum people with Asperger syndrome[2]—which is sometimes classified as high-functioning autism and sometimes viewed as a separate condition (i.e., a nonverbal learning disability[3])—we can say that a "dash of autism"[4] does not necessarily preclude people from enjoying fictional narratives.

Consider Christopher, a bright teenager with Asperger syndrome from Mark Haddon's *The Curious Incident of the Dog in the Night-Time,* a novel drawing on Haddon's previous work with autistic individuals. Although Christopher "mostly [reads] books about math and science" and is not interested in what he calls "proper novels" (4), he does like murder mysteries, appreciating, in particular, their puzzlelike structure. Following the advice of his teacher (a figure based, perhaps, on Haddon), Christopher decides to write his own mystery murder narrative. Christopher's novel will tell the true story of his quest to find the person who killed the neighbor's dog because, as he puts it, "it happened to me and I find it hard to imagine things which did not happen to me" (5).

In describing the story that Christopher wants to write, Haddon attempts to capture the boy's peculiar mind-reading profile. For example, Christopher can figure out, at least partially, some states of mind behind some behavior. Thus he guesses that, when an elderly lady tells him that she has a grandson his age, she is "doing what is called chatting, where people say things to each other which aren't questions and answers and aren't connected" (40). Similarly, Christopher knows that "people do a lot of talking without using any words." As his teacher tells him, "[I]f you raise one eyebrow it can mean lots of different things. It can mean 'I want to do sex with you' and it can also mean 'I think that what you just said was very stupid'" (14–15). This nonverbal communication—which requires reconstructing (and, inevitably, often misconstructing) a mental state behind an ambiguous gesture—is one reason that Christopher finds people "confusing."[5] Consequently, his murder mystery novel is mostly lacking in attribution of thoughts, feelings, and attitudes to its protagonists (we, the readers, supply those missing mental states, thus making sense of the story). Still, as a novel authored by a child with a compromised Theory of Mind (even if this child is himself a fictional character), *The Curious Incident* is a much-needed reminder about the complexity of the issues involved in the relationship between autism and storytelling.[6]

~ 4 ~

"EFFORTLESS" MIND-READING

*A*s we discuss mind-reading as an evolved cognitive capacity enabling both our interaction with each other and our ability to make sense of fiction, we have to be aware of the definitional differences between the terminology used by cognitive scientists and that used by literary critics. Cognitive psychologists and philosophers of mind investigating our Theory of Mind ask such questions as, What is the evolutionary history of this adaptation, that is, in response to what environmental challenges did it evolve? At what age and in what forms does it begin to manifest itself? What are its neurological foundations? They focus on the ways "in which mind-reading [plays] an essential part in *successful* communication."[1] When cognitive scientists turn to literary (or, as in the case below, cinematic) examples to illustrate our ability for investing fictional characters with a mind of their own and reading that mind, they stress the "effortlessness" with which we do so. As Daniel Dennett observes, "[W]atching a film with a highly original and unstereotyped plot, we see the hero smile at the villain and we all swiftly and effortlessly arrive at the same complex theoretical diagnosis: 'Aha!' we conclude (but perhaps not consciously), 'He wants her to think he doesn't know she intends to defraud her brother!'"[2]

Readers outside the cognitive-science community may find this emphasis on "effortlessness" and "success" unhelpful. Literary critics, in particular, know that the process of attributing thoughts, beliefs, and desires to other people may lead to *misinterpreting* those thoughts, beliefs, and desires. Thus they would rightly resist any notion that we could effortlessly—that is, correctly and unambiguously, nearly telepathically—figure out what the person whose behavior we are trying to explain is thinking. It is important to underscore here that cognitive scientists and lay readers (here, including literary critics) bring very different frames of reference to measuring the relative "success" of mind-reading. For the lay reader, the example of a glaring failure in mind-reading and communication might be a person's interpreting her friend's tears of joy as tears of grief and reacting accordingly. For a cognitive psychologist, a glaring failure in mind-reading would be a person's not even knowing that the water coursing down her friend's face is supposed to be somehow indicative of his feelings at that moment.[3] If you find the latter possibility absurd, recall that some cognitive psychologists believe that this is how many people on the autism spectrum experience the world, perhaps because their cognitive architecture doesn't automatically narrow their interpretation of behavior and restrict it to typical metnal states.

Consequently, one of the crucial insights offered by cognitive psychologists is that by thus parsing the world and narrowing the scope of relevant interpretations of a given phenomenon, our cognitive adaptations enable us to contemplate an infinitely rich array of interpretations *within* that scope. As Nancy Easterlin puts it, "[W]ithout the inborn tendency to organize information in specific ways, we would not be able to experience choice in our responses."[4] "Constraints," N. Katherine Hayles observes in a different context, "operate constructively by restricting the sphere of possibilities."[5] In other words, our Theory of Mind allows us to connect Peter Walsh's trembling to his emotional state (in the absence of any additional information that could account for his body language in a different way), thus usefully constraining our interpretive domain and enabling us to start considering endlessly nuanced choices *within that domain.* The context of the episode would then constrain our interpretation even further; we could decide, for instance, that it is unlikely that Peter is trembling because of a barely concealed hatred and begin to explore the complicated gamut of his bittersweet feelings. Any additional information that we would bring to bear upon our reading of the passage—biographical, sociohistorical, literary-historical—would alert us to new shades in its meaning and could, in principle, lead us to some startling conjectures about Walsh's state of mind. Note, too, that the description of Walsh's "trembling" may connect to something in my personal experience that will induce me to give significantly more weight to one detail of the text and ignore others, which means that you and I may wind up with wildly different readings of Peter's and Clarissa's emotions "at eleven o'clock on the morning of the day she [is] giving a party."[6] None of this can happen, however, before we have first eliminated a whole range of other explanations, such as explanations evoking various physical forces (for instance, a disease) acting upon the body, and have focused instead solely on the mind of the protagonist.

This elimination of irrelevant interpretations can happen so fast as to be practically imperceptible. Consider an example from Stanley Fish's essay, "How to Recognize a Poem." To demonstrate that our mental operations are "limited by institutions in which we are already embedded," Fish reports the following classroom experiment:

While I was in the course of vigorously making a point, one of my students, William Newlin by name, was just as vigorously waving his hand. When I asked the other members of the class what it was that [he] was doing, they all answered that he was seeking permission to speak. I then asked them how they knew that. The immediate reply was that it was obvious; what else could he be thought of doing? The meaning of his gesture, in other words, was right there on its surface, available for reading by anyone who had the eyes to see. That meaning, however, would not have been available to someone without any knowledge of what was involved in being a student. Such a person might have thought that Mr. Newlin was pointing to the fluorescent lights hanging from the ceiling, or calling our attention to some object that was about to fall ("the sky is falling," "the sky is falling"). And if the someone in question were a child of elementary or middle-school age, Mr. Newlin might well have been seen as seeking permission not to speak but to go to the bathroom, an interpretation or reading that would never have occurred to a student at Johns Hopkins or any other institution of "higher learning."[7]

The point that Fish wants to get across is that "it is only by inhabiting . . . the institutions [that] precede us [here, the college setting] that we have access to the public and conventional senses they make [here, the raised hand means that the person seeks permission to speak]."[8] This point is well taken. Yet note that all of his patently "wrong" explanations (e.g., Mr. Newlin thought that the sky was falling; he wanted to go to the bathroom; etc.) are "correct" in the sense that they call on a Theory of Mind—that is, they explain the student's behavior in terms of his underlying thoughts, beliefs, and desires. As Fish puts it, "[W]hat else could he be *thought* of doing?" (emphasis mine). Nobody ventured to suggest, for example, that there was a thin, practically invisible string threaded through the loop in the classroom's ceiling, one end of which was attached to Mr. Newlin's sleeve and another held by a person sitting behind him who could pull the string any time and produce the corresponding movement of Mr. Newlin's hand. Absurd, we should say, especially since nobody could observe any string hovering over Mr. Newlin's head. Is it not equally absurd, however, to explain a behavior in terms of a mental state that is completely unobservable? Yet we do it automatically, and the only reason that no one would think of a "mechanistic" explanation (such as the string pulling on the sleeve) is that we have cognitive adaptations that prompt us to "see bodies as animated by minds."[9]

But then, by the very logic of Fish's essay, which urges us not to take for granted our complex *institutional* embedment which allows us to make sense of the world, shouldn't we inquire with equal vigor into our *cognitive* embedment which—as I hope I have demonstrated in the example above—profoundly informs the institutional one? Given the suggestively constrained range of the "wrong" interpretations offered by Fish (i.e., all of his interpretations connected the behavior to a mental state), shouldn't we qualify his assertion that unless we read Mr. Newlin's raised hand in the context of his being a student, "there is nothing *in the form* of [his] gesture that tells his fellow students how to determine its significance"?[10] Surely the *form* of the gesture—staying with the word that Fish himself has emphasized—is quite informative because its very deliberateness seems to delimit the range of possible "wrong" interpretations. That is, had Mr. Newlin unexpectedly jerked his hand instead of "waving" it "vigorously," some mechanical explanation, such as a physiological spasm or someone pushing his elbow, perhaps even a wire attached to his sleeve, would seem far less absurd.

To return, then, to the potentially problematic issue of the effortlessness with which we "read" minds: a flagrantly "wrong," from our perspective, interpretation, such as taking tears of grief for tears of joy, or thinking that Mr. Newlin raises his hand to point out that the sky is falling, is still "effortless" from the point of view of cognitive psychologists because of the ease with which we correlate tears with an emotional state or the raised hand with a certain underlying desire/intention. Mind-reading is thus effortless in the sense that we "intuitively" connect people's behavior to their mental states—as in the example involving Walsh's "trembling"—although our subsequent description of these mental states could run a broad gamut from perceptively accurate to profoundly mistaken. For any description is, as Fish tells us on a different occasion, "always and already interpretation," a "text," a story influenced to some extent by the personal history, biases, and desires of the reader.[11]

~5~

WHY DO WE READ FICTION?

I have mentioned earlier that works of fiction provide grist for the mills of our mind-reading adaptations that have evolved to deal with real people, even though on some level we do remember that literary characters are not real people at all. The question of just how we manage to keep track of their "unreality" is very complicated and directly relates to an important issue taken up by cognitive scientists, namely, what cognitive mechanisms or processes make pretence (and imagination as such) possible.[1] I will discuss here only a very limited sample of hypotheses currently on the table, focusing on those that offer, especially when considered together, some interesting insights into the larger question of why we read fiction. The first hypothesis is developed by a cognitive scientist; the second, by a cognitive literary critic.

To explain why autistic children do not engage in spontaneous pretence, Peter Carruthers suggests that they lack access not only to other people's mental states but to their own mental states as well.[2] Carruthers thus argues that the "*awareness of one's mental state* makes possible the *enjoyment* derived from the manipulation of this state*." It could be, then, that "the awareness of the *attitude* of pretending does not even have to include the *content* of what is pretended. Rather, it need only—at most— metarepresent *that it is now pretending.*"[3] Therefore, autistic children "do have the *capacity* for pretence if prompted," but they rarely exercise this capacity. Deprived, through mind-blindness, "of ready access to their own mental states, they are at the same time deprived of the main source of enjoyment present in normal pretending . . . [and] do not find the activity [cognitively] rewarding."[4] And if, as cognitive psychologists argue, "the function of pretend-play is to exercise the imagination," then having so little "practice at imagining," autistic children do it less well than others.[5]

The cognitive rewards of reading fiction might thus be aligned with the cognitive rewards of pretend play through a shared capacity to stimulate and develop the imagination. It may mean that our enjoyment of fiction is predicated—at least in part—upon our *awareness* of our "trying on" mental states *potentially available* to us but at a given moment *differing* from our own.

Keeping this in mind, let us now turn to the second hypothesis. Developed by the influential cognitive literary critic Reuven Tsur, it also focuses, albeit from a different angle, on the pleasure attendant upon our *awareness* of our cognitive functioning. Tsur's larger argument is that fictional narratives affect us by delaying or disrupting "in some other manner"[6] our cognitive processes. Moreover, our *awareness* of those disruptions "indicates to consciousness" that our crucial cognitive adaptations are in good shape (always welcome news). Here is how it works, for example, in the case of one literary genre, jokes:

[Jokes] crucially depend on a cognitive mechanism of shifting mental sets. *Mental set* is the readiness to respond in a certain way. It is, obviously, an adaptation device of great survival value. It is required for handling any situation in a consistent manner. Of no less great survival value is the adaptation device called *shift of mental sets*. This may be defined as the *shift* of one's readiness to respond in a certain way. It is required for handling *changing* situations in extralinguistic reality. The use of these two (opposing) kinds of adaptation mechanisms may yield different kinds of pleasure. *Mental set* is a typical instance of gaining pleasure from saving mental energy. The shift of mental sets yields a kind of pleasure that is derived from a certainty that one's adaptation mechanisms function properly. . . . The sense of humor, or the ability to apply wit to difficult life situations, is usually regarded as a sign of mental health. . . . Jokes achieve their witty effects by inducing some marked shift of mental sets, usually involving some changing situations. They are, then, an obvious case in which *an adaptive device is turned to esthetic ends.*[7]

I will turn to the question of aesthetics shortly. First, however, let us see how, played off each other, Carruthers's and Tsur's respective hypotheses illuminate an important aspect of our relationship with literary narrative. Carruthers suggests that we may find pleasing the *awareness* of our attitude of pretending. Tsur argues that jokes are particularly pleasing because they serve as a fast test of one's cognitive well-being (i.e., "I laugh; therefore I must be generally able to shift mental sets quickly"). It is possible, then, that certain cultural artifacts, such as novels, test the functioning of our cognitive adaptations for mind-reading while keeping us pleasantly aware that the "test" is proceeding quite smoothly. That is, when I am wondering if my uncle's inconspicuous social standing will influence Mr. Darcy's view of me as a potential wife—and yet know that what I am really experiencing is a state of mind of Elizabeth Bennet, who is, after all, *not me*—I am being made aware that my Theory of Mind must be functioning quite well. (So perhaps I *will* be all right out there in the real world, where my social survival absolutely depends on being able to imagine—correctly, incorrectly, approximately, self-servingly, bizarrely— other people's thoughts, desires, and intentions around the clock.)

There is a rub, though. Sometimes I get so engrossed by my "test" that I lose sight, at least to some degree, of the fact that neither do I have the lawyer uncle who lives in Cheapside nor am I in love with Mr. Darcy. Or, in a related cognitive slippage, I begin to feel that there is much more to Elizabeth Bennet than meets my eye on the page. Whereas I can shake off the former illusion pretty quickly (unless, that is, I am Don Quixote, but that is the subject of the second part of this book), the latter is much more enduring.

Hence what James Phelan sees as the striking "power of the interpretive habit to preserve the mimetic."[8] And hence, perhaps, our ambivalence toward that habit. For even though, as critics and teachers of literature, we do base both scholarly interpretations and classroom discussions on our "interest in the characters as possible people and in the narrative world as like our own,"[9] we remain wary about our own and our students' tendency to treat fictional personages as real people. We consider this tendency "a sentimental misunderstanding of the nature of literature."[10] We complain, as a colleague of mine did recently, that we "work so hard on illuminating the elaborately wrought artifice of the fictional world, and then [our students] get carried away by debating if Elizabeth Bennet slept with Mr. Darcy before marriage. She didn't because she never existed!"[11] It seems to me that our unease on this occasion stems from our intuitive realization that *on some level* our evolved cognitive architecture indeed does not fully distinguish between real and fictional people.[12] Faced with Elizabeth Bennet and Mr. Darcy, our Theory of Mind jumps at the opportunity (so to speak) to speculate about their past, present, and future states of mind, even as we realize that these "airy forms [and] phantoms of imagination"[13] do not deserve such treatment. The pleasure of being "tested" by a fictional text—the pleasure of being aware, that is, that we are actively engaging our apparently well-functioning Theory of Mind—is thus never completely free from the danger of allowing the "phantoms of imagination" too strong a foothold in our view of our social world.

Note, too, how this complicates a closely connected and very attractive hypothesis advanced by several cognitive literary critics, including Palmer, who argue that one "of the pleasures of reading novels is the enjoyment of being told what a variety of fictional people are thinking. . . . This is a relief from the business of real life, much of which requires the ability to decode accurately the behavior of others."[14] Whereas on the whole I subscribe to this view myself (and will build on it shortly), here is a nuance to consider. On the one hand, we indeed "have frequent direct access to fictional minds"[15] (e.g., we *know* that Mr. Darcy gets over his prejudice and learns to like and respect Elizabeth's uncle for who he is as a person). On the other hand, we tend to compromise our pleasure of "direct access" by believing, like Erich Auerbach, that "the people whose story the author is telling experience much more than [the author] can ever hope to tell."[16] Without pressing this point too strongly, I still want us to see in it something of a cognitive catch-22 situation. Our Theory of Mind allows us to make sense of fictional characters by investing them with an inexhaustible repertoire of states of mind, but the price that this arrangement may extract from us is that we begin to feel that fictional people do indeed have an inexhaustible repertoire of states of mind. Our pleasant illusion that there are at least *some* minds in our messy social world that we know well is thus tarnished by our suspicion that even those ostensibly transparent minds harbor some secrets. (Who knows, after all, what *exactly* went through Mr. Darcy's mind when he was introduced to Elizabeth's uncle and aunt?)

In other words, we may see the pleasure afforded by fictional narratives as grounded in our awareness of the successful testing of our mind-reading adaptations, in the respite that such a testing offers us from our everyday mind-reading uncertainties, or in some combination of the two. No matter which explanation or combination of explanations we lean toward, however, we have to remember that the joys of reading fictional minds are subject to some of the same instabilities that render our real-life mind-reading both exciting and exasperating.

If this is not complex enough, throw in some aesthetics. Some writers are willing to construct rather breathtaking tests of our mind-reading ability—provided we are willing to take those tests. (This "we," by the way, is a complex cultural compound, for it denotes a particularly histori-cally situated reader with a particular individual taste.) After all, the story of Little Red Riding Hood tests our ToM quite well—with all the attri-butions of states of mind to the grandma, to the trusting little girl, and to the Big Bad Wolf that it requires from its readers/listeners. Still, as we grow older, we begin to hanker for different mind-reading fare. For liter-ary critic Wayne Booth, for example, it has to be Henry James, and not just any James, but the one in his later period. Toward *that* James, Booth ends up feeling a profound "gratitude"—gratitude of a self-conscious reader of fiction at a certain point in his life toward an author who suc-ceeded in making him try on a poignantly rich suit of mental states.[17] As Booth puts it, in *The Wings of the Dove:*

[James] has invited me to recreate under his tutelage a beautiful structure—not just any *abstract* structure but a structure of beautifully realized human creatures highlighted miraculously by the artist. He offers me the chances to pretend, for the duration of my reading, that I too live "up there" with him, able not only to appreciate what he has done but to do it myself. Nobody, including James himself[18] has ever lived for long in this empyrean. . . . How can I express my conviction that it is good for me to be required to go through all this, and to know that if I return with similar attentiveness to the other late novels [of James] I'll be invited to similar—but always fresh—recreations. I have no doubt about it myself—I who am so much inclined to preoccupations of far less defensible kinds.[19]

If you happen to be a sneaky cognitive literary theorist, you are only too delighted to hear Booth wondering "how can [he] express [his] conviction that it is good for [him] to be required to go through all this." Why (so you pipe in happily), if a reader's mind-reading profile is constituted like Booth's, there is no doubt that it is "good" for him or her to be "tested" by *The Wings of the Dove*. At every step, the book is telling such a reader, as it were: "*These* immensely complex, multi-leveled, ethically ambiguous, class-conscious, mutually reflecting and mutually distorting states of mind you are capable of navigating. *This* is how good you are at this maddening and exhilarating social game. Did you know it? *Now* you know it!"

Something along these lines must be going on every time we read fictional stories that we enjoy, though the deeper personal meaning of each "conversation" between the story and the reader varies widely depending on the circumstances of the latter and her perception of those circumstances. For example, when I came to this country, about fifteen years ago, I went through one of those periods of reading fiction voraciously, going through a wild mix of novels by authors ranging from Belva Plain to Nabokov and from Muriel Spark to Philip Roth. That battery of "tests" must have been offering me a "guarantee" (illusory, perhaps, but still pleasing) that eventually I would be all right in the English-speaking social world, whose overwhelming difference I could only guess at from the self-encapsulated enclave of San Francisco's Russian Jewish community.

Did it matter to me back then that the states of mind that I tried on with such enthusiasm ranged from those of a young Jewish immigrant (*Evergreen*) to an articulate pedophile (*Lolita*) and from a fascist pedagogue (*The Prime of Miss Jean Brodie*) to a sex-obsessed New York lawyer (*Portnoy's Complaint*)? Apparently not. I might have identified with some characters more than others (though even that was a tricky business, for I think I identified more with Humbert Humbert than Anna Friedman), but the awareness of the personal identification must have been somehow less important than the awareness of my mind-reading wellbeing. The latter was crucial for me, the way I was and the way I thought of myself, particularly at a time when I could not express myself, much less discuss complex states of mind, in coherent English. I remember conducting elaborate conversations about those states of mind—in what I thought was English—but only in my head. I was later surprised to learn that I was not alone in this experience. Several immigrants who came to the United States in their late fifties and sixties told me that they did this too, a habit appearing more poignant in their case because, being of a retirement age, few of them had a real chance to break through the social barrier created by the language barrier.

Many of them read a lot of fiction at that time and still do.

~ 6 ~

THE NOVEL AS A COGNITIVE EXPERIMENT

*H*ow much prompting do we need to begin to attribute a mind of her own to a fictional character? Very little, it seems, since any indication that we are dealing with an entity capable of self-initiated action (e.g., "Peter Walsh has come back") leads us to assume that this entity possesses thoughts, feelings, and desires, at least some of which we could intuit, interpret, and, frequently, misinterpret.[1]

Writers can exploit our constant readiness to posit a mind whenever we observe behavior as they experiment with the amount and kind of interpretation of the characters' mental states that they themselves supply and that they expect us to supply. When Woolf shows Clarissa observing Peter's body language (Clarissa notices that he is "positively trembling"), she has an option of providing us with a representation of either Clarissa's mind that would make sense of Peter's physical action (something to the effect of: "how excited must he be to see her again!") or of Peter's own mind (as in: "so excited was he to see his Clarissa again!"). Instead she tells us, first, that Peter is thinking that Clarissa has "grown older" and, second, that Clarissa is thinking that Peter looks "exactly the same; . . . the same queer look; the same check suit" (40). Peter's "trembling" still feels like an integral part of this scene, but make no mistake: we, the readers, are called on to supply the missing bit of information (such as "he must be excited to see her again") which makes the narrative emotionally cohesive.

Ernest Hemingway, famously, made it his trademark to underrepresent his protagonists' feelings by forcing the majority of his characters' physical actions to stand in for mental states (as, for example, in the ending of *A Farewell to Arms:* "After a while I went out and left the hospital and walked back to the hotel in the rain" [314]). Hemingway could afford such a deliberate, and highly elaborate, in its own way, undertelling for the same reason that Woolf could afford to let Peter's trembling "speak for itself": our evolved cognitive tendency to assume that there *must be* a mental stance behind each physical action and our striving to represent to ourselves that possible mental stance even when the author has left us with the absolute minimum of necessary cues for constructing such a representation.[2]

For a different—and differently striking—example of undertelling the characters' mental states, consider Henry James's *The Awkward Age*. Written in the aftermath of James's disappointing venture into playwriting, *The Awkward Age* experiments with fusing the theatrical and the novelistic modes of mind-reading. Theatrical performance, after all, engages our Theory of Mind in ways markedly different from those practiced by the novel, for it offers no "going behind," in James's parlance, that is, no voiceover explaining the protagonists' states of mind (though in some plays the function of such a voiceover is assumed, to a limited degree, by a Chorus or a narrator figure). Instead, we have to construct those mental states from the observable actions and from what the protagonists choose to report to us (e.g., "*Irina:* I don't know why I feel so lighthearted today"[3]; "*Nina:* I am happy!"[4]; "*Treplev:* I wish you knew how miserable I am!"[5]). Moreover, in the case of the live performance—as opposed, that is, to simply reading the text of the play—this exercise of our mind-reading capacity is crucially mediated by the physical presence of actors and thus the wealth of *embodied* information (or misinformation) about their characters' hidden thoughts and feelings.

The Awkward Age strives to approximate this theatrical "absence of . . . 'going behind'" the protagonists' physical exteriors, as it refuses to "compass explanations and amplifications" of Nanda's, Aggie's, Mitchy's, Van's, Mrs. Brook's, and Mr. Longdon's mental states—refuses "to drag out odds and ends from the 'mere' story-teller's great property-shop of aids to illusion" (12). What we get instead is the account of the characters' feelings as hesitantly implied by a third-person narrator—an arrangement that forces us to reconstruct those feelings by negotiating between the narrator's report (riddled with "it seemed's" and "as if's") and our own observations of the characters' physical actions. For example, when Van and Mitchy talk about the possibility of Mitchy's marrying Aggie (mainly to please Nanda, who loves Van, but not Mitchy, even though Mitchy loves her and is considered by her mother to be a highly eligible suitor), the readers receive a detailed description of the two men's body language along with tentative guesses about what might be going on behind their restless starts, turns, and rises:

> Mitchy had stood a moment longer, almost as if to see the possibility [of Van's eventually marrying Nanda if Mitchy first marries Aggie] develop before his eyes, and had even started at the next sound of his friend's voice. What Vanderbank in fact brought out, however, only made him turn his back. "Do you like so very much the little Aggie?"
>
> "Well," said Mitchy, "Nanda does. And I like Nanda."
>
> "You are too amazing," Vanderbank mused. His musing had presently the effect of making him rise . . . (218)

Looking back at his experience of writing a novel "as if . . . constructing a play" (14), James found it both "perplexing and delightful" (12). It was certainly a challenge to write a 300-page story in the vein of the above-quoted "passage . . . between Vanderbank and Mitchy, where the conduct of so much fine meaning" has to be effected "through the labyrinth of mere immediate appearances" (16). Still, the challenge was met and the conduct of "so much fine meaning" was "successfully and safely effected" (16)—a success, let me stress again at the risk of repeating myself, owing both to James's brilliance and to the workings of our mind-reading capacity.

For it is because we engage in our own constant construction of the possible states of mind of the people we encounter—negotiating among their own reports of how they feel, others' guesses of what they might feel, and our intuitions of what a smile, a turn, a pause, a rise may mean in a given context—that writers such as James can play their games of under-telling and underinterpreting. Though, as James's readers well know, his usual game consists rather in overreporting his characters' thoughts and feelings, saturating us with the nuances of their mental states—a saturation, again, made possible by our evolved hankering to know what other people think. We want to know it so badly (though clearly some of us more badly than others) that we can take (and many of us even enjoy) the intense mind-reporting of *The Wings of the Dove, The Golden Bowl,* and *What Maisie Knew.*

To return to my earlier speculations of why we read fiction, I can say that by imagining the hidden mental states of fictional characters, by following the readily available representations of such states throughout the narrative, and by comparing our interpretation of what the given character must be feeling at a given moment with what we assume could be the author's own interpretation, we deliver a rich stimulation to the cognitive adaptations constituting our Theory of Mind. Many of us come to enjoy such stimulation and need it as a steady supplement to our daily social interactions. Viewed within this context, even the act of misinterpretation of the protagonist's thoughts and feelings does not detract from the cognitive satisfaction allowed by the reading of fiction.[6] To give a new twist to the well-known dictum, from a cognitive perspective, a misinterpretation of a character's state of mind is still very much an interpretation, a fully realized and thus pleasurable engagement of our Theory of Mind.

At the same time, as Phelan rightly points out:

> The misinterpreter of James can still achieve cognitive satisfaction, but chances are that the misinterpretation will yield less satisfaction than the more accurate interpretation. This is so not because the accurate interpretation is always going to offer more cognitive satisfaction, but because, in the case of James, getting him right is going to take us deeper into the relation between behavior and mind, and, thus, offer us richer cognitive satisfactions than we'll typically derive from getting him wrong. For an author whose experimentation with Theory of Mind is not as rich as James's, misinterpretation may end up adding things to the experience of reading that do offer more cognitive satisfaction.[7]

The latter observation rings equally true when we think of a variety of interpretive techniques that allow us to make a given text newly exciting precisely by reading more into its treatment of "the relation between behavior and mind." In fact, it seems that a majority of literary-critical paradigms—be that paradigm psychoanalysis, gender studies, or new historicism—profitably exploit, in their quest for new layers of meaning, our evolved cognitive eagerness to construct a state of mind behind a behavior.

But, as I was asked once after giving a talk on ToM and literature, What about those parts of fictional narratives that ostensibly have nothing to do with reporting or guessing characters' minds? If we like reading fiction because it lets us try on different mental states and seems to provide intimate access to the thoughts, intentions, and feelings of other people in our social environment (even if those people do not really exist and the social environment that we "share" with them is an illusion), what about, say, descriptions of nature? Why interrupt the pleasurable workout of our mind-reading adaptations with passages that either do not prod us toward inhabiting and guessing other people's minds or do it in a pointedly circuitous way (e.g., by anthropomorphizing)?

First of all, descriptions of nature are quite scarce even in those works of fiction in which they seem to be overrepresented. It is possible that our perception of some fictional texts as abounding in such descriptions owes simply to the fact that relatively rare as they are, they stand out and, as such, receive a disproportionate share of our attention. I remember how surprised I was recently, rereading the novels of nineteenth-century Russian writer Ivan Turgenev and looking in vain for all those endless "nature" passages that bored me so desperately in my adolescence (I had finally learned to skip all of them). Turns out that those endless passages are brief, few and far between, and, more often than not, shot through with pathetic fallacy and personification.[8] Moreover, when they do not explicitly ascribe human thoughts and feelings to natural events and objects, they are frequently focalized so as to provide an indirect insight into the feelings of the characters perceiving them. Thus Turgenev's *On the Eve*:

> Passing the ponds, they all stopped to admire [the town] for the last time. The bright colors of the approaching evening blazed all around them; the sky glowed; stirred up by the rising breeze, the leaves glittered iridescently; the molten gold waters flowed in the distance; reddish turrets and gazebos, scattered here and there throughout the garden, stood out sharply against the dark greenery. (341; translation mine)

The passage does contain spots of pathetic fallacy: those stirred-up leaves, that glowing sky. On the whole, however, the glorious colors of Turgenev's early sunset derive their meaning from the social context of the scene, as they set off various emotional uplifts experienced by several characters. Still, seeing their states of mind as accentuated by those colors, skies, leaves, and waters may require a cognitive effort different from the effort involved in a more straightforward imagining of a state of mind behind a character's observable behavior.[9] The reader wishing for a more immediate gratification of her mind-reading adaptations—a fast-food experience of reading fiction—may find the "glowing evening" interlude both superfluous and tedious, as I certainly did at age fourteen.[10] Today, now that my taste has been thoroughly vitiated by such works as Wordsworth's *Prelude* (which makes one work hard for every pleasurable shot of mind-reading that it delivers to our insatiably social mind), I can take Turgenev's nature passages in stride and even enjoy them.

Thus, if we conceive of the fictional narrative as a cognitive artifact in progress—an ongoing thousands-year-long experimentation with our cognitive adaptations—we can say that this narrative constantly diversifies the ways in which it engages our Theory of Mind. Imagined landscapes, with their pathetic fallacies, personifications, and anthropomorphizing, and with their tacit illuminations of human minds perceiving those landscapes, prompt us to exercise our ToM in a way very different from the stories that contain no such landscapes. The relative popularity of such descriptions depends on the specific cultural circumstances in which they are produced and disseminated (a topic which I consider in detail in Part III) as well as on the tastes and life histories of individual readers.

~ 7 ~

CAN COGNITIVE SCIENCE TELL US WHY WE ARE
AFRAID OF MRS. DALLOWAY?

*W*hen we start to inquire into how writers of fiction *experiment* with our mind-reading ability, and perhaps push it to its furthest limits, the insights offered by cognitive scientists become particularly pertinent. Although their investigation of ToM is very much a project-in-progress, enough carefully documented research is already available to literary scholars to begin asking such questions as, Is it possible that literary narrative builds on our capacity for mind-reading but also tries its limits? How do different cultural-historical milieus encourage different literary explorations of this capacity? How do different genres? Speculative and tentative as the answers to these questions could only be at this point, they mark the possibility of a genuine interaction between cognitive psychology and literary studies, with both fields having much to offer to each other.

This section's tongue-in-cheek title refers to my attempt to apply a series of recent experiments conducted by cognitive psychologists studying ToM to *Mrs. Dalloway*. I find the results of such an application both exciting and unnerving. On the one hand, I can argue now with a reasonable degree of confidence that certain aspects of Woolf's prose do place extraordinarily high demands on our mind-reading ability and that this could account, *at least in part,* for the fact that many readers feel challenged by that novel. On the other hand, I came to be "afraid" of *Mrs. Dalloway*—

and, indeed, other novels—in a different fashion, realizing that any initial inquiry into the ways fiction teases our ToM immediately raises more questions about ToM and fiction than we are currently able to answer. My ambivalence, in other words, stems from the realization that ToM underlies our interaction with literary texts in such profound and complex ways that any endeavor to isolate one particular aspect of such an interaction feels like carving the text at joints that are fundamentally, paradigmatically absent.

This proviso should be kept in mind as we turn to the experiments investigating one particular aspect of ToM, namely, our ability to navigate multiple levels of intentionality present in a narrative. Although ToM is formally defined as a second-order intentionality—for example, "I *believe* that you *desire* X," or Peter Walsh thinks that Clarissa "would think [him] a failure" (43)—the levels of intentionality can "recurse" further back, for example, to the third level, as in the title of George Butte's wonderful recent book, *I Know That You Know That I Know*," or to the fourth level, as in "I believe that you think that she believes that he thinks that X," and so forth. Dennett, who first discussed this recursiveness of the levels of intentionality in 1983, thought that it could be, in principle, infinite. A recent series of striking experiments reported by Dunbar and his colleagues have suggested, however, that our cognitive architecture may discourage the proliferation of cultural narratives that involve "infinite" levels of intentionality.

In those experiments, subjects were given two types of stories. One cluster of stories involved a "simple account of a sequence of events in which 'A gave rise to B, which resulted in C, which in turn caused D, etc.'" Another cluster introduced "short vignettes on everyday experiences (someone wanting to date another person, someone wanting to persuade her boss to award a pay rise), . . . [all of which] contained between three and five levels of embedded intentionality." Subjects were then asked to complete a "series of questions graded by the levels of intentionality present in the story," including some factual questions "designed to check that any failures of intentionality questions were not simply due to failure to remember the material facts of the story." The results of the study were revealing: "Subjects had little problem with the factual causal reasoning story: error rates were approximately 5% across six levels of causal sequencing. Error rates on the mind-reading tasks were similar (5–10%) up to and including fourth-level intentionality, but rose dramatically to nearly 60% on fifth-order tasks." Cognitive scientists knew that this "failure on the mind-reading tasks [was] not simply a consequence of forgetting what happened, because subjects performed well on the memory-for-facts tasks embedded into the mind-reading questions."[1] The results thus suggest that people have marked difficulties processing stories that involve mind-reading above the fourth level.[2]

An important point that should not be lost in the discussion of the experiments reported by Dunbar is that it is the *content* of the information in question that makes the navigation of multiply embedded data either relatively easy or relatively difficult. Cognitive evolutionary psychologists suggest the following reason for the ease with which we can process long sequences, such as, "A gave rise to B, which resulted in C, which in turn caused D, which led to E, which made possible F, which eventually brought about G, etc.," as opposed to similarly long sequences that require attribution of states of mind, such as, "A wants B to believe that C thinks that D wanted E to consider F's feelings about G." It is likely that cognitive adaptations that underwrite the attribution of states of mind differ in functionally important ways from the adaptations that underwrite reasoning that does not involve such an attribution, a difference possibly predicated on the respective evolutionary histories of both types of adaptations.[3] A representation of a mind as represented by a mind as represented by yet another mind will thus be supported by cognitive processes distinct from (to a degree that remains a subject of debate) cognitive processes supporting a mental representation, for example, of events related to each other as a series of causes and effects or of a representation of a Russian doll nested within another doll nested within another doll. The cognitive process of representing depends crucially on *what* is being represented.[4]

Writers, comic artists, movie directors, and situation comedy producers (to list but a few) intuitively exploit this particularity of our mind-reading ability. Bruce Eric Kaplan's cartoon in *The New Yorker* features a not-so-happily married couple having a conversation about their relationship (figure 1). The gloomy husband feels compelled to assure the equally gloomy wife: "Of course I care about how you imagined I thought you perceived I wanted you to feel." The joke has many layers and is highly culture-specific, focusing on the married tedium of well-to-do Manhattanites and contemplating that tedium from a very particular point of view associated with this magazine. Moreover, even implicitly guided by that view, different readers may find different reasons for thinking that the cartoon is funny. Still, each of those possible ironic angles would be bound with the apparent impenetrability of the husband's sentiment. Overwrought to the sixth level of mental embedment—the level at which our species is not that cognitively fluent—this statement about mutual sensi-

*"Of course I care about how you imagined I thought
you perceived I wanted you to feel."*

FIGURE 1. "Of course I care about how you imagined I thought you perceived I wanted you to feel." © The New Yorker Collection 1998 Bruce Eric Kaplan from cartoonbank.com. All Rights Reserved.

tivity, caring, and understanding is literally incomprehensible and has to be deciphered with pen and paper, if one bothers to decipher it at all.

On a slightly less exalted level, there is "The One Where Everybody Finds Out" episode from the fifth season of *Friends,* in which Phoebe finds out that Monica and Chandler are "doing it" and decides to play a practical joke on them. Phoebe, who is not in the least attracted to Chandler, begins to act as if she were, knowing that because Chandler does not know that she knows that he is going out with Monica, he will think that Phoebe is actually interested in him and will be both confused and flattered, to the secret delight of everybody who is in on the joke. However, when Monica finds out that Phoebe has made a pass at Chandler (whom, she knows, Phoebe does not find attractive), she realizes that Phoebe is trying to make fun of him and talks Chandler into welcoming Phoebe's advances, so that Phoebe, not knowing that Chandler knows that she knows, will back down at a crucial moment and thus make a fool of herself. However, when Chandler acts according to this plan and responds enthusiastically to

Phoebe's flirting, Phoebe realizes that Chandler must know now that she knows that he knows . . . (and here I begin to lose it, so let us move quickly to the end of this sentence), and so decides that she will never back down first. As Phoebe puts it ever so eloquently, addressing her co-conspirator Rachel and their friend Joey, who has been witnessing Phoebe and Rachel's plotting from the beginning: "They thought they could mess with us! They're trying to mess with *us?* They don't know that we know they know we know! And Joey, you can't say anything!" To this Joey replies, rather reasonably, "I couldn't if I wanted to."

I am afraid that neither could I. Watching this episode, many of us start feeling like Joey, who is generally portrayed as being a bit on the slow side. The situation is really not that complicated, and having live actors play it out helps to render it more comprehensible. Still, at some point, the agglomeration of multiply embedded minds proves too much of a cognitive load, and we begin to think of Phoebe's plotting in segments. We are keeping track, that is, of the two or three most immediate mind-readings (as in "now X doesn't known that Y knows what X does") and not of the whole series (as in "X doesn't know that Y knows that X knows that Y knows that X knows that Y knows what X does").

We certainly laugh as we watch Phoebe, Rachel, Monica, and Chandler navigate enthusiastically those mental labyrinths, but our laughter may have a complex emotional undertow. For we *have* been cognitively overpowered, finding ourselves lagging behind in this social game, with Joey bringing up the rear. On the other hand, our social ineptitude (or, as I prefer to see it, our appealing personal predilection for straight dealing) has been revealed in the safe setting of watching a television sitcom, so perhaps it is amusing after all. In fact, as I speculate in Parts II and III, when cultural representations push our mind-reading adaptations to what feels like their limits (within particular historical milieus, that is[5]), we might find ourselves in rather emotionally suggestive moods. Depending on the context and the genre of the representation (e.g., a cartoon in *The New Yorker,* an eighteenth-century psychological novel, a twentieth-century detective novel), a momentary cognitive vertigo induced by the multiple mind-embedment may render us *increasingly* ready either to laugh or to quake with apprehension.

Let us now turn to a novelistic representation of multiply embedded minds and consider a randomly selected[6] passage from Woolf's *Mrs. Dalloway.* Roughly halfway into the story, the husband of the title protagonist, Richard Dalloway, gets together with his old acquaintance Hugh Whitbread, and they come over to the house of one Lady Bruton, a woman keenly interested in politics. Milicent Bruton needs Richard's and Hugh's assistance to write a letter to the editor of the *Times* which would presumably influence the future of Great Britain. Here is how Woolf describes the process of composing the letter:

> And Miss Brush [Lady Bruton's secretary] went out, came back; laid papers on the table; and Hugh produced his fountain pen; his silver fountain pen, which had done twenty years' service, he said, unscrewing the cap. It was still in perfect order; he had shown it to the makers; there was no reason, they said, why it should ever wear out; which was somehow to Hugh's credit, and to the credit of the sentiments which his pen expressed (so Richard Dalloway felt) as Hugh began carefully writing capital letters with rings round them in the margin, and thus marvelously reduced Lady Bruton's tangles to sense, to grammar such as the editor of the *Times*, Lady Bruton felt, watching the marvelous transformation, must respect. (110)

What is going on in this passage? We are seemingly invited to deduce the excellence of Millicent Bruton's civic ideas—put on paper by Hugh—first from the resilience of the pen that he uses, and then from the beauty of his "capital letters with rings around them on the margins." Of course, this reduction of lofty sentiments and superior analytic skills to mere artifacts, such as writing utensils and calligraphy, achieves just the opposite effect. By the end of the paragraph, we are ready to accept Richard Dalloway's view of the resulting epistle as "all stuffing and bunkum," but a harmless bunkum at that, its inoffensiveness and futility underscored by the tongue-in-cheek, phallic description of the silver pen that had done twenty years in Hugh's service but is still "in perfect order"—or so Hugh thinks—once he's done "unscrewing the cap."

There are several ways to map this passage out in terms of the nested levels of intentionality. I will start by listing the smallest irreducible units of embedded intentionality and gradually move up to those that capture as much of the whole narrative gestalt of the described scene as possible:

1. The makers of the pen *think* that it will never wear out (1st level).
2. Hugh *says* that the makers of the pen *think* it will never wear out (2nd level).
3. Lady Bruton *wants* the editor of the *Times* to *respect* and publish her ideas (2nd level).
4. Hugh *wants* Lady Bruton and Richard to *believe* that because

the makers of the pen *think* that it will never wear out, the editor of the *Times* will *respect* and publish the ideas recorded by this pen (4th level).

5. Richard *is aware* that Hugh *wants* Lady Bruton and Richard Dalloway to *believe* that because the makers of the pen *think* that it will never wear out, the editor of the *Times* will *respect* and publish the ideas recorded by this pen (5th level).

6. Richard *suspects* that Lady Bruton indeed *believes* that because, as Hugh *says,* the makers of the pen *think* that it will never wear out, the editor of the *Times* will *respect* and publish the ideas recorded by this pen (5th level).

7. Woolf *intends us to recognize* [by inserting a parenthetical observation, "so Richard Dalloway felt"] that Richard *is aware* that Hugh *wants* Lady Bruton and Richard to *think* that because the makers of the pen *believe* that it will never wear out, the editor of the *Times* will *respect* and publish the ideas recorded by this pen (6th level).

It could be argued, of course, that in the process of reading, we automatically cut through Woolf's stylistic pyrotechnics to come up with a series of more comprehensible, first-, second-, and third-level attributions of states of mind, such as, "Richard does not particularly like Hugh"; "Lady Bruton thinks that Hugh is writing a marvelous letter"; "Richard feels that Lady Bruton thinks that Hugh is writing a marvelous letter, but he is skeptical about the whole enterprise"; etc. Such abbreviated attributions may seem destructive since the effect that they have on Woolf's prose is equivalent to the effect of paraphrasing on poetry, but they do, in fact, convey some general sense of what is going on in the paragraph. The main problem with them, however, is that to arrive at such simplified descriptions of Richard's and Lady Bruton's states of mind, we have to grasp the full meaning of this passage, and to do that, we first have to process several sequences that embed at least five levels of intentionality. Moreover, we have to do it on the spot, unaided by pen and paper and not forewarned that the number of levels of intentionality that we are about to encounter is considered by cognitive scientists to create "a very significant load on most people's cognitive abilities."[7]

Note that in this particular passage, Woolf not only "demands" that we process a string of fifth- and sixth-level intentionalities; she also introduces such embedded intentionalities through descriptions of body language that in some ways approach those of Hemingway in their emotional blandness. No more telling "trembling," as in the earlier scene featuring Peter and Clarissa. Instead, we get Richard watching Lady Bruton watching Hugh producing his pen, unscrewing the cap, and beginning to write. True, Woolf offers us two emotionally colored words, *carefully* and *marvelously,* but what they signal is that Hugh cares a great deal about his writing and that Lady Bruton admires the letter that he produces—two snapshots of the states of mind that only skim the surface of the complex affective undertow of this episode.

Because Woolf has depicted physical actions relatively lacking in immediate emotional content, here, in striking contrast to the scene in Clarissa's drawing room, she hastens to provide an authoritative interpretation of each character's mental state. We are told what Lady Bruton feels as she watches Hugh (she feels that the editor of the *Times* will respect a letter written so beautifully); we are told what Hugh thinks as he unscrews the cap (he thinks that the pen will never wear out and that its longevity contributes to the worth of the sentiments it produces); and we are told what Richard feels as he watches Hugh, his capital letters, and Lady Bruton (he is amused both by Hugh's exalted view of himself and by Lady Bruton's readiness to take Hugh's self-importance at face value). The apparently unswerving, linear hierarchy of the scene—Richard can represent the minds of both Hugh and Lady Bruton, but Hugh and Lady Bruton cannot represent Richard's representations of their minds—seems to enforce the impression that each mind is represented fully and correctly.

Of course, Woolf is able to imply that her representations of Hugh's, Lady Bruton's, and Richard's minds are exhaustive and correct because, creatures with a Theory of Mind that we are, we *just know* that there *must be* mental states behind the emotionally opaque body language of the protagonists. The relative paucity of textual cues that could allow us to imagine those mental states ourselves leaves us no choice but to accept the representations provided by the author. We have to work hard for them, of course, for sifting through all those levels of embedded intentionality tends to push the boundaries of our mind-reading ability to its furthest limits.

When we try to articulate our perception of the cognitive challenge induced by this task of processing fifth- and sixth-level intentionality, we may say that Woolf's writing is difficult or even refuse to continue reading her novels. The personal aesthetics of individual readers thus could be *at least in part* grounded in the nuances of their individual mind-reading capacities. By saying this I do not mean to imply that if somebody "loves" or "hates" Woolf, it should tell us something about that person's general mind-reading "sophistication"—a cognitive literary analysis does not support such misguided value judgments. The nuances of each person's mind-reading profile are unique to that person, just as, for example, we all have the capacity for developing memories (unless that capacity has been clinically impaired), but each individual's actual memories are unique. My combination of memories serves me, and it would be meaningless to claim that it somehow serves me "better" than my friend's combination of memories serves her. (At the same time, I see no particular value in celebrating the person's dislike of Woolf as the manifestation of his or her individual cognitive makeup. My teaching experience has shown that if we alert our students to the fact that Woolf tends to play this particular kind of cognitive "mind game" with her readers, it significantly eases their anxiety about "not getting" her prose and actually helps them to start enjoying her style.[8])

This point is worth dwelling on because, while writing this book and giving talks on ToM and fiction, I have become aware of the appeal of pop-hypotheses about the relationship between certain types of behavior (including reading preferences) and mind-reading "superiority." I have already mentioned the question that I was asked once about the "slightly autistic" adolescents who choose watching TV over reading novels. In the same vein, it was suggested to me that if somebody prefers Woolf to Grisham; or Grisham to TV; or novels to computer games; or long conversations about one's feelings to discussions of basketball games, it may testify to that person's mind-reading "excellence." I find such speculations misguided no matter how I look at them. Whereas common sense suggests that the mind-reading profile of a person who prefers Woolf to Grisham must indeed be somewhat different from that of a person who prefers Grisham to Woolf, I fail to see what practical conclusions about the person's overall mind-reading "fitness" can be made from the assumption of this commonsensical difference. Given how intensely contextual each act of mind-reading is, I would not be able to predict how a "typical" avid reader of Woolf would conduct herself in a complex social situation as opposed, say, to a "typical" avid reader of *TV Guide*. I had a friend once who delighted in discussing emotions and multiply embedded mental stances and who was, on the whole, what we call a "sensitive" man. Yet he could not stand reading fiction and generally was not fond of *any* reading because of a certain visual impairment that made it difficult for him to focus his eyes on the page. What gives? Theory of Mind makes reading fiction possible, but reading fiction does not make us into better mind-readers, at least not in the way that I can theorize confidently at this early stage of our knowledge about cognitive information processing. (I shall return to this point again in Part III, Section 2, entitled "Why Is Reading a Detective Story a Lot like Lifting Weights at the Gym?")

~ 8 ~

THE RELATIONSHIP BETWEEN A "COGNITIVE" ANALYSIS OF MRS. *DALLOWAY* AND THE LARGER FIELD OF LITERARY STUDIES

*I*t is now time to return to the imaginary conversation that opened this book. Some versions of that exchange did take place at several scholarly forums, where I have presented my research on ToM and literature. Once, for instance, after I had described the immediate pedagogical payoffs of counting, in one of my undergraduate seminars, the levels of intentionality in *Mrs. Dalloway*, I was asked if I could foresee the time when such a cognitive reading would supersede and render redundant the majority of other, more traditional approaches to Woolf.[1] My immediate answer was no, but since then, I have had the opportunity to consider several implications of that question important for those of us wishing cognitive approaches to literature to thrive.

First of all, counting the levels of intentionality in *Mrs. Dalloway* does not constitute *the* cognitive approach to Woolf. It merely begins to explore one particular way—among numerous others—in which Woolf builds on and experiments with our ToM, and—to cast the net more broadly—in which fiction builds on and experiments with our other cognitive propensities.[2] Many of these propensities, I feel safe in saying, still remain unknown to us despite remarkable advances in the cognitive sciences during the last two decades.

However, the current state of the field of cognitive approaches to literature already testifies to the spectacular diversity of venues offered by the parent fields of cognitive neuroscience, artificial intelligence, philosophy of mind, cognitive linguistics, cognitive psychology, and cognitive evolutionary anthropology. Literary scholars have begun to investigate the ways in which recent research in these areas opens new avenues in gender studies (F. Elizabeth Hart); feminism (Elizabeth Grosz); cultural historicism (Mary Thomas Crane, Alan Richardson, Blakey Vermeule); narrative theory

(Alan Palmer, David Herman, Uri Margolin, Monika Fludernik, Porter Abbott); ecocriticism (Nancy Easterlin); literary aesthetics (Elaine Scarry, Gabrielle Starr); deconstruction (Ellen Spolsky); and postcolonial studies (Patrick Colm Hogan, Frederick Luis Aldama).[3] What their publications show is that far from displacing or rendering the traditional approaches redundant, a cognitive approach can build on, strengthen, and develop their insights.

Second, the ongoing dialogue with, for instance, cultural historicism or feminism is not simply a matter of choice for scholars of literature interested in cognitive approaches. There is no such thing as a cognitive ability, such as ToM, free-floating "out there" in isolation from its human embodiment and historically and culturally concrete expression. Evolved cognitive predispositions, to borrow Patrick Colm Hogan's characterization of literary universals, "are instantiated variously, particularized in specific circumstances."[4] *Everything* that we learn about Woolf's life and about the literary, cultural, and sociohistorical contexts of *Mrs. Dalloway* is thus potentially crucial for understanding why this particular woman, at this particular historical juncture, seeing herself as working both within and against a particular set of literary traditions, began to push beyond the boundaries of her readers' cognitive "zone of comfort" (that is, beyond the fourth level of intentionality).

At the same time, to paraphrase David Herman, the particular combination of these personal, literary, and historical contexts, in all their untold complexity, is a "necessary though not a sufficient condition"[5] for understanding why Woolf wrote the way she did. No matter how much we learn about the writer herself and her multiple environments, and no matter how much we find out about the cognitive endowments of our species that, "particularized in specific circumstances," make fictional narratives possible, we can go only so far in our cause-and-effect analysis. As George Butte puts it, "[A]ccounts of material circumstances can describe changes in gender systems and economic privileges, but they cannot explain why *this* bankrupt merchant wrote *Moll Flanders,* or why *this* genteelly-impoverished clergyman's daughter wrote *Jane Eyre.*"[6] There will always remain a gap between our ever-increasing store of knowledge and the phenomenon of Woolf's prose—or, for that matter, Defoe's, Austen's, Bronte's, and Hemingway's prose.[7]

Yet to consider just one example of how crucial our "other" knowledges are for our cognitive inquiry into *Mrs. Dalloway,* let us situate Woolf's experimentation with multiple levels of intentionality within the history of the evolution of the means of textual reproduction. It appears that a written culture is, on the whole, more able than is an oral culture to support the elaborately nested intentionality simply because a paragraph with eight levels of intentional embedment does not yield itself easily to memorization and subsequent oral transmission. It is thus highly unlikely that we would find many (or any) passages that require us to go beyond the fourth level of intentionality in oral epics, such as *Gilgamesh* or *The Iliad*. Walter Benjamin captured the broad point of this difference when he observed that the "listener's naïve relationship to the storyteller is controlled by his interest in retaining what he is told. The cardinal point for the unaffected listener is to assure himself of the possibility of reproducing the story."[8] The availability of the means of written transmission, such as print, enables the writer "to carry the incommensurable to extremes in representations of human life"[9] and, by so doing, explore (or shall we actually say "develop," thus drawing upon Paul Hernadi's recent argument about the evolutionary origins of literature?[10]) the hitherto-quiescent cognitive spaces.

Of course, for a variety of aesthetic, personal, and financial reasons, not every author writing under the conditions of print will venture into such cognitive unknown. Even a cursory look through the best-selling mainstream fiction, from Belva Plain to Danielle Steel, confirms the continuous broad popular appeal of narratives sticking to the fourth level of intentional embedment. It is, then, the personal histories of individuals (here, individual writers and their audiences) that ensure that, as Alan Richardson and Francis Steen have observed, the history of cognitive structures "is neither identical to nor separate from the culture they make possible."[11]

In the case of Woolf, scholars agree that severing ties with the Duckworth—the press that had brought forth her first two novels and was geared toward an audience that was "Victorian, conventional, anti-experimentation" (*Diary* 1, 261)—"liberated [her] experimentalism."[12] Having her own publishing house, the Hogarth Press, meant that she was "able to do what" she "like[d]—no editors, or publishers, and only people to read who more or less like that sort of thing" (*Letters,* 167). Another factor possibly informing the cognitive extremes of *Mrs. Dalloway* was Woolf's acute awareness of the passing of time: "my theory is that at 40 one either increases the pace or slows down" (*Diary* 2, 259). Woolf wanted to *increase* the pace of her explorations, to be able to "embody, at last" as she would write several years later, "the exact shapes my brain holds" (*Diary* 4, 53). Having struggled in her previous novels with the narrator "chocked with observations" (*Jacob's Room,* 67), she has discovered in the process of working on *Mrs. Dalloway* how to "dig out beautiful caves behind [her] characters; . . . The idea is that the caves shall connect, and each comes to daylight at the present moment" (*Diary* 2, 263). Embodying the "exact shapes" of Woolf's brain thus meant, among other things, shifting "the focus from the mind of the narrator to the minds of the characters" and "from the external world to the minds of the characters perceiving it,"[13] a technique that would eventually prompt Auerbach to inquire in exasperation, "Who is speaking in this paragraph?"[14]

Woolf's meditations on her writing remind us of yet another reason that simply counting levels of intentionality in *Mrs. Dalloway* will never supersede other forms of critical inquiry into the novel. When Woolf explains that she wants to construct a "present moment" as a delicate "connection" among the "caves" dug behind each character, the emerging image overlaps suggestively with Dennett's image of the infinitely recursive levels of intentionality. ("Aha," concludes the delighted cognitive literary critic, "Woolf had some sort of proto-theory of recursive mind-reading!") But with her vivid description of the catacomb-like subjectivity of the shared present moment,[15] Woolf also manages to do something else—and that "something else" proceeds to quietly burrow into our (and her) cognitive theorizing.

This brings us to a seemingly counterintuitive but important point underlying cognitive literary analysis. Even as I map the passage featuring Richard Dalloway and Hugh Whitbread at Lady Bruton's as a linear series of embedded intentionalities, I expect that something else present in that passage will complicate that linearity and re-pose Auerbach's question, albeit with a difference: Will it be the phallic overtones of the description of Hugh's pen? Or the intrusion of rhetoric of economic exchange— "credit," "makers," "produce," "capital," "margin"? Or the vexed gender contexts of the "ventriloquism"[16] implied by the image of Millicent Bruton spouting political platitudes in Hugh's voice? Or the equally vexed social class contexts of the "seating arrangements" that hierarchize the mind-reading that goes on in the passage? (After all, Woolf must have "seated" Lady Bruton's secretary, Miss Brush, too far from the desk to be able to see the shape of Hugh's letters so as not to add yet another level of mental embedment by having Miss Brush watch Richard watching Lady Bruton watching Hugh.)

Cognitive *literary* analysis thus continues beyond the line drawn by cognitive scientists—with the reintroduction of something else, a "noise," if you will, that is usually carefully controlled for and excised, whenever possible, from the laboratory settings. The exciting noisy scene—with all its overlapping and competing discourses of class and gender—is the rightful province of a literary critic. Still, as Phelan points out, the study "of the embedded intentionalities has implications for every one of [these discourses] if only because it provides a clearer ground from which to proceed."[17]

~ 9 ~

WOOLF, PINKER, AND THE PROJECT OF
INTERDISCIPLINARITY

C hallenging as it may be, Woolf's prose is so fundamentally rooted in our cognitive capacities that I am compelled to qualify an argument advanced recently by Steven Pinker in his remarkable and provocative *Blank Slate*. Pinker sees Woolf as having inaugurated an aesthetic movement whose "philosophy did not acknowledge the ways in which it was appealing to human pleasure."[1] Although he admits that "modernism comprises many styles and artists, . . . not [all of which] rejected beauty and other human sensibilities" and that modernist "fiction and poetry offered invigorating intellectual workouts," here is what he has to say about modernism as a whole and Woolf in particular:

> The giveaway [explanation for the current crisis in the arts and humanities] may be found in a famous statement from Virginia Woolf: "[On] or about December 1910, human [character] changed." She was referring to the new philosophy of modernism that would dominate the elite arts and criticism for much of the twentieth century, and whose denial of human nature was carried over with a vengeance to postmodernism, which seized control in its later decades. . . . Modernism certainly proceeded *as if* human nature had changed. All the tricks that artists had used for millennia to please the human palate were cast aside. . . . In literature, omniscient narration, structured plots, the orderly introduction of characters, and general readability were replaced by a stream of consciousness, events presented out of order, baffling characters and causal sequences, subjective and disjointed narration, and difficult prose.[2]

As literary critics, we have several ways of responding to Pinker's claims about Woolf. We can hope, together with a representative of *The*

Publications of the Modern Language Association, that not "many students, teachers, theorists, and critics of literature will take [him] seriously as an authority on literature or the aesthetics more generally, especially since he misrepresents both Woolf and modernism."[3] At first sight, this is a comfortable stance. It assumes a certain cultural detachment of literary studies and implies that cognitive scientists should just leave literature alone, acknowledging it as an exclusive playing field for properly trained professionals—us. The problem with this view is that it disregards two facts: first, that more people read Pinker (who "misrepresents" Woolf) rather than, say, *PMLA* (which could set the matter straight); and, second, that as a very special, richly concentrated cognitive artifact, literature already is fair game for scientists, including Pinker, Daniel Dennett, Paul Harris, Robin Dunbar, and others, and it will become even more so as the cognitive inquiry spreads further across cultural domains.[4]

Thus, instead of simply ignoring Pinker's assertion that modernist writers have, by and large, cast aside "the tricks that artists had used for millennia to please the human palate," we should engage his argument, incorporating both insights from our own field and those offered by cognitive scientists. For me, the idea that our cognitive evolutionary heritage structures the ways in which we make sense of fictional narrative is profoundly appealing precisely because it begins to explain why the impulse to cast aside the tried-and-true "tricks" of representation is not at all limited to modernists. Writers, after all, have *always* experimented with the palates of their readers. Press a literary critic for an example of a novel featuring "stream of consciousness, events presented out of order, baffling characters and causal sequences, subjective and disjointed narration," and it is possible that she will come up not with one of the early-twentieth-century novels but with an eighteenth-century one, such as Laurence Sterne's *Tristram Shandy* (1759–67), or a nineteenth-century one, such as E. T. A. Hoffman's *Kater Murr* (1820–22). Press *me* for such an example, and I will say Heliodorus's *An Ethiopian Romance,* a novel written sometime between A.D. 250 and 380. Profoundly experimental in its handling of causal sequences and stories embedded within other stories, *An Ethiopian Romance* can be quite baffling to its readers; my students regularly find it so in spite of its accessible language (they read it in a contemporary translation) and its largely conventional set of adventures. Yet *Romance* has survived for seventeen centuries and has been enormously influential in the European literary tradition.[5]

In fact, the history of such books' reception contains a warning for both a cognitive scientist and a literary critic who are compiling a list of "tricks" that had been reliably delighting readers "for millennia" and were then cast aside by the elitist modernists. Dr. Johnson's confident (and so far wrong) observation that "nothing odd will do long," just like "*Tristram Shandy* did not last" should give pause to any attempt to designate some complex features of the literary narrative as broadly pleasing and thus likely to endure through millennia and other features as odd, elitist, and, thus, most likely, transient.[6] A text can be perceived by some readers as unusual and difficult (and indeed it can *be* genuinely difficult, given, for example, its intensified demands on our ToM adaptations). However, that difficulty may actually heighten its appeal for other readers and—given a conjunction of particular historical circumstances and particular means of textual reproduction—eventually contribute to its lasting popularity.

Moreover, to draw on the respective arguments of Alan Palmer and Monika Fludernik, narratives that challenge their readers' ToM by their unusual and difficult representations of fictional consciousness may offer valuable insights into the workings of our consciousness which is anything but predictable, orderly, and simple. As Palmer puts it,

> [fictional texts are] complex in their portrayal of the fictional mind acting in the context of other minds because fictional thought and real thought are like that. Fictional life and real life are like that. Most of our lives are not spent in thoughtful self-communings. Narrators know this, [even if we may not] have yet developed a vocabulary for studying the relationships between fictional minds and the social situations within which they function.[7]

And furthermore, as Fludernik reminds us, modernists saw themselves not as denying human nature and assaulting the human palate but, on the contrary, as getting closer to capturing the complexity of the real:

> [If] the consciousness novel is being discussed here in its relation to novelistic realism, and surprisingly so for some readers I should think it reflects the very rhetoric of Modernist fiction, which claimed to be truer to life than the realist and naturalist novel could ever hope to be: truer, that is, to the very experientiality of people's subjective involvement with their environment. . . . I propose to treat the consciousness novel as the culmination point in the development of narrative realism rather than its first regrettable lapse into idiosyncratic preoccupations with the non-typical and no-longer-verisimilar of human subjectivity.[8]

Ostensibly experimental texts, such as *Mrs. Dalloway* and *Tristram Shandy*, are thus a boon for an interdisciplinary analysis drawing on cognitive science and literary studies (I say ostensibly because my later chapters will expand significantly our concept of literary experimentation.) The moment cognitive scientists succeed in isolating yet another plausible cognitive regularity (e.g., as Dunbar and his colleagues have done), we can start looking for the ways in which fictional narratives (e.g., *Mrs. Dalloway*) have been burrowing into and working around that regularity, testing and reconfiguring its limits.

By thus paying attention to the elite, to the exceptional, to the cognitively challenging, such as Woolf's play with the levels of intentional embedment, we can develop, for instance, a more sophisticated perspective on the workings of our Theory of Mind.[9] And, as Phelan observes, would not Pinker himself and "those in his audience who view modernist literature as he does be more likely to be persuaded to change their dismissive view of it, if literary critics show that [Woolf's] representations of consciousness, though initially challenging to a reader, are highly intelligible because they capture in their own ways insights that Pinker and other cognitive scientists have been offering (and popularizing)?"[10]

But if it makes sense to use as a starting point the cognitive psychologists' insight into certain regularities of our information processing and apply it to the literary narrative, then the opposite conceptual move can be equally productive. Our intuitive impression (bolstered by Dr. Johnson's pronouncement) that Sterne was indeed doing something odd in his *Tristram Shandy* can prompt both cognitive scientists and literary scholars to inquire into other, not yet formulated, cognitive regularities underlying our interaction with fictional narrative. If Sterne was going against some cognitive grain, we need to understand that grain in terms incommensurably more specific than the ones evoking "structured plots, the orderly introduction of characters, and general readability."

I have returned again to the quote from *The Blank Slate* not to criticize Pinker's endeavor to view literary history from a cognitive perspective but rather to stress our own relative interdisciplinary timidity. Responding to the revolutionary advances made in the last two decades in cognitive psychology, anthropology, linguistics, and the philosophy of mind, Pinker and his colleagues in cognitive sciences grapple with difficult questions about literary narrative that *we* should be grappling with to a much larger extent than we currently do. Pinker may or may not be immediately aware of *Tristram Shandy* or *Kater Murr* when he positions far-reaching experimentation with established forms as a literary development unique to the twentieth century, but his awareness of them is almost beside the point. What is important is that he is venturing into the murky interdisciplinary waters *and* engaging a larger audience with important questions about literature and cognition, whereas we, though beginning to address such questions among ourselves, are hardly reaching out to readers outside of literature departments.

I wonder, then, what exactly are the epistemological and ethical grounds on which we stand when we mock Pinker's claim to being an "authority on literature" if we have not yet made any good-faith effort to meet Pinker halfway and offer our literary-historical expertise to develop a more sophisticated and yet accessible cognitive perspective on modernist representations of fictional consciousness? Paradoxically, it is only while we refuse to "take seriously" the research of cognitive scientists who dare to pronounce "on literature or . . . aesthetics more generally" that we could be made to feel that our contribution to this interdisciplinary exchange would represent little or nothing of value. Once we enter the conversation and engage with respect the arguments of Dunbar, Pinker, Dennett, and others, we realize that because of their ever-increasing—and well-warranted—interest in how the human mind processes literary narratives, our expertise could make a crucial difference for the future shape of the ever-expanding field of cognitive science.

PART 11

TRACKING MINDS

~ 1 ~

WHOSE THOUGHT IS IT, ANYWAY?

L et us turn now to the second key concept of this study: "metarepre-sentation."[1] Introduced in cognitive science in the 1980s, it has since gained wide currency among theory-of-mind psychologists and philoso-phers of mind and has recently become a subject of a wide-ranging collec-tion of essays, *Metarepresentations: A Multidisciplinary Perspective,* edited by Dan Sperber. Sometimes described as "a representation of a representa-tion," a metarepresentation consists of two parts. The first part specifies a source of representation, for example, "I thought . . . ," or "Our teacher informed us. . . ." The second part provides the content of representation, for example, ". . . that it was going to rain," or ". . . that plants photosyn-thesize."

Or, to come back to our *Mrs. Dalloway* passage, the sentence describ-ing Hugh's pen—"It was still in perfect order; he had shown it to the mak-ers; there was no reason, they said, why it should ever wear out; which was somehow to Hugh's credit, and to the credit of the sentiments which his pen expressed (so Richard Dalloway felt) as Hugh began carefully writing capital letters with rings round them in the margin . . ."—is a metarepre-sentation with a specific source. That little tag, "so Richard Dalloway felt," alerts us to that source, that is, the mind behind the sentiment. Knowing *whose sentiment it is* constitutes a crucial aspect of our under-standing of the psychological dynamics of this particular scene and of the novel as a whole. Moreover, as I will demonstrate shortly, our tendency to keep track of sources of our representations—to *metarepresent* them—is a particular cognitive endowment closely related to our mind-reading ability.

This section's discussion of metarepresentations draws on the work of Leda Cosmides and John Tooby, particularly their essay "Consider the Source: The Evolution of Adaptations for Decoupling and Metarepresentation," published in Sperber's collection. I will not try to summarize their carefully nuanced argument here; instead, I will adapt it and selectively quote from it for the purposes of explaining metarepresentation in fiction. To students of literature interested in learning more about our metarepresentational ability and its possible evolutionary history, I strongly recommend reading the original essay.

To grasp the importance of our capacity to form metarepresentations, let us imagine for a minute that we do not have this capacity, that is, that we can entertain representations, but we are not able *to keep track of their sources*. Let us consider how, thus circumscribed, we would conduct ourselves in the three following hypothetical situations, each of which involves our receiving a piece of information ranging from trivial, to fairly important, and to absurd.

(1) Imagine yourself sitting in your office (which incidentally has no windows) and getting ready to teach a class. A colleague, named Eve, drops by and mentions casually that it is raining hard outside. You do not simply "save" this new information in your mind—the mind is not, after all, a computer; instead you assimilate it by integrating various inferences resulting from this representation with what you already know about the world, and hence modify your plans for future behavior. Or, to use Cosmides and Tooby's terminology, the information about the rain is treated by your cognitive architecture as "architectural truth"; that is, it is "allowed to migrate . . . in an unrestricted . . . fashion throughout an architecture, interacting with any other data in the system with which it is capable of interacting."[2] Here are some examples of the thoughts arising in the process of such an integration/migration: "I'd better take an umbrella with me because it is a long walk from here to the building where I will be teaching"; "I should postpone making that announcement about the change in the syllabus until the second part of my lesson because many of my students will be struggling to find parking closer to campus and will be late for class"; "Peaches will be cheaper at the Farmer's Market this weekend because the drought seems to be over, so I should stop by the bank tomorrow and take more cash with me when I go to the Market on Saturday"; etc. As we can see, the range of databases affected by the information provided by Eve is so broad as to be, in principle, infinite.

(2) Next imagine that during her short stay, Eve tells you that a recent addition to the department, named Adam, is a terrible person and a bad

colleague. She has known him from a previous job, and she remembers him as selfish, rude, and incompetent. Again, in the process of assimilating this new representation, you will let it affect all kinds of mental databases. For example, you may decide that you should try to avoid working on the same project with Adam and will in fact cancel the lunch appointment that you had with him for next week. You may further begin to think that your department must be really going downhill—look what kind of people they hire these days!—and so maybe it is time to start looking for another job.

(3) Finally, imagine that as Eve stops by, she informs you that it is raining golden coins outside. Once she leaves your office, you immediately call the department's secretary to cancel your class. You can't teach now: you have better things to do. In fact, the thought of an early retirement has just entered your mind; with all that gold falling into your lap, you may as well leave all the grading and committee work behind you. You frantically look around the office for suitable containers and, having found some, rush outside to gather as much of the golden rain into your bags as you can. Before you leave the office, however, you do manage to make a couple of other phone calls. For example, you contact a car dealer and tell him that you are ready to buy that Mercedes that you have seen on his lot, the one you always wanted but knew that you would never be able to afford. Now you can finally get in touch with that inner conspicuous consumer (unless, that is, the devaluation of gold ensues quickly).

(3a) It is also possible, however, that the information about the golden rain strikes you as so obviously absurd that you just ignore it. You do not take in that representation at all; you do not assimilate it with any of your knowledge stores; you nod politely as Eve tells you about it and simply forget it the moment she is out of your office.

But let us see how these situations change once we have our metarepresentational capacity back and thus are able to consider the source of any new information. The first scenario actually stays the same. If you have no reason to suspect that Eve is misleading you about the rain, you adjust your plans (i.e., about the umbrella, the classroom announcements, and the bank) accordingly. The second and third scenarios, however, are markedly different this time around. When you hear from Eve that Adam is a bad colleague, you feel understandably concerned, but you do not cancel your lunch with him and you do not start looking for another job. Instead you keep Eve's information in mind but wait for further evidence that would either strengthen or weaken her claim. If several weeks or months later you find out that Eve has a long-standing grudge against Adam and that her stories about him might well be untrue, and if, meanwhile, Adam has been impressing you as a perfectly amiable person and a good coworker, it is likely that you will revise that initial bad impression about him that Eve has saddled you with. At the same time, you will not just "discard" Eve's communication as if it never happened; you will still retain the metarepresentation, "Eve told me that Adam is a bad colleague," because now it tells you something important about Eve herself.[3] (On the other hand, if some time later Adam does turn out to be a bad apple, you will come back to the information provided by Eve and consider it once more.)

Finally, in the case of the reported golden rain, once you have ascertained that your colleague is not being ironic ("yea, right, it will rain gold in front of a building housing the English department!") or playing a practical joke on you, that is, once you are convinced that she is serious, you will take her representation, "it is raining golden coins," in by integrating it with what you already know about the world. Only, this time, your inferences will focus mainly on this particular colleague and your future behavior in relation to her. You may decide to double-check *any* information that issues from her in the future, and you may consider not entering into any collaborative projects with her—just in case. Again, you will not just discard the incident (the 3a scenario). Discarding it completely could be dangerous because, however wrong, that information still tells you something important about Eve, something that you are better off knowing now rather than in the future when you are put in a situation in which you depend on her. Of course, in time, you may come to revise and abandon your suspicious attitude toward Eve and consider the "golden rain" remark a single instance of bad judgment or a silly joke; or you may come to believe, based on your later experiences with her, that she is indeed not very mentally stable.

In other words, our metarepresentational ability allows us to store certain information/representations "under advisement." What it means is that we can still carry out inferences on information that we know is incorrect (e.g., "it is raining golden coins") or have certain doubts about (e.g., "Adam is a bad colleague") but that the scope of these inferences will be relatively limited.[4] The "meta" part of the representation, that little "tag" that specifies the source of the information (e.g., "it was Eve who told me that . . .") is what prevents the representation from circulating freely within our cognitive system and from being used as an input to "many inferential processes, whose outputs are inputs to others."[5] Instead of being available to *all* of our stores of knowledge and prompting us to adjust our behavior in numerous ways, some of which could be harmful to us, that information is stored in what Cosmides and Tooby call a "suppositional" format and is thus available to a very selective set of cognitive databases, many of them having to do with the source of information. At the same time, "once [information] is established to a sufficient degree of certainty, source . . . tags are lost . . . e.g., most people cannot remember who told them that apples are edible or that plants photosynthesize."

The concept of metarepresentationality begins to figure in psychologists' discussions of the difference between our episodic memories (i.e., memories tied to specific learning episodes or experiences) as compared with semantic memories (i.e., general knowledge not tied to specific learning experience[6]). It has been suggested that "episodic memories are stored and retrieved via metarepresentations." That is, such memories retain the time-, place-, or agent-specifying source tags and as such are stored as events that have been "experienced by the self at a particular and unique space in time . . , with conscious awareness that 'this happened to me.'"[7] I may thus remember, for example, that it was last Thursday (the time-specifying tag), when I had dinner at my friend's house (the place-specifying tag), that she told me (the agent-specifying tag) that I should try to use shorter sentences in my scholarly writing (the representation or memory itself).

By contrast, semantic memories are representations that are stored without the source tag:

> Semantic memory . . . enables a person to have culturally shared knowledge, including word meanings and facts about the world, without having to recollect specific experiences on which that knowledge was based (e.g., knowing that Sacramento is the capital of California [or, to use the example above, that plants photosynthesize]).[8]

Note, however, that a semantic memory—or a representation stored without any source tag—could acquire a source tag and become a metarepresentation. For example, people used to think that Earth was the center of the universe with other heavenly bodies orbiting around it. Gradually, however, this semantic memory, this culturewide, incontrovertible knowledge, became a metarepresentation with a source tag, "[P]eople used to think that. . . ." Moreover, we can append *any* semantic memory with a source tag and thus turn it into a metarepresentation, if only for the purposes of discussion, for example, "Lisa does not believe that Sacramento is the capital of California." By the same token, throughout our lives, we treat an untold number of semantic memories as absolute truths—for example, if you drop a shoe, it will fall—even though we can imagine conceptual frameworks within which these memories are not true anymore, say, in space, outside of Earth's gravitational field. For practical reasons, however, it does not make sense for us to keep in mind all those alternative frameworks and thus store the representation, "if you drop a shoe, it will fall," with a place tag such as, "on Earth" (unless we are astronauts). What these examples show is that although the distinction between the semantic and episodic memories (or between representations and metarepresentations) is useful both for our cognitive information management and for our discussions of cognition, this distinction is always context-dependent and potentially fluid.

Metarepresentational ability might have evolved in response to a very particular cognitive challenge faced by our ancestors. As Cosmides and Tooby point out, humans stand out "within the context of the extraordinary diversity of the living world" because of their ability to use "information based on relationships that [are] 'true' only temporarily, locally, and contingently rather than universally and stably."[9] On the one hand, this ability to make use of local, contingent facts fuels "the identification of an immensely more varied set of advantageous behaviors than other species employ, giving human life its distinctive complexity, variety, and relative success."[10] On the other hand:

> The exploitation of this exploding universe of potentially representable information creates a vastly expanded risk of possible misapplications, in which information that may be usefully descriptive in a narrow area of conditions is false, misleading, or harmful outside of the scope of those conditions. Exactly because information that is only applicable temporarily or locally begins to be used, the success of this computational strategy depends on constantly monitoring and re-establishing the boundaries within which each representation remains useful. . . . Information only gives an advantage when it is relied on inside the envelope of conditions to which it is applicable.[11]

As a constant monitoring and reestablishment of boundaries (e.g., "Adam is a bad colleague, but only in Eve's representation of him"), our metarepresentational capacity is thus "essential to planning, interpreting communication, employing the information communication brings, evaluating others' claims, mind-reading, pretense, detecting or perpetrating deception, using inference to triangulate information about the past or hidden causal relations, and much else that makes the human mind so distinctive." The lack of such an ability could be characterized as "naïve realism"—a state that Cosmides and Tooby suspect was "an ancestral cognition for all animal minds."[12] They further point out that although cognitive "systems of representational quarantine and error correction" that evolved to differentiate among representations, "storing" some of them with source tags that limit their scope of inferences, "are, no doubt, far from perfect [;]. . . without them, our form of mentality would not be possible."[13]

What is the relationship between Theory of Mind and metarepresentationality? Baron-Cohen and Sperber have argued, separately, that "the ability to form metarepresentations initially evolved to handle the problems of modeling other minds or the inferential tasks attendant to communication."[14] After all, consider how crucial it is for a social species such as ours to be able to attribute thoughts to people around us while keeping track of ourselves as sources of those attributions in case we need to revise them later (e.g., "I thought you wanted to go to the store with me because you got up from the table, but now I know that I was wrong: it seems that you just wanted to stretch a bit").

On the one hand, Cosmides and Tooby agree with these views by stressing that the "restricted applications of inferences," achieved by processing information metarepresentationally, is "not an oddity or byproduct of . . . [ToM], but . . . a core set of . . . adaptations essential to modeling minds of others accurately."[15] On the other hand, they point out that "the problems handled by metarepresentations . . . are so widespread, and participate in so many cognitive processes, that it is worth considering whether they were also shaped by selection to serve a broader array of functions—functions deeply and profoundly connected to what is novel about hominid evolution."[16]

Oliver Sacks's research into the cognitive neuroscience of vision seems to support the latter view. Although Sacks does not use the term *metarepresentation,* here is a resonating quote from his essay describing the experience of an Australian psychologist, Zoltan Torey, who went blind at the age of twenty-one and since then worked hard "to maintain, if only in memory and imagination, a vivid and living visual world":

Tory maintained a cautious and "scientific" attitude to his own visual imagery, taking pains to check the accuracy of his images by every means available. "I learned," he writes, "to hold the image in a tentative way, conferring credibility and status on it only when some information would tip the balance in its favor."[17]

Because the argument of my essay focuses on literary texts, I have so far dealt and will continue dealing with verbal or verbalizable metarepresentations, such as, "Eve says it is raining outside." Torey's emphasis on holding *images* in a "tentative" way—visual metarepresentation, if you will—reminds us that, as Sacks points out, "there is increasing evidence from neuroscience for the extraordinary rich interconnectedness and interactions of the sensory areas of the brain, and the difficulty, therefore, of saying that anything is purely visual or purely auditory, or purely anything."[18] In other words, whether we agree with Baron-Cohen and Sperber, who think that metarepresentational ability evolved primarily to model human minds, or with Cosmides and Tooby, who suggest that its gradual emergence must have responded to a broader variety of cognitive challenges faced by our ancestors, it seems that its functioning today informs our interaction with the world on more levels than we are immediately aware of.[19]

~2~

METAREPRESENTATIONAL ABILITY
AND SCHIZOPHRENIA

I have considered above three conjectural instances of our taking in *any* new information as an architectural truth. Now it is time to ask what really happens when the cognitive mechanisms that allow us to store information under advisement are damaged. A number of neurological deficits, such as autism and schizophrenia, have been linked to the failure of metarepresentational capacity, as have several kinds of amnesia. To begin with the mildest functional instance of such a failure, children develop a mature Theory of Mind around the age of four, and it is suggestive that just before that (typically, from three to four), they can go through so-called childhood amnesia, that is, a tendency to "believe that they actually experienced events that never happened, if they are asked about these (fictitious) events repeatedly," a consequence, perhaps, of having an immature "system for source tagging."[1] (This is not to say, of course, that as adults we are immune to developing false memories through external suggestion. Unless we replace the evolutionary framework with the teleological, no such immunity can be expected when we have an immensely complex system, such as our metarepresentational capacity, functioning in an immensely complex world.)

Then there are also important studies of adult patients with amnesia induced by head trauma. Such patients, it turns out, often "experience highly selective memory loss, typically displaying intact semantic memory with impaired access to episodic memory."[2] Since it has been hypothesized that episodic memories are processed via metarepresentations (that is, by enabling people to form self-reflections, for example, "I thought that I would be afraid of the dog"[3]), the study of such selective impairment may lead to new insights into our metarepresentational ability.

Furthermore, Christopher Frith has suggested that since "self-awareness cannot occur without metarepresentation," that is, the "cognitive mechanism that enables us to be aware of our goals, our intentions, and the intentions of other people," specific "features of schizophrenia might arise from specific abnormalities in metarepresentation."[4] The failure to monitor the source of a representation thus can lead to patients' perceiving "their own thoughts, subvocal speech, or even vocal speech as emanating, not from their own intentions, but from some source that is not under their control," whereas the "inability to monitor willed intentions can lead to delusions of alien control, certain auditory hallucinations, [and] thought insertion."[5]

For example, the metarepresentation, "I intend to catch the bus," could be perceived by a schizophrenic patient as "Catch the bus," and "My boss wants of me 'you must be on time'" as "you must be on time,"[6] thus making the patient experience delusions of control or think that he/she hears disembodied voices talking to or about him/her. The latter, called "a third person hallucination," can result from perceiving a metarepresentation, such as, "Eve believes 'Chris drinks too much,'" as a "free floating notion 'Chris drinks too much,'"[7] and so forth.

Note that although people on the autism spectrum may experience difficulties with exercising metarepresentational capacity, the above delusions associated with failure of source-monitoring are typical for patients with schizophrenia but not for those with autism. Frith and his colleagues explain it by the "markedly different ages of onset" for autism and schizophrenia. The former manifests itself in the first years of life, whereas the latter usually develops in the early twenties, when the patient's theory of patient's theory of mind is already in place:

> The majority of autistic children fail to develop [Theory of Mind]. They are unaware that other people have different beliefs and intentions from themselves. Even if they manage, with much effort and after a long time, to learn this surprising fact, they will be only able to infer the mental states of others with difficulty and in the simpler cases. As a consequence they cannot develop delusions about the intentions of others. Furthermore, they will know, over a lifetime of experience, that their inferences are likely to be wrong and will therefore be ready to accept the assurance of others as to the true state of affairs.
>
> In contrast, schizophrenic patients know well from past experiences that it is useful and easy to infer the mental states of others. They will go on doing this even when the mechanism no longer works properly. For the first 20 years or so of life the schizophrenic has handled 'theory of mind' problems with ease. Inferring mental states has become routine in many situations and achieved the status of direct perception. If such a system goes wrong, then the patient will continue to "feel" and "know" the truth of such experiences and will not easily accept correction.[8]

In Sections 8 and 9 below, I focus on fictional protagonists failing to keep track of themselves as sources of their representations of other people's minds and thus "feeling" the truth of their (wrong) mind-attributions. I show that such failures could be used by the authors wishing to tease their readers by making them unsure of what is really going on in the story and which representations originating in the characters' minds they could trust. However, before I get to the narratives that cultivate this kind of conceptual vertigo in their readers, let us consider a more manageable example of a character clearly marked off by the author as mentally unstable.

Fedor Dostoyevski's novels feature many self-deceiving sufferers. Prominent among them, however, is Katerina Ivanovna Marmeladova (*Crime and Punishment*), a gentlewoman by birth and education, now a desperately poor widow dying of consumption among her starving children. Katerina Ivanovna repeatedly invents stories that enhance her past and future and immediately starts believing in these fantasies herself, to the raucous delight of cruel onlookers. For example, at the funeral of her alcoholic second husband, she comes up with the idea that she will soon receive a pension for him (which can never happen), and she decides to use that pension to open a boarding school for refined young ladies. Some of her listeners are simply amused by such ravings, but others, such as her landlady, find her plans as to how to run the school, which county to locate it in, and whom to hire so convincing (for Katerina Ivanovna herself believes in them) that they begin seriously advising her on how to ensure the hygiene and good morals of her pupils (405).

Katerina Ivanovna does not like the thought of accepting advice from her landlady (whom she considers infinitely beneath herself), and she lets it show. The disagreement between the two women escalates into an ugly fight. At this moment, a temporary lodger enters the room, a respectable well-to-do lawyer Petr Petrovich Luzhin. Earlier, Katerina Ivanovna had told everyone that Luzhin was a friend of her first husband, a protégé of her father, and the very man who would use his significant connections to secure her the pension (all of which is, of course, her invention). Now Katerina Ivanovna turns to this near-stranger for support:

> "Petr Petrovich!" cried she, "at least you protect me! Impress upon that stupid beast that she cannot treat this way a gentlewoman in distress, that there is court and justice . . . I will to the Governor-General . . . She will answer for it . . . In the memory of my father's past hospitality, protect us orphans!"
>
> "Excuse me, Madam . . . I beg your pardon, excuse me, Madam," Petr Petrovich was trying to get past her. "I've never had an honor of meeting your dear father, as you well know yourself . . . beg your pardon, Madam!" (Someone in the room roared with laughter.) "And I have not the least intention to participate in your endless squabbles with [your landlady . . .]."
>
> Katerina Ivanovna stood still, unable to move, as if struck by lightning. She could not comprehend how Petr Petrovich could disavow the hospitality of her dear father. Having once invented that hospitality, she now completely believed it herself. . . . (407–8; translation mine)

I have no intention of "diagnosing" the poor Katerina Ivanovna with selective amnesia or schizophrenia, but I do want to point out that her delusions clearly stem from the failure to monitor properly the source of her representations. Katerina Ivanovna's "I wish I could get a pension for my husband" changes to "I get a pension for my husband," and her "I wish this respectable and influential man (i.e., Petr Petrovich) were a friend of my first husband and a protégé of my father" registers in her mind as "This respectable and influential man was a friend of my first husband and a protégé of my father." Note that because these representations are allowed to circulate freely, that is, without "tags" pointing to herself as their source, in Katerina Ivanovna's mind they produce inferences that can corrupt the already existing stores of knowledge. After all, Katerina Ivanovna's late father *had been* a socially prominent figure, and Petr Petrovich *could have been,* in principle, welcomed in his house, if the two men had ever had a chance to meet. What happens here is that Katerina Ivanovna's original memory of her father's house is now corrupted by the conviction that Petr Petrovich used to be a frequent guest there. (Compare it to the hypothetical situation above, in which the information that it is raining gold, when assimilated without a source-specifying tag, such as, "It was Eve who told me," begins to impact our other knowledge stores and results in harmful behavior, such as canceling classes, quitting the job, maxing out on credit cards, etc.).

~ 3 ~

EVERYDAY FAILURES OF SOURCE-MONITORING

O f course, it is not just the hapless Katerina Ivanovna who invents stories about the state of affairs in the world and begins to act upon them as if they were real. We all do it. In many cases, such self-deception is quite beneficial—as one of the more level-headed (or just differently insane) characters from *Crime and Punishment* observes, "Best lives he who dupes himself the best" (502). But generally, especially if we consider the closely related issue of personal memories, it makes sense to think of our partial failures to keep track of some of the sources of our representations as part of the normal functioning of the metarepresenting brain. When I say "normal," I mean to contrast it both with the sustained, pathological pattern of such failures typical for schizophrenic patients and with the deliberately planned and carefully highlighted instances of such failures in the works of fiction.

I was reminded some time ago about everyday failures of our source-monitoring—failures that we do not even register consciously unless pressed by circumstances—while reading the account of Martha Stewart's trial in *The New Yorker* (Stewart had been accused of insider trading and subsequent lying to federal agents). The author, Jeffrey Toobin, refers to a "curious" testimony by one of Stewart's close friends, Mariana Pasternak, who, at one point, could not identify the source of one of her memories:

Pasternak's appearance ended on a curious note. In her direct testimony, she said that, in another conversation in Mexico, Stewart had commented about [the tip of her broker who had advised her to sell her stocks in the biotech company ImClone]: 'Isn't it nice to have brokers who tell you those things?' But under [the defense lawyer's] cross-examination, she said, 'I do not know if that statement was made by Martha or just was a thought in my mind'—a concession so dramatic that it brought a gasp ·from the spectators. But then, when the prosecution questioned her again, Pasternak said her 'best belief' was that Stewart said it. (70)

I suspect that the main reason Pasternak's concession "brought a gasp from the spectators" is the charged atmosphere of the courtroom and the specifics of this particular case, in which so much hinged on reconstructing who said exactly what and exactly when. Had any of the "gasping" spectators been asked to trace the exact sources of this or that representation of his, it is likely that he would feel just as uncertain about certain aspects of it as Pasternak did.[1]

One may ask, then, why we should posit our metarepresentational ability as a special cognitive endowment when it seems that we are routinely unsure about the sources of our representations. The answer to this question applies equally well to the question of why we should posit our Theory of Mind as a very special cognitive adaptation when in fact we routinely misread, misinterpret, and misrepresent other people's states of mind. To adapt one of Ellen Spolsky's insights, both the metarepresentational ability and the Theory of Mind are not "perfect" in some abstract, context-independent sense. Instead, they are "good enough"[2] for our everyday functioning: however imperfect and fallible, they still get us through yet another day of social interactions.

Thus, in the example above, the trial witness may have difficulties pinpointing the exact source of her personal memory, but even her apparent failure is thoroughly structured by her metarepresentational ability. That is, she knows that the representation, "Isn't it nice to have brokers who tell you those things?" does not simply describe the state of affairs but also expresses somebody's opinion. Even if she strongly agrees with the truth of this sentiment, on some level it has still been processed in her mind with a tag limiting its source to two people, either herself or Martha Stewart. The potential for a misattribution or uncertainty (e.g., "Was it really me or Martha?") falls within the same functional range as (to return to the example from Part I) our mistaken interpretation of tears of joy on our friend's face as tears of grief. In the latter case, our range of readings is drastically and productively limited to the domain of emotions; in the former case, Pasternak's range of attribution is drastically and productively limited to two people (as opposed to, say, 150 other people of her acquaintance).

Though not "perfect" (in some rather abstract way), this is surely a "good enough" cognitive scenario, of the kind that we live with daily. Evolution, as Tooby and Cosmides frequently point out, did not have a crystal ball:[3] the adaptations that contributed, with statistical reliability, to the survival of the human species for hundreds of thousands of years and thus became part of our permanent cognitive makeup profoundly structure our interaction with the world, but *even when they function properly*, at no point do they guarantee a smooth sailing through concrete complicated situations or the instinctive knowing of the exact origins of every aspect of our personal memories.

~4~

MONITORING FICTIONAL STATES OF MIND

*H*owever little we may know at this point about our metarepresentational ability, applying what we do know (or at least hypothesize strongly) to analysis of fiction results in the same embarrassment of riches as does the application of the Theory-of-Mind research. We start realizing that our capacity for storing representations under various degrees of advisement profoundly structures our interaction with literary texts, although, just as with the Theory of Mind, specific historical and cultural circumstances shape the specific forms that such interaction takes. Broadly speaking, whereas our Theory of Mind makes it possible for us to invest literary characters with a potential for a broad array of thoughts, desires, intentions, and feelings and then to look for textual cues that allow us to figure out their states of mind and thus predict their behavior, our metarepresentational ability allows us to discriminate among the streams of information coming at us via all this mind-reading. It allows us to assign differently weighed truth-values to representations originating from different sources (that is, characters, including the narrator) under specific circumstances. The ability to keep track of *who* thought, wanted, and felt what, and *when* they thought it, is crucial considering that the majority of our fictional narratives, from Homer's *The Iliad*, Shikibu's *The Tale of Genji*, and St. Augustine's *Confessions*, to Tolstoy's *War and Peace* and

Achebe's *Things Fall Apart,* center on the characters' *reweighing* the truth-value of various cultural and personal beliefs.

Consider Austen's *Pride and Prejudice.* Elizabeth Bennet (and, through her, the reader) can get over her prejudice toward Mr. Darcy because one of the important representations on which she has based her deep dislike of him—Mr. Wickham's account of how Mr. Darcy had mistreated him in the past—is stored in her (and our) mind as a metarepresentation. The agent-specifying source tag, "Mr. Wickham says that . . .," ensures that the information about Mr. Darcy's cruelty and superciliousness is partially restricted from becoming such an integral part of Elizabeth's worldview that no information to the contrary would be able to make any dent in it.

Similarly, Mr. Darcy is able to reconsider his views of himself, Elizabeth, and Elizabeth's sister's feelings toward his friend Mr. Bingley only because he can see these views as metarepresentations: emanating from himself, at a certain time, and for certain reasons (unlike, say, Dostoyevski's delusional Katerina Ivanovna, who is not aware of herself as the source of some of her representations). For example, Darcy used to believe that Elizabeth's sister, Jane, did not love Mr. Bingley and wanted to marry him only for his money and that, furthermore, in marrying any of the Bennet sisters, a man of his own or Mr. Bingley's position would lower himself in the world. These were the sentiments that informed the letter that he sent to Elizabeth shortly after his unsuccessful marriage proposal to her. Later, however, Mr. Darcy is able to assure Elizabeth that the letter was written "in a dreadful bitterness of spirit" that he does not feel any-more; or, to adapt Elizabeth's own apt description of the situation, "the feelings of the person who wrote [that unpleasant] letter . . . are now . . . widely different from what they were then" (248).[1] In other words, Darcy has revised his previous views because they have been "stored" in his mind with an agent-specifying source tag, such as, "It was me who felt it," and a time tag, such as, "several months ago, when I was angry at Elizabeth Bennet and mistaken in my earlier representations of Jane Bennet's feelings."

(Our inquiry into the workings of our metarepresentational capacity may also shed a new light on the unpleasant and yet undisputable power of *ad hominem* arguments. The subconscious appeal of such arguments is a mirror reflection of our tendency to scrutinize the source of representation once the content of representation becomes suspect. Throw a strong *a priori* doubt on Mr. Wickham's character and see if Elizabeth Bennet will take his stories about Mr. Darcy's iniquity quite so uncritically, *even if she is already predisposed* to dislike Mr. Darcy.)

A different example from the same novel: Austen's famous opening sentence, "It is a truth universally acknowledged, that a single man in possession of a good fortune, must be in a want of a wife," derives at least some of its ironic punch from the play between its status both as representation and as metarepresentation. This sentence activates in its readers two rather different information-processing strategies, for it is framed *simultaneously* as an "architecturally true" statement *and* a statement to be processed under advisement. On the one hand, the tag phrase, "It is a truth universally acknowledged," literally pressures us to let the idea that "a single man in possession of a good fortune must be in a want of a wife" circulate completely freely among our other knowledge stores, thus influencing our future behaviors in a broad variety of ways (and, we assume, influencing with equal intensity the behavior of the novel's characters). On the other hand, phrases such as, "It is a truth universally acknowledged," or "as everybody says," or "as everybody knows," are generally a peculiar lot, for they also tend to alert us to the possible metarepresentational nature of the information that they introduce. Somewhat paradoxically, they can be easily interpreted as implying an interested *source* of representation even as they deny that there is one. They seem to hint that somebody wants to manipulate us into doing something that would benefit him or her by having us take a certain precept as a "universal" truth. What if you *are* a single man in possession of a good fortune, and yet you have no desire for marrying whatsoever? Who is it that wants to coax you into believing that you certainly are "in want of a wife"?

Austen's very next sentence provides an answer to this question, presenting a community of people for whom the idea that a well-off man needs a wife is not a metarepresentation but incontrovertible Truth (a semantic memory, if you will): "However little known the feelings or views of such a man may be on his first entering a neighborhood, *this truth is so well fixed in the minds of the surrounding families,* that he is considered as the rightful property of some one or other of their daughters" (1; emphasis added).[2] The immediately following exchange between Mrs. Bennet and her husband narrows down our suspicions even further: it is the mothers of genteel but poor girls who will benefit if the rich young men of their acquaintance share their own absolute conviction on the subject. Some of the ensuing comedy of the novel is foreshadowed by this outlined-in-the-first-sentence clash between the sensibility that has self-servingly assimilated the idea that a rich man needs a wife desperately and immediately (for many of Mrs. Bennet's antics do result from apparently believing it unconditionally!) and the sensibility that holds this idea as a metarepresentation: under advisement and taking into consideration specific circumstances under which it was brought forth.[3]

My third example comes from Austen's *Persuasion*. I take as my starting point an observation of the literary critic Ellen R. Belton, who notes that when the novel's protagonist, Captain Wentworth, thinks that he is emphatically *not* interested in his former fiancée, Anne Elliot, he is, in fact, deceiving both himself and the reader. Belton argues that although it takes some effort for us to see through Wentworth's self-deception, once we do see through it, our attention shifts toward the ultimate source of that incorrect representation, the author herself:

> Why, we immediately ask ourselves, does Captain Wentworth insist so strenuously on his *not* wishing to marry Anne? . . . It may be that [he] does not know his own mind. The value, therefore, of being allowed inside the mind of such a character is partly an illusion, a device of the author's to make us believe simultaneously that we are being told everything there is to tell and that something crucial is being left out. [Something other than Captain Wentworth's faulty introspection thus has] to provide the missing explanations, to formulate meanings that at this moment are beyond the ability of the characters to understand and, ostensibly, against the will of the author to communicate.
>
> *When the reader recognizes this strategy, he becomes not merely an inquirer into the motives and intentions of the characters, but an inquirer into the motives and intentions of the author herself.* Like detectives, we find ourselves asking forbidden questions: How does her mind work? Why is she telling us this and not that? What is being withheld?[4]

I have added emphasis to the parts of Belton's argument that vividly demonstrate how the insight provided by cognitive evolutionary psychologists can productively converge with that of literary critics, who comment on the tacit shift in our interaction with the text, that is, on our heightened attention to the *source* of representation, once the representation itself has proven less than reliable. Let me recast Belton's analysis in explicit cognitive-evolutionary terms. When we consciously decide that Wentworth's professed indifference toward Anne is really not a "fact" anymore, a certain cognitive adjustment takes place within our system of information management. Wentworth's indifference ceases to be a representation that can migrate with very few restrictions throughout our cognitive architecture, impacting "any other data with which it is capable of interacting."[5] It has become a metarepresentation, framed by a source tag along the lines of, "Wentworth believes that. . . ." As a result, we are now moved to take a closer look at the author—the primary source of our information about Wentworth's mistaken beliefs—and ask ourselves what she is trying to achieve here. Is she trying to emphasize certain aspects of Wentworth's character (say, his relative lack of self-awareness) that could partially excuse his present behavior (e.g., his attention to Louisa Musgrove) and thus qualify him as a not infallible but still a suitable partner for Anne?

In other words, the conceptual adjustment that we go through here is similar to the conceptual adjustment that takes place once we learn that the information provided by Eve is wrong (e.g., "Adam is a bad colleague," "It is raining gold outside"). There, we refocus our attention on Eve. Here, we develop a new interest in reevaluating the sources of information about Wentworth's feelings, such as the story's narrator or its author (more about the relationship between the narrator and the author later). Paradoxically, this process of refocusing our attention both constrains and opens up our venues of interpretation. By beginning to treat the representation, "Captain Wentworth is indifferent toward Anne," as a metarepresentation, we "constrain" the scope of inferences we can draw from this representation and thus limit it largely to the possible motivation of our source of information. By doing so, however, we learn to ask new questions about the intentions of the author (such as, how do we account for Austen's emphasis on Wentworth's lack of self-awareness?) and consequently develop new ways of thinking about *Persuasion*. Our capacity for "monitoring and reestablishing the boundaries within which each representation remains useful"[6] thus underlies crucially our practices of literary interpretation.

The cognitive-evolutionary research into our ability to "consider the source" does more, however, than just substantiate Belton's insightful reading. Thinking in terms of our metarepresentational capacity allows us to see a pattern behind a series of seemingly unrelated conceptual processes informing our interaction with works of fiction. We begin to recognize that the same cognitive predisposition, that is, our ability to process information under advisement, makes possible *both* the metamorphosis of the once-proud or -prejudiced protagonists into romantic lovers *and* the metamorphosis of the formerly trusting readers into "detectives" querying the author's motives.

Furthermore, such an approach allows us to make certain predictions about the "chess game" that could take place between the reader and the writer. The author who gives his or her readers a good reason to doubt a representation considered hitherto true in the context of the narrative can reliably expect the reader to start scrutinizing the source of that representation. For example, once the readers of Vladimir Nabokov's *Pale Fire* realize that Charles Kinbote's account of the country named "Zembla" contains serious contradictions and lapses, they *have to* begin wondering who Charles Kinbote really is and what about his life and past makes him tell such strange stories. Such a "guarantee" of what the reader will be thinking of and looking for offers the writer the possibility of calibrating, if he is so inclined, the kind and amount of information about the source of representation that the writer sees fit to provide. Nabokov responds to the carefully anticipated shift in the reader's attention by providing cues about Kinbote's real personality, and, although these cues remain maddeningly inconclusive, the author knows that the reader will return to them again and again as Kinbote's chronicles of Zembla become both further divorced from reality and peculiarly reconnected to it. Of course, all of this is done intuitively—neither readers nor writers think in terms of "information stored under advisement"—but the intuition does tend to follow a suggestive pattern. Some writers are particularly fond of choreographing this particular mental game, which may explain, at least in part, the not-altogether-unpleasant feeling that we sometimes get after reading their novels, which is that the writer had somehow anticipated and even planted some of our smart interpretive gambits.

~ 5 ~

"FICTION" AND "HISTORY"

*H*ere are some questions that must have occurred to you while reading my discussion of source-monitoring and that I have actually elided as long as possible to keep my argument under some semblance of control: Aren't works of fiction themselves metarepresentations with source tags pointing to their authors? And, if they are, what allows us to consider *any* information contained in them, even the apparently incontrovertible, "Lydia ran away with Wickham," a "fact" or an "architectural truth"? Should not we try to envision a much more intricate system of degrees of metarepresentational framing that would allow for such nuances? Thinking through these questions inevitably means raising a series of far-reaching inquiries into the ways cognition structures and is in turn structured by culture. In the remaining sections of Part II, I map out a few parts of this forbidding territory and point briefly to some of its landmarks (a more detailed discussion deserves a separate book).

Commenting on the special metarepresentational status of fictional texts, Cosmides and Tooby observe that it is likely that stories explicitly labeled as fiction (e.g., *Little Red Riding Hood*) are never stored "without a source tag. The specificity of the source tag may be degraded, from (say) 'Mother told me [story X]' to 'Someone told me [story X],' . . . but . . . insofar as source tags are an important part of a self-monitoring system, one would expect them to be retained in some form as well."[1] In other words, works of fiction, at least those clearly defined as such, seem to be metarepresentations par excellence, perennially stored with either variously implicit source tags, such as "folk" in the case of *Little Red Riding Hood* and as "Anglo-Saxon bard(s)" in the case of *Beowulf,* or explicit source tags, such as "Jane Austen" in the case of *Pride and Prejudice.*

We can speculate, then, that it is our awareness that there is a *source behind the representation* that legitimates a variety of personal and institutional endeavors to resituate, reinterpret, and reweigh every aspect of a literary text. One may feel a bit nervous and yet somehow justified in questioning what so recently seemed to be the widely accepted view—for example, the notion, based on Austen's own direct assertion, that Captain Wentworth does not wish to marry Anne—because as long as we keep track of the source of a representation that involves complex human interaction (or of the mind behind the "gossip," so to speak), no aspect of that representation is completely safe from a reevaluation.

Consider in this context the poststructuralist concept of the "Death of the Author," first advanced by Roland Barthes in 1968, elaborated by Michel Foucault in 1969, and assuming since then a prominent place in literary theory. The concept refers not to the actual demise of the writer (who could be dead or alive at the time of discussion—it does not matter) but to the rejection of the traditional view of the author as the main agency and the "ultimate 'explanation' of a work."[2] As Barthes puts it, "[T]he birth of the reader must be at the cost of the death of the Author,"[3] meaning that the reader, at liberty to choose whatever interpretation (or interpretations) of the text strikes him or her as most compelling, assumes the position of authority formerly reserved for the writer.

As a literary-theoretical credo (versus, that is, an obituary notice), "the Author is dead" strikes a cultural nerve, and for a good reason. It seems to demand a conceptual readjustment peculiarly challenging for our meta-representing mind: the erasure of the figure of the author calls for some kind of suspension—or deferral—of the process of source-monitoring. It is possible, then, that as a conceptual experiment, "the Author is dead" is exciting because it allows us to consider various implications of such a suspension of source-monitoring even if on some levels this suspension remains unattainable.

For, ingenuous as the concept of the "Death of the Author" appears to be, note its essential cognitive conservatism. The source behind the fictional text is not really eliminated—it is merely substituted by another source. It is the reader who now emerges as an author or one of many authors of the narrative—a game of substitutes testifying to, among other things, the tenaciousness with which we cling to the idea that there must be some source (e.g., an author, a reader, multiple authors, multiple readers) behind a narrative that bears distinct marks of fiction.

Of course the idea that fictional narratives are always stored in a metarepresentational format is useful only as long as it is carefully qualified. Cosmides and Tooby begin such a qualification by pointing out that "the falsity of a fictional world does not extend to all of the elements in it, and useful elements (e.g., Odysseus's exploits suggest that one can prevail against a stronger opponent by cultivating false beliefs) should be identified and routed to various adaptations and knowledge systems." They further assert that the "fact that fiction can move people means that it can serve as input to whatever systems generate human emotions and motivation,"[4] which is to say that at least on some level those systems "don't care" if the whole emotionally moving bundle of representations is stored with a source tag identifying it as an "invention" of somebody known as Jane Austen. (I will return to this issue of "not caring" later in my discussion of detective novels.)

But even if on some level we are ready to weep and laugh at a story that we know to be somebody's willful invention, on a different level we can be very sensitive to any attempt on the part of the writer to pass his or her fantasy as a "true" and not a "meta" representation. As Cosmides and Tooby observe, even though "'false' accounts may add to one's store of knowledge about possible social strategies, physical actions, and types of people, in a way that is better than true, accurate, but boring accounts of daily life, [this] does not mean that falsehoods are, other things being equal, preferred. True narratives about relevant people and situations—'urgent news'—will displace stories, until their information is assimilated."[5]

Moreover, the attempts to pass fictions for such "urgent news" would be decried. Consider, for example, the indignation of the early readers of Daniel Defoe's *Robinson Crusoe* (1719), who had been promised by the title page of the first edition "a just history of fact" but had then been given what they perceived as a "feign'd" story. Responding to the heated charges of "lying like the truth," Defoe felt compelled to tell his "ill-disposed" critics that his "story is not "feign'd" and "though Allegorical, [it] is also Historical, [because it contains] Matter of real History."[6] And, indeed, Defoe's novels contain plenty of information that could be stored either with no scope-limiting source-tagging at all or with a *relatively weak* tagging (note the importance of introducing the concept of gradation to our discussion of source-tagging; I shall come back to it later). For example, *Robinson Crusoe* contains information fully compatible with our basic ontological assumptions about causation, naïve physics, mental states, and so on, as well as the information compatible with culture-specific semantic knowledge, for example, that eighteenth-century Englishmen engaged in overseas trading, that they used slave labor, that they followed their primogeniture laws. This is not to mention that *Robinson Crusoe* is also a good source of potentially useful inferences of the kind indicated by Cosmides and Tooby in their "Odysseus" example above, such as that one can survive even in the direst circumstances by exercising resourcefulness and self-reliance, or that wanderlust may come at a serious cost. Strictly speaking, the presence of all this ontologically, semantically, and emotionally true information allowed Defoe to claim that his novels were "true histories" because they contained "matters of fact," and yet his critics felt justified in accusing him of lying and violently discarded his "matters of fact" claim. Their outrage[7] seems to indicate a strong conviction that certain representations should be publicly acknowledged as fictions *as a whole* even if many of their constituent parts satisfy a broad range of truth-value requirements.[8]

Other epochs and cultural settings offer examples of a similar drive to differentiate the "true stories" from "feign'd," even if the criteria and indeed the very vocabulary of "truth" are different in each case. The famous fourth-century B.C. entry in Chinese *Zuozhuan* (the commentary on *Spring and Autumn Annals,* which covered the reigns of the twelve Dukes of the state of Lu from 722 to 491 B.C.) tells of the three historians who chose to be killed, one after another, rather than agree to falsify the account in the same *Zuozhuan* that recorded the murder of Duke Zhuang of Qi by his chief minister. Although *Zuozhuan* undoubtedly contains some "falsification of records, precisely to suit those in position of power," its testimony about the heroic historians clearly intends to impress upon the readers that the commentary would not sponsor the promulgation of political myths, even if the word *myth* itself did not exist in ancient China.[9]

Similarly, a sixth-century B.C. Greek historian, Hecataeus, ridiculed other people's tales as "absurd" and presented "his own accounts . . . as true" (*alethes*), and in the following generation Thucydides distanced "himself from those whose accounts are 'more suited to entertain the listener than to the truth.'" As being beyond scrutiny (*anexelegktos*), such stories, wrote Thucydides, "won their way to the mythical" (*muthodes*), a term, that, as G. E. R. Lloyd observes, "clearly acquires pejorative undertones" when used "in a collocation associated with unverifiability."[10]

Finally, as a more familiar example, think of our own bookstores' commitment to carefully demarcating shelves containing fiction from those containing nonfiction, even though the former offer plenty of information that deserves to be assimilated by our cognitive systems as architecturally true, and the latter contain a broad variety of cultural fictions (just consider treatises on dating and dieting!).

A cognitive perspective on "fiction" and "history" allows us to qualify the argument sometimes made by my colleagues in literary studies that the notion of "truth" is a relatively recent Western invention and that other epochs and cultural settings do not share our preoccupation with that elusive entity. To support this argument, they typically point out that other peoples' notions of "history" and "fiction" are very different from ours; for example, something that we certainly classify today as a myth could be considered, say, 2,000 years ago, a historical truth about the origins of a nation. What my examples from eighteenth-century England, fourth-century B.C. China, and sixth-century B.C. Greece demonstrate is that although on some level, *some* of our cognitive systems do not distinguish between actual situations and deliberate fictions—for example, the tears that we shed while reading a touching novel are real enough—on another level, people have *always* cared deeply about the difference between "true" and "feign'd" stories and were even willing to die for their right to call the myth a myth.

On the other hand, my colleagues are right in their skepticism about some *universal* notion of "history" and "fiction," because on the practical level there is really very little universality to our enduring quest for truth. The criteria and definitions of truth shift on every imaginable level, cultural, contextual, and personal—they *have to shift*, in fact, if we consider this process from the perspective outlined by Cosmides and Tooby. If our metarepresenting mind is constantly busy "monitoring and re-establishing the boundaries within which each representation remains useful," then our universal "quest for truth" is really a universal quest for temporary, local, intensely contextual truths that are reliable only within "the envelope of conditions to which [they are] applicable."[11] This is to say that the constantly changing boundaries and definitions of truth are not the casualty of the social-historical change but rather the key condition of the functioning of the human brain. By adjusting and redefining what constitutes the "truth" at every new social, cultural, and personal junction, we exploit, build on, develop, fine-tune, struggle with, tease, and train a broad variety of cognitive mechanisms underlying our evolved metarepresentational capacity.[12]

This constant hunt for truths supposes a constant delicate interplay between energy costs and benefits. Our brain is a very "expensive" device: compared with muscle tissue, it consumes sixteen times as much energy per unit weight. Monitoring and reestablishing the boundaries for truths is crucial for our existence, and yet, in some specific situations, doing it *again and again on the same material* could become too costly.

For example, it may be that once readers have decided on the relative truth-value of a complex cultural artifact, such as *Robinson Crusoe,* or, to put it differently, once they have integrated it with a relatively weak metarepresentational tagging (as a "true story"), they may experience a broad gamut of negative emotions, ranging from disappointment to anger, when they realize some time later that they have to expend more cognitive energy on drastically reassessing their initial valuation and on reintegrating *Robinson Crusoe* with a very strong metarepresentational tagging (as a "feign'd" story) instead. Some readers may be more amenable to this kind of reassessment, which involves revising numerous knowledge databases affected by the initial processing of the story, whereas others may find this call for the extra expenditure of mental energy irksome.

Of course I am speculating here, but the question that I am grappling with is a serious cognitive issue that has to be addressed and cannot be simply dismissed. On the one hand, we can say Defoe's readers were unhappy about his having exploited their strong preference for what Cosmides and Tooby call "urgent news"—the "true narratives about relevant people and situations." But, on the other hand, think about it: why, in principle, should readers feel so angry about realizing that a story about a person whom they have never met is really a story about a person whom nobody has ever met, especially since it contains so much otherwise true and useful information?

Similarly, a cost-benefit analysis may enter into a discussion of the tenacity with which our bookstores cling to the separation between "fiction" and, say, "history," in their shelving practices. Can it be that imperfect as it is, this separation saves the customers a significant cognitive effort of "deciding" (subconsciously, of course), when they begin to read a book, how much of metarepresentational tagging each little element of the story will need? Once a book is placed on the "fiction" shelf, the decision about its overall truth-value has been made for us, so to speak.[13] We have the cognitive luxury of knowing, as we pick up such a book, that the story it contains is, *as a whole,* a metarepresentation that needs to be stored with a permanent source tag pointing to the author. We can then enjoy it as such, processing some constituent parts of it with a much weaker or no metarepresentational framing at all (including the parts that conform to our general knowledge and the parts that have a real emotional effect on us and/or teach us important life lessons).

Compare the experience of picking up a book from a shelf labeled "history." We open such a book with a subconscious expectation that *as a whole* it could be assimilated with a much weaker metarepresentational tagging than a book from a "fiction" shelf. Of course we can change our mind in the process of reading and decide, for example, that the given treatise contains more propaganda than accurate historical information and thus store it with strong metarepresentational tagging. But again, the preliminary cognitive work has been done for us (or is claimed to have been done for us) by the publisher, who has provided enough external markings to alert us to the intended truth-value of the book, and by the bookstore's clerk, who has put it on the designated shelf.

Furthermore, once we begin to think of how cultures satisfy, reinforce, struggle with, and manipulate our cognitive predispositions, such as our constant monitoring of the boundaries of truth, we may realize, for example, that there is something deeply paradoxical in the position of historian both today and in the time of Thucydides. On the one hand, a historian strives to diminish the amount of metarepresentational framing that her readers would deploy in assimilating her book, which, taken to its logical extreme, means removing herself from readers' consciousness altogether. The ultimate goal of the historian is to have her readers store the information that she provides simply as "X," and not as "Thucydides says that 'X,'" or as "Linda Colley says that 'X.'" On the other hand, the historian's own personality (e.g., her academic degrees, her other books, the names of publishing houses that she associates with) becomes an important factor in persuading the reader that the information contained in her book has a high truth-value, that is, that it should be assimilated with a relatively weak source-tagging.

Thucydides thus had to puff himself up and put down his competitors as liars and myth-peddlers (all the while claiming that his work "is no mere piece produced for a competition"[14]) in order to *disappear* from his work, that is, to encourage his readers to perceive a historical account penned by Thucydides as simply "the" historical account or "the every-reasonable-person's" historical account. The martyrdom of the three Chinese historians bound them inextricably to *Zuozhuan* and *as such* contributed to making *Zuozhuan* an infinitely more trustworthy, that is, low-on-source-tagging, book. The concept of "Death of the Author" sounds titillating precisely because it is really not that cognitively feasible (i.e., there is *always* an author behind a *fictional* text, even if her name is lost to us); by contrast, the concept of "Death of the Historian" sounds rather unexciting because the expectation of the historian's fading-out (and I don't mean physical annihilation) is implicitly built into each historical account aspiring to the high truth-value.

The phenomenology of source-monitoring may sound complicated and look complicated, but don't let that fool you: it really *is* complicated. The scope of issues raised by introducing the concept of metarepresentationality, as defined by cognitive psychologists, into literary and historical studies can be truly staggering. Our evolved cognitive ability to store representations under advisement; to reweigh their architectural "truth"; and to refocus our attention on a source of a given representation in proportion to our intuitive perception of that representation's relative truth-value, structures an untold variety of cultural practices.

Of course, we are still quite a way off from figuring out what is actually going on in our brains/minds when we discriminate among the levels of truth-value associated with a given representation, such as *Pride and Prejudice; Zuozhuan;* or, for that matter, a toothpaste commercial—that is, when we somehow decide on the relative truth-value of the representation *as a whole* and on the relative truth-value of its components. For the purpose of the present discussion, however, we can agree on the following pragmatic observation. Our cognitive makeup allows us to store a given representation with a very strong, perhaps permanent, source tag (e.g., *Beowulf* will always remain a story "feign'd" by somebody, and so will *Pride and Prejudice*). Once we are decided on the overall metarepresentational framing of the given story (a decision mediated by a variety of cultural institutions), we can process its constituents as so many architectural truths, including the truths about emotions experienced by its characters and our own feelings in response to their emotions. The next section will thus take for granted the larger metarepresentational status of the given literary text and focus on the interplay of metarepresentations and variously weighted architectural truths *within* its fictional world.

~6~

TRACKING MINDS IN BEOWULF

*B*ecause this book will eventually focus on several particular instances of the novelists' experimentation with our metarepresentational ability, here is an important point worth repeating and worth clarifying. Throughout my argument, I frequently say that this or that fictional text experiments in a certain way with our Theory of Mind and/or our metarepresentational ability. What I do not want you to infer based on such statements is that I believe that some texts *do not* experiment with these cognitive predispositions. They *all do* insofar as every single act of writing and reading fiction deploys our ToM, and the overall cognitive outcome of such deployment is never fully predictable. Thus when I refer to Woolf's or Richardson's or P. D. James's experimentation with their readers' ToM and/or metarepresentational ability, what I really claim is that they push to their limits certain aspects of the *general, constant, ongoing experimentation* with the human mind that constitutes the process of reading and writing fiction.

To illustrate my point about this constant experimentation, let us turn to the text that I used in Part I as an example of a work of fiction that *does not* (and perhaps could not, due to material realities of its time's textual reproduction) play with multiply embedded levels of intentionality the way Woolf's *Mrs. Dalloway* does—an Old English epic *Beowulf. Beowulf* may never be able to embed more than three levels of intentionality, but it still engages our Theory of Mind in ways that vary—within certain parameters—from one moment to another and from one reader to another.

When the protagonist of the poem, the great Geat hero, Beowulf, first arrives to Heorot to save it from the terrible monster Grendel, he is taunted by one of the local men, Unferth, who (we infer, using our ToM) must be jealous of the attention and respect heaped on the newcomer. Later, however, after Beowulf has defeated Grendel and starts preparing for the fight with that monster's vengeance-breathing mother, Unferth lends him a powerful weapon, "a rare and ancient sword named Hrunting" (64).

Because the anonymous author takes particular care to inform us that it was Unferth and not some nameless drunkard in the crowd who ridiculed Beowulf about his presumed past misadventures, the present act of sword-giving can be read as a sign of a grudging change of heart in the character who initially envied the Geat hero and distrusted him.

Here is why I see this as an example of the text's experimentation with our metarepresentational ability. On the one hand, the poem clearly relies on our tendency to monitor sources of representations (e.g., "It was Unferth who initially said that Beowulf was a loser"). Similarly, the general thrust of our interpretations of Unferth's change of heart is guided by the text's emphasizing some social nuances more than others (e.g., "It looks like Unferth is somebody whose opinion will not necessarily carry the day, but it won't be completely ignored, either"). On the other hand, *within these constraints,* the exact effect that each particular instance of source-monitoring may have on the reader's understanding of the text remains unpredictable.

For instance, there is no certainty that when, utilizing my ToM and my metarepresentational ability and gauging Unferth's relative social importance, I register his new attitude, my reaction to his behavior will be the same as yours, or even the same as my own after five minutes of thinking further about the poem.[1] I can say that Unferth is a good guy who has been led astray by drink and then came to his senses; OR, that he is a calculating fellow who can see in which direction the wind is blowing after Beowulf's first victory, and wants to be in the good graces of the winning warrior; OR, that he is one of the rare characters in the poem who actually intuits Beowulf's vanity but is powerless to do anything about this intuition, for Beowulf is destined to live out the flaws of his character, now gloriously, now tragically.

In other words, our interpretation of Unferth's and Beowulf's behavior and personality *will certainly be structured* by our metarepresentational ability: for the poem calculatedly feeds this ability by implying, first, that there is an important difference between the states of Unferth's mind *then* and *now* and, second, that Unferth's opinion matters to a certain degree within the social world of the poem. Still, the exact effect of this exploitation of the particular cognitive capacity remains dependent on the state of mind of the specific reader in the specific moment.

Thus any fictional gestalt (or, were I to broaden this discussion, I would say any utterance[2]) that deploys our Theory of Mind and/or our metarepresentational capacity experiments with these cognitive adaptations insofar as the effect of such a deployment on the reader is never fully determined: it differs from one mind to another and from one mind now and five minutes, five hours, or five years from now. Any fictional text is profoundly experimental because the brain that interacts with this text is a dynamic system. (Hence, perhaps, the pleasures of rereading: no two close encounters with the same fictional text are ever truly the same, for the brain that responds to the text changes ever so slightly with every thought and impression passing through it.)

~7~

DON QUIXOTE AND HIS PROGENY

*A*lthough all fictional texts rely on and thus experiment with their readers' ability to keep track of *who* thought, wanted, and felt *what* and under what circumstances, some authors clearly invest more of their energy into exploiting this ability than others. Indeed, we can speak of several overlapping and yet distinct literary traditions built around such exaggerated engagement with our metarepresentational capacity. In the rest of this book I focus on two such traditions: one, exemplified by the story of Don Quixote, is the subject of Sections 7–11; another, exemplified by detective stories, will be dealt with in Part III (Sections 1–4).

From a cognitive psychological point of view, Cervantes's protagonist suffers from a selective failure of source-monitoring. He takes in representations that "normal" people store with a restrictive agent-specifying source tag such as "as told by the author of a romance" as lacking any such tag. He thus lets the information contained in romances circulate among his mental databases as architectural truth, corrupting his knowledge about the world that we assume has hitherto been relatively accurate. Among other literary characters belonging to this tradition are Arabella, the heroine of Charlotte Lennox's *The Female Quixote* (1752),[1] who takes the fantastic events described in French romances as the accurate representation of reality, as well as the already mentioned Katerina Ivanovna from Dostoyevski's *Crime and Punishment* and Charles Kinbote from Nabokov's *Pale Fire,* both of whom wax delusional by failing to keep track of themselves as the sources of their fanciful representations about the world.

The category of such "Quixotic" protagonists can be further expanded if we consider characters whose source-monitoring is somewhat compromised, though not to the degree that renders them unquestionably mad, such as Richardson's Lovelace (*Clarissa*) and Nabokov's Humbert Humbert (*Lolita*).[2] For a literary critic exploring fictional narrative's manipulation of our metarepresentational capacity, such characters as Lovelace and Humbert are particularly fascinating: not only do they conflate their visions of reality with the more "real" reality, but they also drag their readers along into that perceptual quagmire.

That's what such novels do then. If in *Don Quixote* and *The Female Quixote,* the failure to keep track of sources of certain types of representations was restricted to the title characters, making them the locus of madness, *Clarissa* and *Lolita* diffuse this fascinating failure among characters *and* readers, making us experience if not a bout of insanity then still an occasional feeling of mental vertigo. This feeling, captured in part by the literary-critical term *unreliable narrator* (more about this term later), is predicated upon our anxious (though not, of course, articulated in these terms) realization, as we read on, that we have been tricked by the narrative into losing track of sources of certain representations.

Consider *Lolita* and its first-person narrator, Humbert Humbert. We realize (so to speak) that going back and retroactively turning representations into metarepresentations by supplying source tags such as, "*It was Humbert's idea* that Lolita has been sexually interested in him, for in reality she has not," is a treacherous undertaking. What if she *has been,* a little bit? Whom can we trust now in figuring that out? Which source tags should we retain? Which discard? Which reweigh as to their relative truth-value? Having processed some representations as architectural truths within the world of the novel, are we now supposed to scrap the results of that processing? And if we do, where is the guarantee that our new assignment of truth-values will hold for the next fifty pages in this kind of story? Some writers never fully resolve the source-monitoring ambiguity cultivated by their narratives, leaving it to those readers who appreciate this kind of mental game to enjoy *Lolita* and *Pale Fire;* others may grudgingly settle on decidedly battered and compromised versions of the "real."

Of course a reader who hated *Lolita* yesterday because she felt that there is no stable ground in the story from which to judge the truth-value of any given episode (read: no reliable source of information; too much metarepresentational ambiguity) may start liking it tomorrow, influenced, for example, by her classmates' discussions of the novel. Circumstances change, minds change, readers change. But even as we reinvent ourselves every second, we still cannot help monitoring sources of our representations and constantly reweighing the relative truth-value of those representations based on the incoming information about the apparent trustworthiness of their sources. The interplay between the unpredictability, on the one hand, and the unavoidable regularities of our information-processing cognitive systems, on the other, is what makes it possible for such writers as Cervantes, Lennox, Dostoyevski, and Nabokov to play with us in millions of ever new ways, degrees, and combinations, and it is what ensures that the game of fiction is still going strong after thousands of years.

~8~

SOURCE-MONITORING, ToM, AND THE FIGURE OF THE
UNRELIABLE NARRATOR

I am pleased to report that there seems to be an affinity between my take on an unreliable narrator as a function of textual experimentation with our source-monitoring and the view first introduced by Jonathan Culler and then explored by Monika Fludernik and Ansgar Nunning. As Nunning has argued recently, the critic may account

> for whatever incongruousness s/he may have detected by reading the text as an instance of dramatic irony and by projecting an unreliable narrator as an integrative hermeneutic device. Culler . . . has clarified what is involved here: "At the moment when we propose that a text means something other than what it appears to say we introduce, as hermeneutic devices which are supposed to lead us to the truth of the text, models which are based on our expectations about the text and the world."[1] . . . [Similarly, as] Fludernik has shown so convincingly [in a related context,] the projection of an unreliable narrator can be seen as "a result or effect of the reader's pragmatic interpretation of textual elements within their specific literary context."[2]

At the same time—although I agree with Nunning that we import the figure of an unreliable narrator because we need to frame in familiar social terms a perceived pattern of textual ambiguities—I am less troubled than he is by all the anthropomorphizing that goes into it. From the point of view of cognitive theory, it is not terribly surprising that we conjure up an extra mental presence when we intuit that the narrative is monkeying around with our source-monitoring capacities. There is a very short step—thanks to our Theory of Mind, which is ever hungry for more material to work on—from starting to suspect that the text is fooling us, to ascribing a whole host of other states of mind to that wily typographic entity. As Uri Margolin observes in a different context, "[S]ince we cannot but conceive of narrative agents as human or human-like, it is a basic cognitive requirement of ours that we attribute to them information-processing activities and internal knowledge representations."[3]

It is not accidental, then, that Phelan's recent exploration of unreliable narrators, *Living to Tell about It,* describes different types of fictional unreliability in terms of specific behavioral patterns *on the part of the text* as well as on the part of its readers. Phelan defines unreliable narration thus:

> Narration in which the narrator's reporting, reading (or interpreting), and/or regarding (or evaluating) are not in accord with the implied author's. There are six main types of unreliable narration: misreporting, misreading, and misregarding, underreporting, underreading, and underregarding. The two main groups can be differentiated by the activity they require on the part of the authorial audience: with the first group—misreporting, misreading, and misregarding—the audience must reject the narrator's words and reconstruct an alternative; with the second group—underreporting, underreading, and underregarding—the audience must supplement the narrator's view.[4]

Indeed, given what we know about the workings of our metarepresentationality and Theory of Mind, we should be able to have our theoretical cake and eat it too. That is, I have no qualms about thinking of the unreliable narrator as first and foremost a function of the textual engagement of our cognitive adaptations for source-monitoring while at the same time appropriating, for the rest of my argument, Phelan's excellent (and anthropomorphic) classification.

A given narrator, Phelan observes, "can be unreliable in different ways at different points in his or her narration."[5] For example, Frankie, the child-narrator of Frank McCourt's *Angela's Ashes,* both misreads and misregards what is going on around him, whereas Nabokov's Humbert misregards, misreports, and underreports his actions and Lolita's responses to them. Likewise, Mr. Stevens, the protagonist of Kazuo Ishiguro's *Remains of the Day,* misreports and misregards certain events of his story as well as underreports and underreads his own motives.[6] When "Stevens says that 'any objective observer' will find the English landscape 'the most deeply satisfying in the world,' he demonstrates a misperception analogous to his saying that 'any objective observer' would find the English cuisine the most satisfying in the world."[7] He thus exhibits unreliability both "on the axis of knowledge/perception" (misreading) and "on the axis of ethics and evaluation" (misregarding).[8]

Note that Stevens is perfectly sincere in his belief about the "objective" superiority of the English landscape. This belief (Phelan suggests) might be rooted in his "mistaken value system,"[9] which takes as a given certain subjective assumptions about the world. From the point of view of cognitive theory, by considering his take of the English landscape universal, Stevens loses track of himself as a source of this representation. To "reject the narrator's words and reconstruct an alternative,"[10] the reader thus has to become aware of the missing source tag—"Stevens thinks that . . ."— and to reapply it.

Every step in this process engages and titillates our metarepresentational capacity: We come into the awareness of the missing source tag. We reapply the tag. We contemplate various ramifications of the difference between the two representations ("the English landscape is the most deeply satisfying in the world" vs. "Stevens thinks that the English landscape is the most deeply satisfying in the world") that jostle against each other in our readerly consciousness. We begin to wonder what other representations within the story may also be missing their source tags. As Phelan points out, "[O]nce any unreliability is detected all the narration is suspect"[11]—in some narratives, the game of the missing source tags is never *really* over. We close such books with a strange feeling that the state of cognitive uncertainty that they induced in us may never be fully resolved. We continue guessing which representations within the story deserve to be treated as "true" and which have to remain metarepresentations with a source tag pointing to the first-person narrator.

~ 9 ~

SOURCE-MONITORING AND THE IMPLIED AUTHOR

A similar kind of guessing game (whom to trust and how much?) takes place when literary critics contrast such figures as the "real" author of the text, its narrator (especially when unreliable), and its "implied author." If you are unfamiliar with the latter term, Gerald Prince's *Dictionary of Narratology* defines it as "the implicit image of an author in the text, taken to be standing behind the scenes and to be responsible for its design and for the values and cultural norms it adheres to."[1] Students of narrative have been debating the added value of this concept at least since the publication of Wayne Booth's *The Rhetoric of Fiction,* in which Booth suggested that the category of implied author captures our "intuitive apprehension of a completed artistic whole" of a given text.[2] (For a good summary of critical grapplings with "this anthropomorphized phantom," see Nunning.[3]) Among cognitive narratologists, Palmer remains skeptical of the possibility of maintaining the distinction between the narrator and the implied author, observing that though "clear in the case of first person narrators, [this distinction] can be problematical in other cases." As Palmer sees it, when it comes to practical discussion of many novels, it is not even possible to maintain a "coherent distinction between the agency that is responsible for selecting and organizing the events (as Prince describes the role of the implied author), and the voice that recounts them (the narrator)."[4]

On the one hand, I see Palmer's view as broadly corroborated by what we are learning about our metarepresentational capacity. Constantly keeping track of the difference between the implied author and the narrator means in effect retaining a source tag behind every minute instance of narration and, moreover, doing so *after* you have already bracketed the whole story as a metarepresentation pointing to the author. It means, for example, saying to yourself as you read *Pride and Prejudice* and come across Lydia Bennet's elopement with Wickham: "Austen claims that Lydia ran away with Wickham"—a kind of micro source-tracking[5] that is simply too cognitively expensive and as such is not a default mode of our reading process. It seems to me that it is precisely because we do *not,* in our everyday reading practices, trace back to the author every single representation contained in the text (once we have bracketed off the *whole* fictional text as a metarepresentation) that the writers fond of unreliable narrators can play their complicated games with their readers.

On the other hand, I am not really that invested in debating either the overall usefulness of the category of the implied author or the cognitive feasibility of maintaining such a category. What I find more fascinating is the cultural history of the figure of the implied author. Susan Lanser has characterized its introduction into the narratological discourse in the early 1960s as a "problematic compromise." As she sees it, the figure of the implied author "not only adds another narrating subject to the heap but it fails to resolve what it sets out to bridge: the author-narrator relationship." At the same time, at a "crucial moment in literary history the word 'implied' did provide a respectable prefix with which the mention of the author became permissible."[6]

Lanser is referring to the time when the terms *author* and *reader* had "all but disappeared from the analysis of point of view, because they were not considered properly textual personae." By 1960, "Anglo-American New Criticism had taken as a basic tenet the autonomy of the text as a concrete linguistic object; thus it became virtually taboo to speak of the text as an act of communication among real people in the real world."[7] I find Lanser's account of the compensatory function of the term *implied author* particularly gratifying from the cognitive perspective I champion here. It appears that, prevented from speaking about the "real" author behind the fictional narrative, critics nevertheless found a way of *still* retaining a source tag behind this narrative—by introducing the category of the "implied" author. Compare this act of cognitive compensation to the one that I described earlier, when talking about Barthes's-Foucault's concept of the "Death of the Author." Here, the author is substituted by the "implied" author; there, the author was substituted by the reader. It seems that a culture *will* find a way to insinuate a source tag into its perception of a representation that is a metarepresentation. A work of fiction *has* to have an agent-specifying source tag affixed to it, however extravagant (e.g., "dead" or "implied") that agent may seem at certain historical junctures.

Let us give this screw yet another turn. The implied author is alive and well and entering his/her forties. As a heated discussion at a recent meeting of the Society for the Study of Narrative Literature demonstrated, this figure continues to exercise a strong pull on critics' imagination, with some of my colleagues questioning our need for such a concept and others reaffirming its usefulness. I am tempted to see such debates as a function of the source-monitoring ability played out in a very particular social environment, that is, among the people self-selected to pay attention to textual ambiguities. Here is how it works:

Our source-monitoring adaptations are generally on the lookout for material to work on, ready to seize on any evidence that a given representation could be processed as a metarepresentation. Nothing is sacred, nothing is safe from being turned from "truth" to a representation accompanied by a source tag and thus processed under advisement ("Chocolate is good for you." "Says who?"), although different ideological climates may actively encourage some types of metarepresentational processing and discourage others. Combine this general cognitive tendency with the professional training of a literary critic, and it is not unlikely that this individual would be more attuned to the possibility of seeing not just *one* source behind *Pride and Prejudice* (i.e., Jane Austen) but a rich hierarchy of sources (i.e., the "real" Jane Austen, the "implied" Jane Austen, the "narrator" of *Pride of Prejudice,* and so forth). In other words, whereas our shared cognitive adaptation for source-monitoring makes it in principle possible both for me and for my first-year students to see those multiplying authors behind the text, it might be easier for me than for them (at least initially) to achieve such a split vision. I think of the relative ease with which it comes to me as my cognitive-professional hazard.

~10~

RICHARDSON'S *CLARISSA*: THE PROGRESS OF THE ELATED BRIDEGROOM

*W*hen I think of fiction and cognition in literary-historical terms, attempting to reconstruct, in particular, the development of the motif of the "Quixotic" imagination from Cervantes to Nabokov, I inevitably return to Samuel Richardson's novel *Clarissa* (1747–48). *Clarissa* has been deservedly admired by numerous literary critics, and it is currently going through a pedagogical renaissance, being increasingly taught, even in its forbidding 1,500-page entirety, in a variety of graduate and undergraduate college courses. With the advent of a "cognitive" approach to literature, however, it also ought to be acknowledged as a massive and unprecedented-in-Western-literary-history experimentation with the readers' Theory of Mind and metarepresentational ability, experimentation that certainly made possible the later-day mind-games played by *Lolita* and *Pale Fire*.[1]

In this section I argue that in *Clarissa,* Richardson created a kind of protagonist that we today would call an unreliable narrator. I follow a series of episodes in the novel that increasingly force the reader to doubt the trustworthiness of at least one of its two narrators, and I discuss the cognitive effects of being confronted with a character who seems to believe his own lies. I suggest, in particular, that the presence of such a personage induces in us a state of metarepresentational uncertainty, thus providing a rich stimulation for our Theory of Mind.

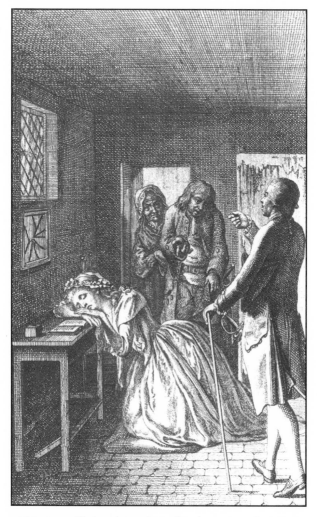

FIGURE 2. Clarissa dying. Reproduced courtesy of McMaster University Library.

(a) Mind-Games in Clarissa

Clarissa is a story of two brilliant young people, Clarissa Harlowe and Robert Lovelace, fatally misreading each other's minds in the course of their deeply troubled courtship. Lovelace, a paradigmatic eighteenth-century "rake," committed to seducing and subsequently abandoning incautious virgins, and Clarissa, a paragon of beauty, piety, and foresight, live out the eighteenth-century version of the "ultimate challenge": will Clarissa convert Lovelace to her exalted system of values and prove that "the reformed rake makes the best husband," or will Lovelace sweet-talk, cheat, and intimidate Clarissa into cohabitation without marriage, his "darling scheme" and his sign of "triumph" over the whole female sex and their pretensions to "virtue"?

Structured as a series of epistolary exchanges between Clarissa and her confidante, Anna Howe, Lovelace and *his* confidante, John Belford, and the occasional letters from and to their respective families, the novel is simultaneously claustrophobic and boundless. The protagonists are mostly confined to their writing-desks, reporting to their respective friends in painstaking detail their endeavors to guess, second-guess, plant, anticipate, and interpret each other's thoughts. The outcome of this obsessive mind-reading is such that Clarissa and Lovelace stop communicating altogether and die, or, rather, commit what could be considered thinly veiled acts of suicide. Clarissa wills herself to die (figure 2), possibly out of commitment to her developing view of herself as a tragic heroine—indeed, a martyr—who moves inexorably toward her terrible and instructive end,[2] possibly from depression induced by Lovelace's manipulation of her reality, a manipulation that makes her feel that none of the mainstays of her moral world—familial love, compassion of the strong for the weak, communal ties—can survive when confronted with playful but determined evil. Lovelace dies because he came to be so emotionally invested in her that he cannot go on after she passes away.

Before I turn to examining Richardson's experimentation with our metarepresentational capacity, let me make a point that may sound like old news to you by now. This point, however, cannot be repeated often enough in a book that hopes to put the cognitive-evolutionary concept of the Theory of Mind on the map of contemporary literary studies. Clarissa and Lovelace may be preternaturally adept at planning and deflecting each other's mental gambits, an intellectual one-upmanship that marks them as exceptional among other characters in the novel and justifies the appellations of "genius" generously bestowed upon them throughout the narrative. And yet the truly amazing and sustained feat of mind-reading takes place not when Clarissa "sees through" Lovelace's new contrivance or when Lovelace anticipates her seeing through it and prepares a plan B. It takes place when we as readers of Richardson's novel attribute the generous capacity for thoughts and desires to each fictional character, however tenuously delineated, and then proceed to interpret his or her behavior in terms of his or her underlying mental world, supplying a myriad of absent links, assumptions, and tacit explanations that allow us to see the story as a rich and emotionally coherent whole. In our interactions with *Clarissa* (or any other work of fiction), we take our own mind-reading capacity completely for granted and notice it no more than we notice oxygen when we wake up in the morning, an obliviousness which does not, however, render either oxygen or our ToM less important for our everyday life.

Back to *Clarissa* and metarepresentationality. One of the central premises of Richardson's novel is that its male protagonist is a consummate liar. The intellectual one-upmanship between Lovelace and Clarissa that I have just mentioned is set in motion by his constant endeavors to deceive her. He plots behind her back to set her own family against her; he introduces to her as seemingly respectable people a bevy of prostitutes and criminals; he forges her letters; he dons disguises and draws unsuspecting strangers into assisting him in tricking her.

But, you may point out, a lying protagonist is hardly news for a fictional narrative. How is Lovelace different, say, from Milton's Satan, who manipulates his fellow fallen angels, assumes different identities to deceive the guardian angels of Paradise, and, finally, lies to Eve?

The difference between Milton's and Richardson's antiheroes is Satan's ability to keep track of himself as the source of his representations of the world. That is, when he lies, he (mostly) knows that he lies. Moreover, Milton's poem features an omnipresent narrator who provides a running commentary on Satan's misrepresentation of reality. For example, when Satan approaches Eve in the garden in the guise of a snake, he is said to begin "his fraudulent temptation" (IX; 531); when he ends that fateful speech, the narrator observes that "his words replete with guile / Into [Eve's] heart too easy entrance won" (IX;11. 733–34). This commentary helps us to see the difference between the world "as it is," or at least as perceived by that omnipresent narrator, and the world as represented by Satan. Our cognitive predisposition to monitor sources of information thus enables us to make sense of the poem; when Satan, "enclosed in serpent" (IX;11. 494–95) tells Eve that he was miraculously "endued . . . with human voice" (1. 561) after eating the forbidden fruit, we know that he, and only he, is the source of that false representation, and we know that he knows it, too.

The same cognitive predisposition, however, could be used to disorient the reader, as in *Clarissa.* To begin with, Lovelace seems to have a selective problem with monitoring sources of his representations, regularly failing to keep track of himself as the source of his fantasies about the world. In other words, unlike Milton's Satan, when Lovelace lies, he at times appears not to know that he lies. Moreover, because *Clarissa* is an *epistolary* novel (unlike, for example, *Don Quixote,* which also features a self-deceiving protagonist), we do not have here an omnipresent narrator who would alert us to the glaring discrepancy between Lovelace's version of what is going on and an alternative, perhaps truer, version. Instead, *Clarissa* is, in effect, a first-person narrative split between the two main protagonists. Consequently, it takes us some time—about five hundred pages or even much longer—to realize that one of the narrators of the story is misleading not just Clarissa but also himself and, consequently, us.

What it all adds up to is that in Lovelace we have an early instance of an unreliable narrator (a literary device typically associated with modernist and postmodernist fiction). As discussed in previous sections, the presence of such a narrator forces us to begin to question at some point during our reading numerous pieces of information that we would have otherwise processed as true within the fictional world of the story. Worse yet, since the narrator himself seems to believe in what he is saying and marshals evidence that supports his version of events, we may never find out what has "really" happened. We thus close the book with a strange feeling that the state of cognitive uncertainty that it induced in us will never be fully resolved. We will never know which representations within the story deserve to be treated as "true" and which have to remain metarepresentations with a source tag pointing to the first-person narrator.

Let us see now how *Clarissa* draws us into this state of metarepresentational uncertainty. Writers wishing to spring an unreliable narrator onto their readers frequently begin with a sly maneuver of establishing him/her as not only quite reliable but also *more* reliable than other characters in the story. As Ronald Blythe puts it, "[C]harmers must charm before the charmed begin to smell a rat."[3] That's exactly what Richardson does in *Clarissa.* He opens the novel with a description of a familial turmoil that spins out of control, and he then introduces Lovelace as somebody who sees clearly into the messy passions of everybody else and can tell us what is really going on.

Here is what happens. Clarissa's parents, siblings, and uncles are angry at her because she refuses to marry an obnoxious wealthy suitor of their providing. Her rejection of that man, they are convinced, stems from her secret preference for Lovelace. The argument escalates quickly, with both parties afraid and mistrustful of each other. Clarissa is grounded, denied the right to correspond with her best friend, all but disowned by her mother and father, threatened with forced marriage, and physically assaulted by her brother. It matters little that she proclaims her indifference to Lovelace and her willingness to abide by the wishes of her elders if only they don't make her marry the man that she abhors. For reasons that she cannot fathom—for she has been an obedient and truthful child all her life—they don't believe her.

After about one hundred pages of this family drama, we (but not Clarissa) finally learn why they don't. We are made privy to a letter (the first of many) from Lovelace to his friend Belford, in which he explains what fuels the fear and anger of the elder Harlowes. It turns out that he has been inflaming the passions of Clarissa's parents and siblings by bribing one of their own servants and using him to feed them information about Clarissa's supposed intention to elope with Lovelace. Lovelace has it all figured out. Persecuted by her own family—who would not believe her protestations of innocence since they listen to the servant who presumably knows her real intentions—Clarissa would soon be forced to run away from them. And whom would she run to, if not Lovelace, who has all the while been assuring her of his love and respect and begging her to take refuge from her unfeeling relatives with his own family? To get Clarissa out of her father's house and into his sole power is the goal toward which Lovelace is working with patience and prescience. He is the mastermind behind the commotion at the Harlowes—after hearing from him, we finally understand their motives fully.

Having thus established Lovelace as our privileged source of information about the tangled situation, Richardson proceeds to deepen that impression by demonstrating Lovelace's unusual perceptiveness when it comes to figuring out other people's states of mind. Roughly one-third into the novel comes a "Miss Partington" episode, which confirms Lovelace as not only an inveterate plotter but also an insightful mind-reader. Here is how Richardson builds up to it:

Lovelace has finally tricked Clarissa into leaving her family and eloping with him. He then manipulates her into staying together in rented apartments in London, at a house that, as he told Clarissa, is owned by a respectable widow of an Army officer, who lets rooms and takes care of her two nieces. In reality, the house is a brothel; the owner, "Mrs. Sinclair," is a madam; and her nieces are prostitutes, turned into such by Lovelace who had earlier seduced and abandoned them. Clarissa is introduced to the inhabitants of the house as Lovelace's wife, when, in fact, both Mrs. Sinclair and her nieces are convinced that Lovelace does not want to marry Clarissa and instead intends to make her his kept mistress. Lovelace explains to Clarissa that since they spend so much time together, they have to pose as a married couple (even though they keep separate bedrooms) in order not to scandalize the (presumably) respectable inhabitants of the house. However, the real reason that he wants Clarissa to address him as a husband in front of Mrs. Sinclair and her "nieces" is that if he then happens to rape Clarissa, he would have the witnesses who could testify in the court of law that Clarissa considered herself married to him and thus cannot possibly complain of any sexual liberties he has taken with his "lawfully wedded" wife.

One evening Lovelace throws a party to which he invites four of his equally debauched male friends and another former mistress of his, one Miss Partington (now, too, a prostitute), who is presented to Clarissa as a young lady of good family, wealth, and virtue. Miserable as she is about perpetuating the lie about her marriage, Clarissa is prevailed to continue posing as "Mrs. Lovelace" in front of his friends, not knowing that they are all apprised of the true state of affairs and of Lovelace's motives for making Clarissa believe that they all think that she is married to him. Later that night, Clarissa is asked if Miss Partington can stay in her room for the night, for Mrs. Sinclair has presumably run out of beds to accommodate her illustrious guests. Although, on the surface of it, there is nothing strange about such an application, particularly as Miss Partington is supposed to be a woman of birth and virtue, the "over-cautious" Clarissa, not even knowing exactly what she is afraid of, but mindful of the house full of the intoxicated "gentlemen of free manners" (546), turns the request down. As readers soon find out (Lovelace explains it all in his letter to Belford), Clarissa was correct in her fears. Lovelace planned to use Miss Partington to open Clarissa's door at night and let him into her bedroom, after which, had he raped her, she would have had even fewer chances to sue him later since now not only Mrs. Sinclair and her "nieces" but also four of Lovelace's friends could testify that she went by the name of his wife.

On the morning after the failed Miss Partington scheme, Lovelace asks Clarissa what it was that Miss Partington and Mrs. Sinclair wanted from her last night. He then reports in his letter to Belford that Clarissa "*artfully* made lighter of her denial of Miss for a bedfellow than she *thought* of it, I could see that; for it was plain she supposed there was room for me to think she had been either over-*nice,* or over-*cautious*" (552; emphasis in the original).

Note, first of all, the multiple levels of intentionality embedded in this sentence. We can map them as follows:

Lovelace *intends* Belford (and with him, the readers) to be *believe* that

Clarissa *did not want* him to *think* that she did, in fact, *suspect* that he *had some ulterior motives* in having Miss Partington spend a night in her room.

Depending on how we count, this sentence embeds from four to six levels of intentionality. This, as I have argued in Part I, makes it somewhat more challenging for the reader and, subsequently, subtly heightens our admiration of the ease with which the clever and observant Lovelace can figure out what other people, including Clarissa, are thinking.

It is the tragedy of both Lovelace and Clarissa, however, that their occasionally accurate readings of each other's states of mind never translate into the actual meeting of the minds. Paradoxically, the better Lovelace "reads" Clarissa, the more persistently he misinterprets her and the more assuredly he embarks upon the course of action destined to destroy any chances for their happiness together. In this particular case, Lovelace uses his insight into Clarissa's fear and her reluctance to let him see her fear to justify his intensified plotting against her. As he reasons now in his imaginary conversation with her, "[S]ince thou reliest more on thy own precaution than upon my honour; be it unto thee as thou apprehendest, fair one!" (553).[4]

Needless to say, the more Lovelace plots, the less Clarissa wants to marry the heartless liar. This effectively renders impotent the main lever that Lovelace could hope to use to control her (and any other woman): his alleged intention to be "reformed" and to make the heroic woman who succeeds in reforming him his wife. Feeling how the source of power is slipping away from him, Lovelace grows both more desperate and cruel in his treatment of Clarissa, which, of course, makes her even more adamant in her decision to escape him.

Richardson's novel thus articulates, with a hitherto-unprecedented intensity and detail, the theme of the correlation between arduous mind-reading and tragic misunderstanding. Remaining prominent in the later-day novels adhering to what I call the Quixotic tradition, such as *Lolita,* this theme is inextricably bound with our metarepresentational ability. Mind-reading is a crucial aspect of our everyday existence, but a character too occupied with figuring out other people's states of mind, and, worse, flaunting his ability to "see though" other people, runs a grave metarepresentational danger: he can easily lose track of himself as the source of his representations of the other person's mental world. He may take what really is a *meta*representation *with himself as a source tag*—for example, "*I think* that Clarissa is blushing in response to my half-hearted marriage proposal because she badly wants to marry me, poor dear, but is ashamed to acknowledge it" (to paraphrase one of Lovelace's typical sentiments) as a representation *without any source tag*, for example, "Clarissa is blushing in response to my half-hearted marriage proposal because she badly wants to marry me, poor dear, but is ashamed to acknowledge it."

Of course, this is by definition an impoverished and frequently quite wrong ascription of Clarissa's state of mind. In this particular case, Clarissa is blushing in response to Lovelace's lukewarm proposal not because she desperately wants to marry him—as a matter of fact, she doubts more and more that he would *ever* be able to make a suitable husband for her—but also because she is thinking of her friend Anna's most recent letter, in which Anna pragmatically advises her to take Lovelace up on his first word and marry him out of hand in order to avoid being censured by the world for eloping with a rake. Clarissa's blushing is indicative of a complex amalgam of feelings, for she is aware of the truth of Anna's advice, angry with herself for putting herself in such an ambiguous situation, and half-ashamed at realizing that, in spite of everything, she is still attracted to Lovelace.

It is only natural that Lovelace would have no access to these complex feelings—he is not, after all, telepathic—but what is more important is that by losing track of *himself* as the source of his representations of Clarissa's mind, he is foreclosing any potential for thinking that Clarissa may have complex feelings not accessible to him and thus subsequently revising his past misconceptions. By keeping track (that is, as much as we can, for sometimes it is not that simple) of ourselves as sources of our representations of other people's minds, we remain humbly aware of the possibility of making a mistake in our interpretation of their thoughts. So in *Pride and Prejudice*, Mr. Darcy can change for the best and deserve happiness with Elizabeth Bennet because he is aware of himself as the source of his misinterpretation of Jane Bennet's mind (i.e., his former belief that she did not really love his friend Mr. Bingley). By contrast, Lovelace does not correct, until it is too late, his readings of other people's states of mind—he would rather try to correct reality to fit his delusions.

Any manifestly successful instance of mind-reading then becomes a trap for the person whose ability to keep track of himself as a source of his representations of other people's mental stances is somewhat compromised. Although I am not interested in diagnosing Lovelace as mildly schizophrenic, I do want to apply here, albeit tentatively and perhaps more metaphorically than literally, Frith's suggestion that the reason schizophrenic patients go on reading minds even though they do it all wrong is that, unlike individuals with autism, who know that "their inferences [of mental states] are likely to be wrong," schizophrenics "know well from past experiences that it is useful and easy to infer the mental states of others [and] will go on doing this even when the mechanism no longer works properly."[5] Lovelace's dangerous propensity to ignore himself as the source of his representations of Clarissa's mind and instead perceive these representations as accurate reflections of her mental stances is so persistent because it gets positive reinforcement on the occasions when he does read her mind quite correctly, as so happens, for example, in the above-discussed episode of Miss Partington as Clarissa's intended bedfellow. Like schizophrenic patients—and, again, I am using this comparison guardedly—Lovelace knows from his "past experiences" that he can be very perceptive in inferring mental states of others and has clearly benefited from doing so in his endeavor to seduce one virgin after another. With these memories of past and present successes alive in his mind, he will continue to treat his interpretations of other people's mental states as objectively true, even if this strategy backfires again and again in his relationship with Clarissa and finally makes any amicable communication between them impossible.

(b) Enter the Reader

At this point, we have to start considering the effect that Lovelace's peculiar brand of unreflective mind-reading has on the reader of the novel. Strictly speaking, I have already implicitly introduced the reader into the discussion above when I said that Lovelace happens to infer correctly Clarissa's mind in the Miss Partington episode. *We know* that Lovelace's inference is correct because we have access to Clarissa's letter to Anna Howe—in which Clarissa explains why she did not let Miss Partington share her bed—whereas Lovelace merely *thinks* that he is right simply because he is convinced that he is never wrong in his assessment of other people's mental states. In other words, we, the readers, are tacitly coerced by the novel into accepting Lovelace's assessment of Clarissa's thoughts as rather accurate, in fact, more accurate on many occasions than the assessment offered by Clarissa herself in her letters to Anna. Clarissa, after all, has to sound invariably proper and virtuous, whereas Lovelace is under no such obligation and can be as cynical and straightforward as he wishes.

Lovelace's fraught tendency to ignore himself as the source of his representations of the world thus becomes *our* tendency, too, especially in the early parts of the story, when we turn to his letters to find out what has *really* transpired.

Establishing Lovelace as a relatively trustworthy source of our representations—that is, drawing us into temporarily forgetting that his account of the events should be processed with a source tag, such as, "Lovelace claims that . . ."—is a crucial part of the metarepresentational game that the novel plays with the reader. The more we trust Lovelace as a privileged source of information, the greater is our shock and disorientation when in the second third of the novel we start coming across sentiments that imply that Lovelace may be losing it and, in fact, may have never had it together in the first place.

Here is one such moment. Clarissa's loyal servant Hannah had been earlier taken away from her. Lovelace has just heard that Hannah might be available once more to serve her lady. Lovelace cannot let her come near Clarissa because, to advance his scheme of seduction, he has to keep her friendless and surrounded by his agents. Lovelace muses in a letter to Belford:

> I have just now heard that her Hannah hopes to be soon well enough to attend her young lady, when in London. It seems the girl has had no physician. I must send her one, out of pure love and respect to her mistress. Who knows but medicine might weaken nature, and strengthen the disease?—As her malady is not a fever, very likely it may do so—But perhaps her hopes are too forward. Blustering weather in this month yet—And that is bad for rheumatic complaints. (554)

Lovelace has been plotting and scheming, and manipulating everybody before, but this is the first time he contemplates sending an *assassin* (i.e., a doctor who would administer a poison) to do in an inconvenient person. But perhaps this is just an empty talk: he is simply kidding, keeping up the image of the All-Powerful Rake he's been cultivating in his letters to Belford. But does *he* know that he is kidding? Reading the passage, we get the unsettling impression that Lovelace might have temporarily lost the ability to experience the difference between the world as imagined by Lovelace—in which he is indeed the most gorgeous, powerful, and dangerous man alive, with corrupt doctors at his disposal and no law to stop him—and the world outside of his imagination. This impression becomes even stronger as we read on and realize that Lovelace implies that God himself, by ensuring that the weather stays "blustering," is helping Lovelace along in his plans.

Again, knowing Lovelace's lively sense of humor (of which he is inordinately proud, too), we may hope that he is joking when he makes God one of his agents. The passage, however, gives no positive reassurance to our hopes. Had Richardson intended to provide such a reassurance, it would have been easy enough. Lovelace could have added to his musings about Hannah, physicians, and blustering weather something to the effect of, "or so I tell myself as I sit here and figure out how to subdue this proud beauty" (i.e., Clarissa). Because he does not say anything like it, we as readers have two options. We can make our lives easier and insist—in spite of the absence of any clear textual evidence—that Lovelace is ironic and knows it. We can remind ourselves that, after all, he is writing a letter to one of his friends and admirers and thus has to sustain his tone of swaggering self-assurance in order to impress his addressee. We can hope that this addressee, John Belford, is such a close friend that Lovelace can count on Belford's knowing which of his bizarre claims should be taken at their face value and which should not. Thus, with a bit of effort, we can read all this comforting information into the text and decide that Lovelace is joking. Alternatively—and much less comfortably—we can remain suspended in a state of uncertainty, not quite understanding how seriously we should take anything that Lovelace says at this point.

Moreover, as the story goes on, Richardson begins to downright ply us with similar instances of Lovelace's conflating *his* version of reality with reality itself and forcefully imposing his conflation on his audience. (One effect of such a conflation is that we begin to experience a feeling of mental vertigo not dissimilar to the one induced upon Clarissa, who is not able to tell, at least for a while, what is really going on around her.) Soon after the failed Miss Partington ploy, Lovelace conceives of another stratagem, different in design but tending to the same end. The women of the house are instructed to start a small, manageable fire in the middle of the night, a fire that could be easily put out, but not before the terrified and half-dressed Clarissa unlocks her door and steps out, afraid of being burned. *Then* Lovelace can enter her room on the pretence of saving her and calming her down, and stay in that room for the rest of the night.

At the appointed hour, as Lovelace sits at his writing-desk rereading a letter from his friend, he hears a commotion outside his rooms, the first stirrings of the "fire" scenario that he had himself carefully planned with the women of the house. Here is Lovelace's account of his immediate reaction:

Soft, oh virgin saint, and safe as soft be thy slumbers!—

. . . But, what's the matter! What's the matter! What a *double*—But the uproar abates! What a *double coward* am I?—Or is it that I am taken in a cowardly minute? for heroes have their fits of *fear;* cowards their *brave* moments; and virtuous ladies, all but my Clarissa, their moment *critical*—

But thus coolly enjoying thy reflections in a hurricane!—Again the confusion's renewed!—

What! Where!—How came it!—

Is my beloved safe!—

Oh wake not too roughly my beloved!—(722)

To understand how the passage works our metarepresentational ability, we first need to realize that Lovelace is uncharacteristically nervous about the immediate prospect of forcing himself into a young woman's bed. Hence every mention of "confusion," "hurricane," and the "uproar" can be read as describing both the fake turmoil among the inhabitants of the house prompted by the fake fire and the real turmoil in Lovelace's soul.

Lovelace is surprised by his feelings—"What's the matter? . . . What a double coward am I?"—and wants to rally his spirit. One way of psyching himself up for going through with his plan is to work himself into the state of mind of somebody who is as surprised and frightened by the fire as Clarissa herself is. If Lovelace can convince *himself* that he and Clarissa were thrown together in the middle of the night by the accident and not by his premeditated plan, it would be easier for him to act more naturally in Clarisssa's room, thus taking some edge off his presently unbearable anxiety. (Believing in one's own lie could be cognitively liberating because it frees up the energy spent on processing that extra level of metarepresentational framing stipulated by oneself as a source tag.) Consequently, when Lovelace wishes "soft slumber" to his Clarissa, he knows well that her slumber will be rudely interrupted this very minute, and yet he *endeavors* to sound as if he did not know it. Similarly, when Lovelace perks up at the noise and asks anxiously, "What's the matter? "What's the matter?" and then, when he does not hear anything else for a couple of seconds and notes with relief that "the uproar" has apparently "abated," he is faking the natural reaction of the person disturbed by strange sounds around the house but then lulled back to the feeling of security by the temporary quiet. When the "confusion's renewed," Lovelace responds as a man frightened and surprised anew ("What! Where!—How came it!"), moreover as a man who is so dedicated to his "beloved" that her safety is the first thing that comes into his mind even when his own life is apparently in danger ("Is my beloved safe!") and who is determined to spare her any unnecessary anxiety upon this life-threatening occasion ("Oh wake not too roughly my beloved!").

This sequence of spontaneous and noble emotional responses is, of course, the exact opposite of what must be really going on through Lovelace's head, for the whole point of the "fire" plot is to terrify and disorient Clarissa to such a degree that she would have no strength to withstand his sexual attack. But again, as in the earlier episode, in which Lovelace contemplates sending an assassin to Hannah, the text offers us no reassurance that he is consistently aware of his role-playing. He might be so in the beginning of the scene, when he comments first on his nervousness and then on his ability to "coolly" enjoy his "reflections in a hurricane"; but toward its end ("What! Where!—How came it!"), he has, as far as we know, completely taken on his make-believe personality. It *might be* that by the time Lovelace begins to implore some figment of his imagination ("Oh wake not too roughly my beloved"), he is thinking to himself, as it were, "I pretend that I am a perfect lover caught unawares by fire"— a metarepresentation with himself as a source of representation. But as readers we get very little indication that he *is* thinking this, and we see instead a man who appears, at least for the time being, to sincerely believe his own lie, an *unreliable narrator* par excellence.

One of the most striking instances of this elimination of himself as a source of his fantasies comes when Clarissa, shortly after the fire episode (which, indeed, frightens but does not subdue her) escapes the hateful brothel and breaks free of Lovelace. Though desperate at first at having lost the object of his obsession, Lovelace is soon cheered up by finding out that she is residing in the neighboring town of Hampstead (Clarissa cannot simply go back to her family because she has completely antagonized them by eloping with the rake). Lovelace is even disappointed at the ease with which he has located his victim: had she concealed herself better, his game of pursuit would have been more exciting.

As he is getting ready to go to Hampstead to retrieve Clarissa, Lovelace calls for the assistance of one of his numerous agents, a "vile and artful pander" to his "debaucheries" (38), Patrick MacDonald, a wanted criminal, kept from prosecution only through the intervention of the rich and well-connected Lovelace. MacDonald has earlier appeared before Clarissa in the guise of a respectable gentleman, one Captain Tomlinson, presumably sent by her uncle, Antony Harlowe. As the fake "Captain Tomlinson" claims, Mr. Harlowe wants to see his niece respectably married to the man (i.e., Lovelace), who, for all that the world knows, has already seduced her, as a prerequisite to negotiating the truce between Clarissa and her estranged parents. Mr. Harlowe has thus asked his dear old friend, the Captain, to meet with Mr. Lovelace and Clarissa and find out how the matters stand between them. All these are lies, of course, invented by Lovelace to subdue Clarissa. Lovelace brings in the sham Captain because he desperately needs Clarissa to still want to marry him, if no longer out of love for him, then as the means to be reconciled with her beloved uncle and later the rest of her family. As long as she still wants—for *any* reason— to become his wife, he can have some source of emotional power over her.

Obeying Lovelace's urgent summons, MacDonald, a.k.a. Captain Tomlinson, hastens to Mrs. Sinclair's house ready to accompany Lovelace on his trip to Hampstead. Lovelace's description of Captain Tomlinson's arrival and their subsequent conversation emerges as downright surreal if we keep in mind that every person in the house knows who MacDonald really is and what he is doing here, and the only "spectator" who would have benefited from keeping up the pretence is Clarissa, and she is gone. In the long quote below, I have interspersed Lovelace's full account of the Captain's entrance and their subsequent trip to Hampstead with my comments in italics:

A gentleman to speak with me, Dorcas?—Who can want me thus early? [*Dorcas is one of Lovelace's "agents" employed to keep an eye on Clarissa and posing, for Clarissa's benefit, as a poor relative of Mrs. Sinclair. She certainly knows who the "gentleman" is, and Lovelace knows that she knows. Why then does he keep up the pretence in front of her?*]

Captain Tomlinson, sayest thou! Surely he must have traveled all night!—Early riser as I am, how could he think to find me up *thus* early? [*MacDonald certainly did not travel all night, for he resides nearby to be on hand when Lovelace needs him to play his role in front of Clarissa, and he is here "thus early" because Lovelace would have destroyed him had he not obeyed his summons immediately. Again, Dorcas knows all this, and Lovelace knows that she knows, and yet the role-playing goes on.*]

. . . Dear captain, I rejoice to see you: just in the nick of time . . . Strange news since I saw you, captain! Poor mistaken lady!—But you have too much goodness, I know, to reveal to her uncle Harlowe the errors of this capricious beauty. It will all turn out for the best. You must accompany me part of the way. I know the delight you take in composing differences. But 'tis the task of the prudent to heal the breeches made by the rashness and folly of the impudent.

[Lovelace's pretence in front of MacDonald does have one logical explanation: he needs to "instruct" him on how to view what has happened between Lovelace and Clarissa, that is, on how the real Captain Tomlinson, had such a person existed, might have perceived the situation, without knowing what is really going on. We may say, thus, that Lovelace performs the role of the bridegroom injured by his capricious bride in front of MacDonald to make it psychologically easier for the latter to later perform his role of a respectable peacemaker in front of Clarissa. Still, when we read this passage—for I am concerned here primarily with the effect that Lovelace's deep play has on the reader—we cannot help feeling that on some level Lovelace believes in what he is saying.]

And now (all around me so still, and so silent) the rattling of the chariot-wheels at a street's distance do I hear!—And to this angel of a lady I fly!

Reward, oh God of Love (the cause is thy own); reward thou, as it deserves, my suffering perseverance!—Succeed my endeavors to bring back to thy obedience, this charming fugitive!—Make her acknowledge her rashness; repent her insults; implore my forgiveness; beg to be reinstated in my favour, and that I will bury in oblivion the remembrance of her heinous offence against thee, and against me, thy faithful votary.

[This is Lovelace's "prayer" as he is ready to board his chariot to go to Hampstead. This part is particularly unsettling because here Lovelace is presumably speaking to himself and thus truly has no reason to pretend that Clarissa is the one who was rash, insulted him, and needs to implore his forgiveness, and not the other way around. It is possible that, as in the earlier episode with the fake fire, Lovelace is nervous about his forthcoming meeting with Clarissa and needs to work himself up into the state of mind of the injured bridegroom; that is, he needs to temporarily forget that he himself is the source of his representation, "I am an injured bridegroom." However, we get no direct textual evidence of his nervousness, and all we see instead is a man fully committed to his version of reality. Richardson explicitly and brilliantly articulates here, for the first time in Western literary history, the mental stance of the stalker. This stance is crucially bound with the stalker's tendency to eliminate himself as a source of his representation, "She loves me and she wants me, but she is coy and she is hurting me by her excessive coyness, so she needs to be punished and then forgiven," and instead perceive this representation as an objective reflection of what is going on.]

The chariot at the door!—I come! I come!—

[Lovelace is fully in his role of an eager bridegroom on the way to attend his beloved, who, he is joyfully confident, will soon make everything right between them.]

I attend you, good captain—

Indeed, sir—

[This is MacDonald speaking.]

Pray, sir—civility is not ceremony.

[We infer from this exchange that Lovelace is treating the fake Captain with an exaggerated courtesy, perhaps bowing and politely inviting him to walk through the door before himself. Had MacDonald been who he and Lovelace pretend he is—a respectable gentleman who does not approve of Lovelace's libertine ways but has to deal with him to oblige his old friend, Antony Harlowe—Lovelace's humble behavior would have made some sense. Given, however, that Lovelace is a rich aristocrat and MacDonald a proscribed criminal, sold to Lovelace soul and body, Lovelace's obeisance looks decidedly out of place. It is possible that Lovelace is ironic, but, considering the overall tone of the scene, it is also possible that the fictitious scenario that he has created has temporarily replaced any other reality for him.]

And now, dressed like a bridegroom, my heart elated beyond that of the most desiring one (attended by a footman whom my beloved never saw), I am already at Hampstead! (761)

This last sentence introduces an interesting variation on Lovelace's delusional reasoning. Lovelace is still stubbornly treating his own fantasy of the passionate romance between him and Clarissa as a true representation of reality. At the same time, his interjection about the footman whom his "beloved" never saw shows that he is aware that Clarissa will not be happy to see her "bridegroom" at all. Lovelace knows that the moment she saw her torturer's servant at Hampstead, she would flee again—hence his precaution about taking along the man she has never met. As any successful stalker, Lovelace thus retains some ability to see the world through the eyes of his victim, even though on a certain level his capacity for monitoring the source of his representations is compromised. And, contrary to what we often assume, seeing the world through another's eyes does not necessarily translate (it certainly does not in Lovelace's case!) into feeling compassion for that person. As cognitive psychologist Robert W. Mitchell observes in a related argument about the relationship between a successful deceiver and his/her victim:

Surprisingly, such ability to take the part of the other demonstrated in acumen need not result in any *sympathetic* or compassionate response to another's turmoil at being deceived. The deceiver can invent reasons why the other deserves to be deceived even while the deceiver recognizes that the victim would be psychologically better off without the deception. So the same imaginative propensity which allows someone to take the perspective of the other also allows the person to imagine the other from a perspective which discounts the other's perspective.[6]

Though coming from a different research angle, Mitchell's observation about the possibility of a "perspective which discounts the other's perspective" is compatible with the present argument about the "selectively compromised" metarepresentational ability of a stalker such as Lovelace. Richardson makes Lovelace constantly balance between making accurate assessments of given situations and pointedly ignoring the possibility that some parts of his assessment reflect primarily his own wishful thinking about what is going on. To a degree, we all engage in such balancing acts in our everyday life, which is why, when taken to the extreme, as in *Clarissa,* they remain both emotionally alien and unsettlingly recognizable.

Let me clarify the stakes of my twofold claim that Lovelace's metarepresentational ability is selectively compromised and that the novel cultivates the scenes that make the reader uncertain of whether Lovelace is fully aware that his representations of other people's mental states are, at least on some level, his own self-serving inventions. As I have pointed out earlier, I am not interested in diagnosing Lovelace as slightly schizophrenic. Neither am I invested in figuring out exactly which version of reality Lovelace *truly* believes in. Lovelace does not exist. The reader does exist, however, and so does the novel as massive and focused experimentation with that reader's cognitive adaptations. Thus, from the perspective of cognitive theory, the ultimate reason that Lovelace goes through his elaborate and peculiarly flawed mind-games is that it allows the narrative to engage, train, tease, and titillate our metarepresentational ability. Our brain is the focus of the novel's attention, its playground, its raison d'être, its meaning, whereas Lovelace, Clarissa, Dorcas, MacDonald, and all other characters are but the means for delivering this kind of wonderfully rich stimulation to the variety of cognitive adaptations making up our Theory of Mind.

Thus we may completely miss one level of Lovelace's manipulation of his reality or add another level, one that Richardson never intended. You may vehemently disagree with my interpretation of what Lovelace thinks, or of what he thinks that he thinks, or of what he wants Clarissa to believe, or of what Dorcas thinks MacDonald knows, and so on. We may profitably historicize Lovelace's mind processes, arguing, for example, that his lack of empathy with Clarissa and her middle-class kin is symptomatic of the general crisis of the aristocratic worldview during the Industrial Revolution, or that Richardson's particular interest in "sentiments" (i.e., feelings and their bodily and verbal expressions) was predicated upon certain developments in eighteenth-century natural philosophy. Every single one of our interpretations, honest mistakes, willful inventions, disagreements, and historical groundings will be imperceptibly but inescapably enmeshed with our ability to keep track of *who* in this novel *thinks what and when.* (If you doubt it, try making a single argument interpreting *Clarissa* within *any* framework of your choice without implicitly relying on such source-monitoring!) Because of its obsessive, unrelenting focus on people's representations of other people's mental states, *Clarissa* continues to structure our interpretations in this particular way (which is not to say that it renders them predictable—quite the opposite!).

By the same token, our ongoing arguments over historical, aesthetic, and personal meanings of *Clarissa* themselves expand the range of the novel's engagement with our metarepresentational ability. As we take in any given innovative reading of Richardson's magnum opus, it latches onto our individual metarepresentational ecology in a myriad of unpredictable ways. *Clarissa* thus reenters culture with every new interpretation because it is peculiarly geared to its exclusive environment: the responsive, dynamic, learning, and changing, but always metarepresenting, human mind.

~ 11 ~

NABOKOV'S *LOLITA*: THE DEADLY DEMON MEETS AND DESTROYS THE TENDERHEARTED BOY

The writer who creates an unreliable narrator runs an exciting and terrible risk: his or her readers may wind up believing the narrator's version of events. That is what happened to the author of *Clarissa* when he depicted Lovelace as apparently losing track of himself as the source of his fantasies. For most of the novel, Lovelace speaks of Clarissa not as his victim whom he hounds into depression and drives to suicide, but rather as his Juliet, his Beatrice, and his intended. If Richardson hoped that his discerning readers would mentally supply the source tags that Lovelace was shedding (e.g., "*Lovelace claims* that Clarissa is his intended"), he was quite mistaken. To his surprise and disappointment, eighteenth-century audiences (particularly the novel's target audience, women) bought Lovelace's version of reality. They fell in love with the rake and started demanding of the author that he end the story with a happy marriage between the angelic Clarissa and the man whom Richardson saw as a consummate stalker and rapist. In response to such demands Richardson prepared a revised edition of *Clarissa* (1751). It contained new scenes and pointed editorial notes, all of them tending to the same end—"blackening" the image of Lovelace[1] so that no future readers would be so naïve as to see him as a misguided, wretched, star-crossed but still romantic and desirable lover.

To see how much these efforts availed Richardson, take a look at the back cover of the most popular modern edition of the novel (Penguin, 1985).[2] It describes Lovelace as "easily the most charming villain in English literature" and claims that in this "fatally attracted pair, Richardson created lovers that haunt the imagination as Romeo and Juliet do, or Tristran and Isolde." Lovelace would have certainly been happy with this blurb. Didn't he strive mightily to persuade his audience that he is a new Romeo or Tristan even if his Isolde is occasionally unwilling to live up to her part?

An eerily similar fate (down to the phrasing of the cover blurb) awaited Nabokov's *Lolita,* another novel that challenged its readers' metarepresentational capacity with its figure of the unreliable narrator. *Lolita* features a sexual predator who tells the story of his "relationship" with a twelve-year-old girl by portraying himself as an ultimate star-crossed lover, doomed both by the social unacceptability of his love and by the stubborn unwillingness of the underage object of his passion to rise up to his transcendent feelings. "Betrayed" and "abandoned" by her—for, like Clarissa, Lolita manages to escape her jailer—he discovers new depths of feeling. He is ready to "shout [his] poor truth" to the cruel world until he is "gagged and half-throttled" by philistines, for he insists "the world know how much [he] loved [his] Lolita," even when she outgrew the tender age which made her attractive to pedophiles and turned into a seventeen-year-old woman, "pale and polluted, and big with another's child" (278).

Many readers swallowed Humbert Humbert's "poor truth" hook, line, and sinker. As Brian Boyd reports, one early reviewer saw the book's theme not as "the corruption of an innocent child by a cunning adult, but the exploitation of a weak adult by a corrupt child."[3] Another admitted that he had "come virtually to condone the violation . . . [for he] was plainly not able to muster up the tone of moral outrage. . . . Humbert is perfectly willing to say that he is a monster; we find ourselves less and less eager to agree with him."[4] Peter Rabinowitz highlights critical reactions to *Lolita* that strike me as particularly reminiscent of responses to *Clarissa*. He cites one distinguished critic who characterized Lolita and Humbert as "lovers" and their relationship as a "love affair," and another who saw Lolita as Humbert's "Juliet" (a "trivial" and "complicit" one, but still a Juliet).[5]

Like Richardson before him, Nabokov felt compelled to correct his readers' misperception. He pointed out that Humbert Humbert is a "vain and cruel wretch who manages to appear touching" (*Strong Opinions*, 94). Also like Richardson, Nabokov did not altogether succeed in his corrective endeavor.

I know that he did not, based on my own first experience of reading *Lolita* in my early twenties. I was profoundly touched by this story of Humbert's "impossible love." I felt deeply sorry (I say it now without any irony) for the witty, imaginative, and sensitive protagonist. As I was moving deeper and deeper into the novel, and Humbert was offering for my consideration one highly suspect supposition after another—that is, that some adolescent girls are demonic "nymphets" and that, though unaware of her special powers, one such "demon child" enchants the vulnerable Humbert into a mistimed and misplaced but poignant love affair—I *ought to* have started questioning the truth of such suppositions. I *ought to* have contemplated the possibility that Humbert is, as Nabokov righteously puts it, "a vain and cruel wretch," a ruthless pedophile, who exploits and victimizes the twelve-year-old orphan girl. Yet I did not.

Looking back at my first impression of the novel, I realize, to quote Boyd again, that I had "accepted only Humbert's version of himself." I responded to "Humbert's eloquence, not Nabokov's evidence." Boyd observes perceptively that by "making it possible to see Humbert's story so much from Humbert's point of view, Nabokov warns us to recognize the power of the mind to rationalize away the harm it can cause: the more powerful the mind, *the stronger our guard needs to be*" (232; emphasis added).

Understood within the context of a cognitive-evolutionary discourse, Boyd's notion of the "strong guard" corresponds, of course, to the concept of strong source-monitoring. In order not to be duped by liars, such as Lovelace and Humbert, who regularly lose—or seem to lose!—track of themselves as sources of their lies, we need to keep reapplying a very strong source tag, "Lovelace claims that" or "Humbert claims that," to every, however innocent and casual, observation such characters make and thus store it under the highest degree of advisement.

The trouble with this ideal stance of readerly vigilance is that it presupposes a constant state of suspicion that is difficult to maintain both in real life and in our engagement with the literary narrative. Note that there *is* a genre built around the hypertrophied readerly mistrust—the detective story—but it deploys a particular set of markers to signal to us early on that certain—by no means all!—information within it has to be stored with a high degree of metarepresentational framing. (I return to this issue again in Part III, dedicated to the detective novel.) By contrast, *Lolita* (although it *can* be read as a kind of a detective story) offers us little in the way of such markers. We do not realize until well into the novel, and sometimes not even then, that no information offered, however casually, by Humbert was safe from his manipulation and misrepresentation.

A novel featuring a first-person unreliable narrator thus exploits a particular niche in our cognitive makeup. Although source-monitoring *is* an integral part of our information management, *exaggerated and unrelentingly strong* source-monitoring can be rather cognitively expensive and thus not our default state of mind. It seems that we are not automatically open to incurring this large cognitive cost. Once we have bracketed the given fictional narrative *as a whole* as a metarepresentation par excellence stored with the perpetual source tag pointing to its author, we are not necessarily prepared to treat with suspicion the majority of representations that we encounter *within* it. That is, we *could,* but we need some reason for it. We need some indication that a given character (i.e., a source of this or that representation) is untrustworthy.

It follows, then, that *Lolita* manages to trick us into accepting Humbert's perspective on his relationship with his victim not because we are such gullible, naïve, undiscerning readers walking around like happy idiots with our mental guards down, but rather because Nabokov makes the most of certain regularities of our cognitive system of information management. The "powerful mind" against which Boyd warns us is really our own.[6]

(a) "Distributed" Mind Reading I:
A "comic, clumsy, wavering Prince Charming"

Here is one specific strategy that Nabokov uses to turn our source-monitoring ability to Humbert's advantage as he constructs his initial account of his and Lolita's "love affair." Nabokov "distributes" Humbert's version of events through the multiple minds within the narrative.[7] That is, he makes other characters indirectly tell Humbert's story the way he wants it to be told. The effect of this distributed representation is such that instead of dealing with just one source of information—Humbert, whose credibility we could have sized up pretty quickly—we are encouraged to perceive that we are dealing with multiple sources of information. Some of those sources—most of them, in fact—are introduced and removed so fast that we simply have no opportunity to evaluate their trustworthiness and even to realize that such an evaluation is necessary.

The minds through which the story is told in such a distributed manner include the mind of the implied reader, of Lolita, of her friends and family, and of the numerous people they meet on their travels. Typically, we would get Humbert's report of what happened to him and Lolita (e.g., they were stopped for speeding), followed by a representation of participants' thoughts and feelings (e.g., what the patrolmen who stopped the couple thought of them). The representation in question is supplied by Humbert in such a calculatedly quick, casual, and assured manner that we rarely pause and attempt to separate the observed behavior (here, of patrolmen) from Humbert's interpretation of a mental stance behind that behavior. Instead of registering the information as "Humbert claims that" (one crucial source tag) "when patrolmen stopped their car they thought" (another source tag) "X" (the representation itself), we instead register it as a representation with just *one* agent-specifying source tag: "when patrolmen stopped their car they thought X." Even if at this point in the narrative we have good reasons to mistrust Humbert, we have no reasons to mistrust the patrolmen we have just met (so to speak). We thus swallow the false representation because it is presented to us with an apparently trustworthy or, at least, *not conspicuously untrustworthy* source tag.

And, of course, whatever patrolmen and other strangers are thus reported to think or feel, their thoughts and feelings tacitly corroborate in a broad variety of ways Humbert's tale of the oversexed little demon seducing the innocent adult. The overall effect of those accumulating snapshots of states of mind is that the "vain and cruel wretch's" version of the story imperceptibly worms its way into the reader's consciousness.

The novel does contain several strategically chosen occasions on which we are allowed a glimpse at Humbert as the source of our representations of the characters' thoughts and feelings. The accretion of such occasions toward the end of the story finally forces us to start doubting what we have until now considered trustworthy reports of mental states. Many of these doubts, however, are never completely confirmed or cleared up. As in *Clarissa,* we are left with a feeling of a mental vertigo[8] induced by the author's consummate manipulation of our source-monitoring ability.

To begin to appreciate the range of strategies Humbert uses to erase himself as the source of every mental state reported by the novel, consider his early attempt to ascribe a certain memory to his readers. Here is Humbert telling us about his childhood on the Riviera:

> My very photogenic mother died in a freak accident (picnic, lightning) when I was three, and, save for a pocket of warmth in the darkest past, nothing of her subsists within the hollows and dells of memory, over which . . . the sun of my infancy had set: surely you all know those redolent remnants of day suspended, with the midges, about some hedge in bloom or suddenly entered and traversed by the rambler, at the bottom of a hill, in the summer dusk; a furry warmth, golden midges. (10)

As a matter of fact, we do *not* know "those redolent remnants of day suspended, etc." (unless we happen to be Lewis Carroll scholars, familiar with the "summer midges, each in its own golden afternoon" from his essay "'Alice' on the Stage"). Or to be more exact, we *did not* know them a moment ago. Humbert is addressing us with the complete assurance of somebody who simply helps us to bring back our own personal memories, when in fact he is planting those memories in our heads, for after we have read the sentence and tried to visualize that "hedge of bloom" and maybe even imagined ourselves as that "rambler" who traverses it at the bottom of the hill, it can be said that we do know what Humbert is talking about, sort of. Since it is very early in the novel and even the most discerning reader has little reason to treat with suspicion everything that Humbert says, we do not make a particular point of storing the representation of those blooming hedges with a strong source tag such as, "Humbert claims that we all remember that. . . ." Instead, we let those hedges be *almost* our memory, with just a whiff of a source tag pointing to the book.

Nabokov's strategy here is the same as Richardson's, when early on in *Clarissa* he establishes Lovelace as a penetrating mind-reader and thus our privileged source of information. The unreliable narrator has to initially come across as not only reliable but also quite unordinary in his/her ability to see through things and to articulate his/her visions. The eloquent, intelligent, and imaginative Humbert helps us to recover the warm and golden memories that we *almost* had all along even if we did not know that we had them. (And if we *do* catch the Carroll allusion, it may make us further appreciate the distinguished literary company we are thus invited to join.) Don't we want to surrender to such a promising narrator and just go along with his story? After all, he may regale us with more reconstructions of lovely if half-forgotten representations of our past.

But if we do surrender to such a narrator, pretty soon we find other states of mind imputed to us that are far less warm and pleasant, even if at that precise moment, we may not realize what exactly is being read "into" us. For example, when Humbert tries to come up with the best phrasing for the telegram that he has to send to a hotel to reserve a room in which he hopes to molest the drugged Lolita, he describes his difficulties as follows: "How some of my readers will laugh at me when I tell them the trouble I had with the wording of my telegram! What should I put Humbert and daughter? Humbert and small daughter?" (109). Going over these sentences quickly, one may miss Humbert's construction of "some of his readers" as cynical and experienced pedophiles.[9] For, on the one hand, we can all certainly relate to the feeling of momentary panic and uncertainty induced by the challenge of quickly translating our messy everyday comings and goings into an informative and respectable language required by some official form.[10] On the other hand, however, given the context of this particular act of translation, only a veteran pedophile would wholeheartedly "laugh" at Humbert's predicament, remembering, apparently with conscious superiority, all those occasions on which he himself (i.e., the implied reader) had to send such telegrams to hotels and knew exactly how to frame them so as not to excite the receptionists' suspicions.

This imputation of a state of mind to the reader happens so quickly that many of us do not register its implications the first time around: I certainly did not. The effect of not fully comprehending what Humbert is really saying here is that we half-consciously acquiesce to his view of himself as a babe in the woods, a romantic soul, not knowing the ways of the world and as such deserving our compassion. Note that there are plenty of occasions in the novel on which Humbert describes himself in precisely those terms. He talks of himself as "pathetic" (63); "mawkish" (109); "unpractical" (175); "comic" and "clumsy" (109); "weak," "not wise," and held "thrall" to a "schoolgirl nymphet" (183); "guilty," but still "great" and "tenderhearted" (188); in possession of a "credulous, simple, benevolent mind" (200); and altogether a "fond fool" (229). Ubiquitous as they are, standing on their own, such epithets would have been less convincing than when complemented by characterizations issuing seemingly from the minds of his readers, such as the one discussed above. This is what I see as one striking instance of the novel's "distribution" of the sources of its representations—we certainly hear about Humbert's sweet naïveté not only from him (one source of our representations) but also from some of his implied readers (a source seemingly independent from the first).

Here is another of those instances of the reader's "independent" testimony to Humbert's goodness. Having finally checked into that coveted hotel, having in fact gotten to Lolita's bed, lying next to her and not daring, yet, to touch her, Humbert apostrophizes thus:

> Please, reader: no matter your exasperation with the tenderhearted, morbidly sensitive, infinitely circumspect hero of my book, do not skip these essential pages! Imagine me; I shall not exist if you do not imagine me; try to discern the doe in me, trembling in the forest of my own iniquity; let's even smile a little. After all, there is no harm in smiling. For instance (I almost wrote "frinstance"), I had no place to rest my head, and a fit of heartburn . . . was added to my discomfort. (129)

To make us feel Humbert's (but not Lolita's!) pain in this passage, Nabokov has to manipulate us into not fully comprehending what kind of reader (or readers) his rhetoric implies here. For isn't it true that only a hardened pedophile would respond with "exasperation" to Humbert's lack of decisive action in the bed of his stepdaughter?[11] And isn't it only in contrast to this kind of reader/rapist that Humbert may appear "tenderhearted, morbidly sensitive, [and] infinitely circumspect"? To prevent us from facing squarely that reader (for how trustworthy can such an utterly repugnant source of the sympathetic representation of Humbert really be?), Nabokov has to distract our attention. He accomplishes it by suddenly ratcheting up the emotional intensity of the scene. Immediately upon introducing the flattering image of his "tenderhearted" self, Humbert turns to us with the desperate—and really rather unwarranted in its urgency—cry of "Imagine me! . . . I shall not exist if you do not imagine me!" The interactive drama of the moment engrosses our attention. It might be a bit incoherent—"let's smile a little . . . there is no harm in smiling . . . I had no place to rest my head . . . [I had] a fit of heartburn"—but it is still gripping. We emerge from this flailing emotional rollercoaster with the vague vision of Humbert as a "trembling doe," a lost soul whose childlike innocence is underscored by his use of teenage parlance ("frinstance"), and rarely do we turn back to examine more closely the reader implied by the opening of the paragraph.

My last example (though not the novel's!) of Nabokov's using the implied reader to promote a positive view of the protagonist comes from the later part of the story. Having just lost Lolita to the yet-unknown rival, Humbert tries to trace him through the registers of various hotels in which the "fiend" stayed as he followed Humbert and Lolita on their last car journey across America. "Imagine me," implores Humbert, turning to us once more in an apparent overflow of emotions:

> Imagine me, reader, with my shyness,—my distaste for any ostentation, my inherent sense of the *comme il faut,* imagine me masking the frenzy of my grief with a trembling ingratiating smile while devising some casual pretext to flip through the hotel register . . . (247)

Again, understood in practical cognitive terms, Humbert's present plea "Imagine me!" is nothing less than a "prompt" for the reader to perceive *herself*—and not, that is, Humbert—as the source of her positive representation of the protagonist. And given that the novel does manage to lull many of us into a kindly view of Humbert—such a shy foreigner, such a tortured soul, such a man *comme il faut*—this strategy of implied minds/distributed sources must be working. It must be working in spite of our knowing all the while that since Humbert tells us the story, every representation within the story originates with *him* and not with other minds that he lines up for us. Apparently, our tendency to register possible sources of representations and to subconsciously keep track of them overrides our conscious awareness that all of those sources are spurious, nonexistent, fabricated by the crafty narrator who wants to win us over to his side.

More attempts to "outsource" his flattering representation of himself take place during Humbert's last encounter with Lolita, when summoned by her unexpected letter he comes to visit her in "Coalmont," where she lives with her husband, "Dick Schiller." As Humbert sits on the divan in the Schillers' squalid parlor, we get a glimpse of him, presumably through Lolita's eyes:

> She considered me as if grasping all at once the incredible—and somehow tedious, confusing and unnecessary—fact that the distant, elegant, slender, forty-year old valetudinarian in velvet coat sitting beside her had known and adored every pore and follicle of her pubescent body. (272)

Note the rhetorical sleight-of-hand promulgated by this passage. Both the reader and Lolita are ostensibly asked to grasp the "incredible . . . fact" that Humbert once knew and adored every pore of Lolita's body. While we obligingly consider this fact, weighing it this way and that, Humbert manages to slide by us as the casual given that Lolita perceives Humbert as "the distant [and] slender . . . valetudinarian." Now, this is indeed the image of himself that Humbert wants to cultivate on the last pages of his narrative: his purported elegance and slenderness would soon provide the most useful contrast to the swinish appearance of Quilty whom Humbert murders. Similarly, the intimation of Humbert's failing health could garner extra sympathy for the murderer. However, when we look at this scene closely, there is no evidence at all that Lolita indeed sees Humbert as distant, slender, and ailing. Given, however, that our attention is distracted (for, remember, we are still busy "grasping" the incredible fact, etc.), we hardly pause to realize that we are presented with yet another fake source of our sympathetic image of Humbert.

Immediately after, Humbert brings up the same image again—now using as its source the mind of Lolita's husband and that of his friend, Bill, who enter the parlor and thus have to be introduced to Lolita's "dad": "The men looked at her fragile, *frileux,* diminutive, old-world, youngish but sickly, father in velvet coat and beige vest, maybe a viscount" (273). The representation of Humbert as a refined, vaguely aristocratic valetudinarian acquires more and more validity as it is presented to us as originating in *three* different minds (Lolita's, Dick's, and Bill's) almost simultaneously.

The novel closes with the protagonist feeling that his "slippery self [is] eluding [him], gliding into deeper and darker waters than [he cares] to probe" (309). Still, he is trying desperately to extort the last appealing image of that elusive self from the minds of his readers. Wishing to "make [Lolita] live in the minds of later generations," and thus "thinking of aurochs and angels, the secret of durable pigments, prophetic sonnets, the refuge of art," Humbert quietly upstages his "immortal love" in those not-yet-born minds with his assertion that "this is the only immortality you and I may share, my Lolita" (309). In other words, when future readers remember Humbert, they will not think of sexual enslavement, emotional abuse, rape, and murder; instead they will think of angels and of sonnets, and of the miraculous endurance of love and art. And the strangest thing about this last manipulative sentiment of Humbert's is that he is right—at least in so far as *Lolita* is considered to be "the only convincing love story of our century." (I am quoting now from a book blurb on the cover of the Vintage International edition of *Lolita* and attributed to *Vanity Fair.*)

(b) "Distributed" Mind Reading II:
An "immortal daemon disguised as a female child"

Throughout the novel, Humbert promotes our view of the heroine as a nymphet, a sexually precocious little girl, a demon who seduces men without even trying—a view that effectively absolves Humbert and turns him into *her* victim. To convince the reader of the truth of this perspective, Humbert uses the same strategy that he used to convince us that he is a sensitive, noble, kindhearted, if a bit naïve, man: he obliterates himself as the source of our representations of Lolita and presents us instead with snapshots of other minds (including Lolita's own) that support his interpretation of events.

Consider one early instance of Humbert's assured mind-attributing strategically aimed at confirming Lolita's oversexed nature. When Lolita comes to visit Humbert in his room at her mother's house and, "studying somewhat shortsightedly, the piece of paper [from his desk] innocently [sinks] to a half-sitting position upon [his] knee," Humbert reports Lolita's thoughts as follows:

> All at once I knew I could kiss her throat or the wick of her mouth with perfect impunity. I knew she would let me do so, and even close her eyes as Hollywood teaches. A double vanilla with hot fudge—hardly more unusual than that. I cannot tell my learned reader . . . how the knowledge came to me; perhaps my ape-ear had unconsciously caught some slight change in the rhythm of her respiration—for now she was not really looking at my scribble, but waiting with curiosity and composure—oh, my limpid nymphet!—for the glamorous lodger to do what he was dying to do. (48)

The plausibility of Humbert's claim that Lolita is waiting for him to kiss her is bolstered by the pounding repetition of the words "knew" and "knowledge." Imagine substituting these particular words with their close correlatives, for example, "all at once I *thought* I could kiss her throat . . . I *thought* she would let me do so . . . I cannot tell my reader how the *idea* came to me." The wimpy "I thought" would strongly imply Humbert as the source of our representation of Lolita's mind, whereas "I knew" works toward obliterating this source, especially this early in the novel, when we do not yet have a good reason to doubt every one of Humbert's claims to knowledge. And so we go along with Humbert's elucidation of Lolita's thoughts, an elucidation that, on this particular occasion, could be correct but (a possibility that, lulled by Humbert's rhetoric, we do not consider!) could also be completely wrong.

Much of Humbert's unflinching mind-reading is aimed at construing a world responsive in numerous subtle ways to the demonic presence of nymphets. Here is Humbert reporting his solitary trip to the department store where, newly initiated in the intricacies of teenage prêt-a-porter, he buys a new wardrobe for Lolita. As Humbert moves from counter to counter, accumulating "bright cottons, frills, puffed-out short sleeves, soft pleats, snug-fitting bodices and generously full skirts" (107), "an only shopper in that rather eerie place," he senses "strange thoughts form in the minds of the languid ladies" (108) who assist him in his enchanted shopping quest. Readers rarely pause at this mention of Humbert's "sensing" the salesgirls' thoughts, for we easily guess what thoughts Humbert is intuiting. "Oddly impressed by [his] knowledge of junior fashions" (108), the salesgirls must be wondering about his relationship with the person for whom he is buying all this stuff, perhaps even guessing at some unwholesome sexual inclinations lurking behind the "elegant" (108) façade that this customer presents to the world. And yet, just as in Humbert's earlier report of Lolita's feelings when she sits on his lap in his study presumably waiting for him to kiss her, we have absolutely no evidence for the salesgirls' "strange thoughts" other than Humbert's barefaced assertion. For all that we know, they may be admiring the caring father who has to shop for his teenage child on his own (a widower, perhaps?). So taken, however, are we by Humbert's confident tone—for who could argue with the visceral authority of "sensing"?[12]—that we do not consider this alternative possibility.

Humbert's quick, casual, and, as it turns out on the second reading, groundless attributions of mental states to strangers are ubiquitous. On a different occasion, he mentions in passing that during his and Lolita's journey across the United States they are regularly accosted by "inquisitive parents," who, "in order to pump Lo about [him], would suggest her going to a movie with their children" (164). If we append this sentence with the simplest of the agent-specifying source tags, such as, "Humbert thinks that . . .," we would easily recognize this piece of mind-reading for what it is—plain paranoia and inability to imagine a state of mind not centered on Humbert's august persona and his enviable possession of a nymphet. The idea that the only reason one parent after another would invite a girl clearly starved for the company of her peers to go to a movie with his or her own child is to "pump" her about her father is ridiculous once we restore the missing source tag. We do not, however, realize that the tag is missing when we first read the book and thus unwittingly acquiesce to the Humbertian vision of the world.

And in that world, the snooping parents are followed by sexually frustrated policemen. Stopped for speeding in a small town, Humbert notices that the patrolmen peer at Lolita and him with "malevolent curiosity."

However, once Lolita smiles at them "sweetly," the officers turn "kind" (171) and let them go, apparently gratified by the little sexpot's homage to their uniformed masculinity. Or so Humbert makes us imagine, for unless we consciously supply the missing source tag, "Humbert thinks that . . ," we indeed believe there is something "malevolent" and darkly intrusive in the patrolmen's rather ordinary act of reconnaissance.

In fact, no male can come in contact, however fleeting, with Lolita's "special languorous glow" without falling under her nymphetic spell. Humbert easily penetrates the minds of various "garage fellows, hotel pages, vacationists, goons in luxurious cars, [and] maroon morons near blue pools" and informs us matter-of-factly that they were all thrown into "fits of concupiscence" (159) at the mere sight of the sexy girlie. Losing track of the source tag pointing back to Humbert, we actually buy this mass attribution of mental states.

And we have already swallowed Humbert's confident prediction that two teenage boys who happen to share a pool with Lolita for a couple of minutes one afternoon will be aroused by the mere thought of "the quicksilver in the baby folds of her stomach . . . in recurrent dreams for months to come" (162). Not only does Humbert know what strangers he meets are thinking *now*, but he also knows what they will be dreaming about for months to come! Their dreams will naturally resemble his own, testifying once again to Lolita's irresistible, bewitching sexuality.

(c) How Do We Know When Humbert Is Reliable?

Like Richardson's *Clarissa,* Nabokov's *Lolita* contains episodes that imply that the narrator might have crossed over to that near-schizophrenic realm where self-awareness breaks down. For instance, when Lolita finally escapes Humbert, he spends some time in what he calls a "Quebec sanatorium" (a mental institution of some kind), where he composes a poem, featuring the following lines:

> Where are you hiding, Dolores Haze?
> Why are you hiding, darling?
> (I talk in a daze, I walk in a maze,
> I cannot get out said the starling). (255)

Humbert's sentiments on the occasion are eerily reminiscent of those of

Lovelace, who, when Clarissa has fled him for good, apostrophizes, "Oh return, return, my soul's fondledom, return to thy adoring Lovelace!" (1023)—a stalker and rapist apparently unaware of the fact that the overpowering vision of himself as a romantic and suffering lover and of his victim as a cruel coquette has originated in his own brain and has no support in the external reality. Like Lovelace before him, Humbert seems to be unable to comprehend why his "darling" would hide from him, though his unwavering focus on his own sufferings ("*I* talk in a daze, *I* walk in a maze") may also imply a vague Lovelacean threat (i.e., "she is hurting me; she ought to pay for it").

It is peculiarly appropriate that to comment on his predicament, Humbert draws on the famous sentimental emblem of the second part of the eighteenth century—an image of a trapped bird[13]—put into cultural circulation by the author himself particularly fond of experimenting with his readers' source-monitoring ability (for how trustworthy, for example, is a narrator who tells the story of his conception and his mother's pregnancy and labor as if he were present on all of these occasions?[14]). Already by the early nineteenth century, a writer could imply that a character takes herself a touch too seriously by having that character liken herself to the Sternean starling (as does Maria Bertram in Austen's *Mansfield Park*), but we get no indication in *Lolita* that Humbert is aware of this ironic tradition. His portrayal of the caged self is yet another in a series of images showing him as trapped and enslaved by his irresistible nymphet, and, on this occasion, we have no way of knowing whether he can put a critical distance between this vision of his plight and the reality of his relationship with Lolita. In Phelan's terms, Humbert misregards his reality, manifesting unreliability "on the axis of ethics and evaluation."[15]

Yet, scattered throughout the novel—and growing more persistent toward its end—are Humbert's apparently *reliable* assessments of that relationship. Their presence eventually enables us to reread *Lolita* not as a "love story" but as a story of a "vain and cruel wretch," who has been misleading himself and his audience about the true meaning of his actions and is now beginning to face that true meaning, albeit gradually and reluctantly. This crucial dual perspective of *Lolita* is possible only because it is firmly grounded in our metarepresentational capacity. Nabokov intuitively exploits this capacity *both* to deceive and to disabuse his readers. Here is how it works:

I have shown already how, to convince his audience of his version of events, Humbert distributes representations testifying to his tortured virtue and Lolita's demonic sexuality via different, seemingly independent and disinterested, sources throughout the narrative. Because we register those sources (can't help doing so—metarepresenting species that ours is!), we are amenable to buying into the false perspective that they tacitly and tirelessly convey. But then something else happens, too. Nabokov splits his narrator in two—Humbert *before* he started writing the "Confession of a White Widowed Male" and Humbert who *is* writing his "Confessions" and rethinking his story—a phenomenon that Phelan characterizes as the "dual focalization"[16] of the novel. The "present-tense" Humbert is forced to see things that the "past-tense" Humbert managed/chose not to see, and this painful new "sightedness"[17] renders him an increasingly, if fitfully, *reliable* narrator.

In other words, to *deceive* us, the novel triggers our metarepresentational capacity by alerting us to the *source tags* of certain representations (i.e., agent-specifying source tags pointing to policemen, garage-fellows, hotel pages, vacationists, salesgirls, the implied reader, Dick, Bill, etc.), whereas to *undeceive* us, it triggers our metarepresentational capacity by alerting us to the *time tags* of certain representations (i.e., source tags pointing to Humbert "then" and Humbert "now"). Let us consider some instances of the latter, using as a starting point Phelan's analysis of *Lolita* in *Living to Tell about It*.

To show that *Lolita* contains frequent shifts between the perspectives of the pre-"Confessions" protagonist and the protagonist who is now writing his "Confessions," Phelan turns to Humbert's description of his first intercourse with Lolita. This description is introduced by Humbert's claim that he is "not concerned with so-called 'sex' at all," but is inspired instead by a "greater endeavor": to "fix once and for all the perilous magic of nymphets" (134). What follows, however—and belies this claim of higher purpose—is a series of fragmented images highlighting Humbert's sexual "desire . . . and pleasure" as well as his "selfish violence and Dolores's pain."[18] Attempting to convey what transpired between him and Lolita through an impressionistic mural that he (ever a creative soul) might have painted, Humbert conjures up a "catalogue of fragments"[19] that includes, among other images, "a fire opal dissolving within a ripple-ringed pool, a last throb, a last dab of color, stinging red, smarting pink, a sigh, a wincing child" (135). As Phelan argues,

> through the very act of telling his story, the effort of perceiving and mis-
> perceiving himself and Dolores, [Humbert] is changing his relation to the
> story as well as to himself, to Dolores, and to his audience. . . . [During]
> the first intercourse, he has seen her wincing, stinging, and smarting, and

during his two years with her, he has seen the kind of suffering that led to her sobs in the night, but during those years, he refused to let those sights affect his behavior. . . . The first time Humbert gives the account of the intercourse, he succeeds in keeping his eyes averted from Dolores's pain [hence his claim that he was not concerned about 'so-called sex']. But [as the images that follow suggest] the act of telling leads him to begin to face much of what he had previously turned away from. The more he allows himself to see, the less he can pursue his exoneration, and so the motive for his telling shifts.[20]

It shifts to Humbert's increasing willingness to condemn rather than exonerate himself. In contrast to the self-exonerating Humbert—the one who has forced us to see his version of events as coming from other sources throughout the novel—the self-condemning Humbert is a reliable narrator. And it is by following *his* text—by uncovering, that is, the parts of *Lolita* that can be traced to *this* Humbert—that we are able to reconstruct the true story of the relationship between the man and the girl.

Of course, this "present-tense" Humbert, who begins to face Lolita's suffering and thus may regain (at least some of) his readers' trust, does not totally break with the "past-tense" Humbert, who had refused to register those sufferings. Humbert still regularly "reverts to the kind of rationalization that [he] has engaged in before"[21] to justify his abuse of Lolita. One important effect of such parallel narratives is, as Phelan observes, to make Humbert the narrator (i.e., "present-tense" Humbert) more sympathetic than Humbert the character (i.e., "past-tense" Humbert):

> Nabokov uses this present-tense story and the technique of dual focalization to add a significant layer to the whole narrative: the ethical struggle of Humbert the narrator. The struggle, at the most general level, is about whether he will continue to justify and exonerate himself or shift to admitting his guilt and accepting his punishment. . . . [And this struggle] becomes a significant part of our interest, even as it becomes increasingly painful to see what he sees about his past behavior.[22]

Phelan believes that "the story of Humbert's gradual move toward greater clear-sightedness is a move toward greater reliability along the axis of evaluation" and that by "the end of the narrative he has stopped trying to hoodwink both himself and his audience and has instead confessed to his crimes against Dolores and condemned himself for them."[23] If we indeed allow ourselves (for not all readers do) to trust the "present-tense" Humbert, we can go back and reread the story looking for the early and not-so-obvious traces of that slowly and painfully emerging reliable narrator. It is then that we realize that the two different appeals to our source-tracking adaptations often do their insidious work side-by-side, sometimes even in the same sentence. That is, the same sentence may prompt us to see certain representations—corroborating the "past-tense" Humbert's version of events—as issuing from other independent sources, while, at the same time, alerting us to the voice of the "present-tense" Humbert competing, so to speak, with the voice of the "past-tense" Humbert.

Let me illustrate this point by returning to (and now quoting in full) one already discussed instance of Humbert's using the minds of strangers to insinuate his view of Lolita into readers' consciousness:

> Oh, I had to keep a very sharp eye on Lo, little limp Lo! Owing perhaps to constant amorous exercise, she radiated, despite her very childish appearance, some special languorous glow which threw garage fellows, hotel pages, vacationists, goons in luxurious cars, maroon morons near blued pools, into fits of concupiscence which might have tickled my pride, had it not incensed my jealousy. (159)

It is easy to see how on our first reading we subconsciously use the "testimony" of hotel pages and maroon morons to corroborate Humbert's vision of Lolita. Lacking though they must be that creative insight which allows Humbert to recognize a nymphet when he sees one, these men still cannot help feeling that there *is* something special about that "little limp" girl and respond accordingly by falling into "fits of concupiscence." We trace what is really Humbert's representation of Lolita as a little oversexed "daemon" to the minds of aroused multitudes and, for the time being, buy that representation wholesale.

Snuggled in the middle of Humbert's ravings about the garage fellows' carnal wishes, is, however, a quiet observation that Lolita in fact had a "very childish appearance." Upon our first reading, the "past-tense" Humbert's assured tone as he divines the thoughts of strangers prevents our realization that with her "childish appearance" Lolita is unlikely to affect people the way that the "past-tense" Humbert claims she does. When we are rereading the novel, however, the description of Lolita as a mere child begins to sound like something that the "present-tense" Humbert might have written and thus "faced" (to use Phelan's insight) for the first time.

Of course, he must have faced it only askance. For the "present-tense"

Humbert is at this point quite a way from finishing writing his "Confessions" and thus attaining that painful clear-sightedness with which Phelan credits him. Still, the sentence can be profitably read in terms of a tacit tension generated by the two source-monitoring strategies that compete for its overall meaning. When we pay more attention to the distributed sources of representation of Lolita as a nymphet, we are being sold, more or less, on Humbert's lie. When we focus instead on the time tags and think in terms of "Humbert then" vs. "Humbert now," we begin to perceive the text as telling us the truth in spite of itself.

I see the same tension sustained until the very end of *Lolita*. It is this tension that makes possible very different critical responses to the novel's closing sentences, in which Humbert speaks about "the refuge of art" as the only shared immortality that could be granted to him and his (still his!) Lolita. I have earlier read this sentiment as typical of Humbert's manipulation of his readers' source-monitoring ability. If Humbert wants us to think that "the minds of later generations"—a series of seemingly independent sources—will indeed unite him with "his" Lolita, his project of self-exoneration is apparently far from over, and manipulation and deceit go on. In contrast, Phelan, whose interpretation can be seen as geared more toward registering the time tags implicitly present in the novel (i.e., Humbert then vs. Humbert now), reads the same passage very differently. He considers it a "statement of noble purpose," pointing out that "the very last line shows that [Humbert] harbors no illusions about his own redemption: the implication of where he expects to spend eternity—in contrast to where he expects Dolores to spend it—is very clear."[24]

Is there a way to combine the two readings by trusting and distrusting Humbert *at the same time?* Sustaining such an ambivalent state of mind is generally challenging, as Dorrit Cohn observes in her analysis of a "historical pattern that recurs time and again in critical responses" to novels featuring unreliable narrators. As she puts it:

A first phase of their reception—sometimes lasting for decades—takes the narrator at his word, in a manner that makes for a fully concordant reading; and a second phase understands this same narrator as discordant—producing a reading that is itself at first received with surprise and disbelief, but that is before long widely accepted. I would propose that this second phase might ideally be followed by a third—one that is actually quite rare in practice: a self-conscious reading that understands the choices involved, a reading aware of the fact that there are choices involved, that the problems created by certain types of narrators—

narrators in whom one can spot incongruities in their evaluation of the events and characters of the story they tell—can be resolved in different ways.[25]

Though Cohn sees the third phase as "quite rare," I wonder if focusing on the ways in which a given text manipulates our cognitive predispositions may make it easier for us to sustain that challenging state of "self-conscious reading." Specifically in the case of *Lolita*, if we realize that the novel encourages us to gravitate now toward one type of source-monitoring and now toward another (sometimes switching between the two in the same sentence), can we maintain for some time that strange mental stance of simultaneously believing and disbelieving Humbert?

And if we can do it with *Lolita*, what about Nabokov's other novels, such as *The Eye, The Real Life of Sebastian Knight,* and *Pale Fire*? For it seems that by tirelessly probing and teasing and stretching our tendency to monitor sources of our representations, Nabokov made the cultivation of a mental vertigo in his readers into his trademark as a writer. Will our reading experience change as we gradually articulate the ground rules of the cognitive games that his novels play with us? Will we start putting a premium on consciously prolonging and cultivating those moments of cognitive uncertainty when we both believe and disbelieve, know and don't know, see and don't see?

Though, of course, we are already doing this, or something very close to this, when we are reading fictional chronicles of mayhem and murder, lies and thievery (i.e., narratives more immediately accessible and less disturbing than *Lolita*). Nabokov's novels are sometimes called "metaphysical" detective stories.[26] Let us turn now to the "plain" detective stories and see how the research into the workings of our metarepresentational capacity clarifies the affinity between the two and generally begins to explain the pleasure that we derive from being intensely aware that we are being lied to.

PART III

CONCEALING MINDS

~ 1 ~

ToM AND THE DETECTIVE NOVEL: WHAT DOES IT
TAKE TO SUSPECT EVERYBODY?

L et us remind ourselves what a *strange* affair a typical detective novel is. Here is one of the masters of the genre, Dorothy Sayers, on the integrity of the craft:

> There you are, then: there is your recipe for detective fiction: the art of framing lies. From beginning to end of your book, it is your whole aim and object to lead the reader up the garden; to induce him to believe some harmless person to be guilty; to believe the detective to be right where he is wrong and mistaken where he is right; to believe the false alibi to be sound, the present absent, the dead alive and the living dead; to believe in short, anything and everything but truth.[1]

In other words, we open a detective novel with an avid anticipation that our expectations will be systematically frustrated, that we will be repeatedly made fools of, and that for several hours—or even days, depending on how fast one reads—we will be fed deliberate lies in lieu of being given a direct answer to one single simple question that we really care about (i.e., who done it?). Ellen R. Belton observes that the reader of the detective story is motivated "by two conflicting desires: the desire to solve the mystery ahead of or at least simultaneously with the investigator and the desire not to solve it until the last possible moment in order to prolong the pleasures of the mystery situation."[2] The desire "to prolong the pleasures of the mystery situation" rings immediately recognizable and true, and yet how can we explain this perverse craving? After all, what is so "pleasurable" about remaining in the dark for a long time about something sinister and threatening that you really, desperately, passionately want to know *now?* I do not think that many of us would find such a suspended state particularly delectable in real life.

One way to approach this question is to suggest that the enjoyment we derive from whodunits is akin to the enjoyment some people derive from watching/reading suspense thrillers: they get to experience the emotional thrill of danger, of chase, of relief, and then, perhaps, of a renewed danger, all the while remaining safe and warm and not at all threatened by a homicidal maniac posing as a kind next-door neighbor one has known for five years (hmm . . .). Moreover, we can stand being kept in the dark for three hundred pages because we know from our previous experience and from certain cultural conventions associated with this genre that ultimately the mystery will be fully explained. What makes suspense largely unpleasant in real life is that there is no guarantee that we will ever get a complete, or even a partially true, answer to any perplexing question. We can thus enjoy being lied to in the highly structured world of a murder mystery because it offers us a *safe setting* in which to relieve our anxieties about the uncertainties and deceptions of real life. Or, as Erik Routley puts it, it is the "matter of . . . assurance: it's . . . being allowed for a space to go out of the draught of doubt—that's what the detective story reader thanks his author for."[3]

I cannot argue with this explanation or with many other fine explanations put forth by literary critics and aficionados of the detective genre in the last hundred or so years. But neither can I pretend to be satisfied with them, for each of them feels incomplete once you start probing deeper. For example, the concept of "relieving-our-anxieties-about-real-life-deceptions" in a safe setting of the novel is useful because it allows us to make some immediate sense of the apparent paradox inherent in our interaction with detective stories, but it does not have any predictive capacity. Postulating that as readers we enjoy dwelling in a state of cruel uncertainty which we would by all means try to avoid in real life implies that, everything else being equal, we should derive pleasure from reading about *any* activity or about *any* state of mind that makes us anxious in reality. To a certain limited extent this is true,[4] but it sets no boundary condition for its truth. It cannot predict or explain why reliving some of our numerous anxieties in fiction could be a pleasure and reliving others is a nightmare. Even more important, it does not explain why this experience should differ so radically from one reader to another, for plenty of people cannot stand whodunits and thus apparently derive no pleasure, to quote Routley again, from "being allowed" this particular literary "space to go out of the draught of doubt."

This part of the book develops an explanatory framework that can be used to address some of the very basic and yet at the same time very complex issues informing our interaction with detective novels. I approach the question of why some people may enjoy being lied to in the context of the detective narrative by arguing that, although any narrative engages our metarepresentational ability, whodunits tend to "work out" certain aspects of this ability in a rather focused way. I then speculate on the larger implications of this argument, considering the possibility that our genre designations, such as "detective" or "romance," could be viewed as shorthand expressions of our intuitive awareness that certain texts engage one particular cluster of cognitive adaptations to a slightly higher degree than another. Finally, I check my argument about metarepresentationality and the detective novel against John Cawelti's warning about the dangers of reducing a literary text to psychological factors, and I discuss an important difference between a more traditional psychological approach to fiction and the one made possible in the context of cognitive framework.

~ 2 ~

WHY IS READING A DETECTIVE STORY A LOT LIKE LIFTING WEIGHTS AT THE GYM?

Poirot smiled at me indulgently. "You are like the little child who wants to know the way the engine works. You wish to see the affair . . . with the eye of a detective who knows and cares for no one—to whom they are all strangers and all are equally liable to suspicion."

"You put it very well," I said.

"So I give you then a little lecture. The first thing is to get a clear history of what happened that evening—always bearing in mind that the person who speaks may be lying."

I raised my eyebrows. "Rather a suspicious attitude."

—*Agatha Christie,* The Murder of Roger Ackroyd, *111*

*B*ringing in what we currently know about our metarepresentational ability can begin to explain our strange hankering for being deceived again and again as part of our experience of reading detective novels. I suggest that detective stories "work out" in a particularly focused fashion our ability to store representations under advisement and to reevaluate their truth-value once more information comes in.[1] They push this ability to its furthest limits, first, by explicitly requiring us to store a lot of information under a very strong advisement—that is, to "suspect *everybody*"—for as long as we can possibly take it and, then, as the story comes to an end, to readjust drastically much of what we have been surmising in the process of reading it.

Let me return very briefly to the arguments of Part II to clarify how what I said there about fiction and our metarepresentational ability differs from what I am saying here. There, I considered the possibility that certain fictional stories (especially those featuring unreliable narrators) play in a particularly focused way with our ability to monitor our sources of information. They portray protagonists who fail, on some level, to keep track of themselves as sources of their representations of their own and other people's minds, and, by doing so, they force the reader into a situation in which she herself becomes unsure of the relative truth-value of any representation contained in such a narrative. Detective stories, I propose in this chapter, play a slightly different game with our metarepresentational ability. Rather than encouraging us to *believe* what a given protagonist (e.g., Lovelace or Humbert) is saying, only then to slap us with a revelation that we should not have trusted him in the first place, the detective stories want us to *disbelieve,* from the very beginning and for as long as possible, the words of pretty much every personage we encounter. The two types of narratives thus build on the *same cognitive capacity for storing information under advisement,* but they approach it from different angles.

One may argue, then, that detective stories literally exist for assiduously cultivating what Dr. Sheppard would consider a "rather . . . suspicious attitude" in the reader. In this respect, whodunits can be enjoyable and even addictive in the same way as weightlifting can be enjoyable and addictive: the more you train a certain muscle, the more you feel that muscle and the more you want to train that muscle. Note that I am using the far-from-perfect bodybuilding analogy on purpose to stress that just as not everybody is an avid bodybuilder—though everybody has a body and is in principle able to lift weights to train isolated muscles—so also not everybody is an avid detective-novel reader or is even remotely interested in detective narratives. Those of us who do not work out with weights still get enough indirect exercise from our everyday activities to keep our muscles from atrophying, and, similarly, those of us who do not read detective stories (or even much of any fiction) still get plenty of relevant interaction with our environment to keep our metarepresentational capacity "in shape." The assumption that reading detective stories works out our metarepresentational capacity thus allows us to account both for the enjoyment that we derive from such stories and for the fact that such enjoyment is *not* universal.

Furthermore, even if weightlifting makes one generally stronger, and detective-novel-reading makes one a veritable expert in the genre, both experiences still remain in many ways decoupled from reality. Just as overdeveloping one's triceps, biceps, and trapezoids generally does not give the bodybuilder any particular advantage in her everyday activities[2]—it certainly does not make one more adept at handling such crucial items as a pen, a laptop, a phone, and a fork—so keeping on a steady diet of detective stories does not make one a particularly discerning social player. It does not help me see through somebody's lies and it does not help me to know which "clues" to pay attention to in order to get to the truth of a given matter. In fact, applying what I have "learned" from a murder mystery to my everyday life could make me a social misfit: there is an important difference between being able, in principle, to revise one's views based on new evidence and going around deliberately suspecting everybody of being not what they seem, "just in case." In this respect, detective narratives may be said to parasitize on our metarepresentational ability: they stimulate it without providing the kind of "educational" benefit that we still implicitly look for in what we read. Delight they do, but instruct they don't, or at least not in the traditional sense of the word *instruction*.[3]

The detective narrative's emphasis on exploring the furthest limits of our metarepresentational ability is the reason I prefer to focus on the novel and not on the classical form of the genre, the short story. Literary critic Jacques Barzun has suggested that the short story remains the "true medium of detection," for turning an elegantly economic piece into a "tangled skein of 150,000 words" accomplishes little else than adding the "artificial bustle and bulge" of false leads. Note, though, that put in "cognitive" terms the difference between the short story and the novel acquires a new meaning. Unlike its shorter counterpart, the detective novel veritably luxuriates in mind-reading; it adds more minds for the reader to consider and more metarepresentational framing to keep track of (or, as Jack Womack puts it on a different occasion, "the difference between the stories and the novels is the difference between coffee and methedrine"[4]). Of course, one of the founding fathers of the genre, Edgar Allen Poe, was already quite aware that his short stories were all about mind-reading, for as the narrator of "The Purloined Letter" famously discovers, figuring out the crime requires the "identification of the reasoner's intellect with that of his opponent" (13). Generally, however, the format of the short story limits the number of minds that could be read in-depth and titillatingly misread.

However heavy-handed it may be, the parallel between detective fictions and weightlifting works on yet another level: in a culture that does not have a concept of weight-training facilities, *or* that considers muscular bodies ugly, *or* that frowns upon women exercising in such an "unfeminine" fashion, *or* that thinks that there is something unbearably ridiculous about setting aside significant amounts of time and money for lugging around pieces of iron, weightlifting of the kind currently widespread in this country would not exist. By the same token, there is nothing historically inevitable about the emergence, wide cultural acceptance, and long-term prospects of the detective genre, however apt this genre happens to be in stroking our metarepresentational ability.

This emphasis on historicizing is crucial for the cognitive-evolutionary approach to literature championed by this study, and one of its broader ramifications applies not just to the detective genre. As we learn more and more about our metarepresentational ability, this knowledge may allow us to account, at least on some level, for certain fascinating regularities that we encounter in *already existing* cultural representations, such as literary texts, but it will never *predict* what cultural representations we are bound to have or cannot have in the future. Those are grounded in future history and as such are unpredictable even if they build on the same cognitive predispositions that have been with us for hundreds of thousands years.

Thinking of the detective narrative as engaging in a particularly focused way our metarepresentational ability and yet being anything but historically inevitable puts on a stronger footing our project of historicizing the "rise of the detective story" phenomenon. Briefly, critics have offered explanations for the emergence and cultural entrenchment of the genre that range from sociopolitical (e.g., Howard Haycraft's hypothesis of the relationship between the detective genre and democracy) and scientific (e.g., Ronald R. Thomas's correlation of the rise of the detective story with the development of forensic technology), to ideological (e.g., Routley's argument about the relationship between the detective story and the English puritan tradition) and aesthetic (Joyce Charney's view of the detective novel as a latter-day response to the same set of aesthetic needs that used to be addressed by the English novel of manners). The endeavor to historicize the nineteenth- and twentieth-century detective story is often complicated, however, by the acknowledgment that we can find "proto-detective" narratives in much earlier epochs, from Daniel's interrogating of the elders in the biblical story of Susanna in the garden to Sophocles' *Oedipus* and Voltaire's *Zadig.*[5] Such acknowledgments seem to undercut, at least on some level, our attempts to situate the detective story in the nineteenth-century or the twentieth-century historical milieu and to explain its popularity by specific sociocultural developments of the moment. For if there is a detective story already present in the Bible, how can we speak about its "emergence" in, say, the 1840s, with the stories of Poe?

The cognitive framework lets us address this issue directly. It suggests that if (some form of) the metarepresentational ability has been with us since the dawn of the human species, then people have always had the potential for being interested in the stories that engage this ability. Consequently, by completely vindicating our suspicions that we have "always" had some sort of detective narratives lurking in our cultural history, the cognitive framework allows us to move on, so to speak, and to focus on the sociohistorical and aesthetic factors that might have contributed to the appearance, in the nineteenth century, of the detective story as a culturally recognizable, new, and special literary genre.

Furthermore, our perspective on the permutations of this genre from the nineteenth century until today may, too, change once we posit as the key underlying characteristic of the detective story its tendency to engage in a focused way our evolved cognitive ability to store information under advisement. That is, we can begin to see the recent history of the detective narrative as a cultural chronicle of writers' experimentation with our metarepresentational ability and our Theory of Mind, pushed to their limits in several different directions. In the process of such experimentation, writers learn to negotiate and redirect cognitive challenges that may have first appeared insurmountable for their readers.

A detective story seems to be particularly fit for such an analysis because the genre is relatively young, and we have access to the feedback received by the experimenting authors. That is, we know what initially caused an uproar in the audience but gradually became widely accepted and what, on the other hand, continues to constitute a problem even as generations of authors have tried their hand at circumventing it. The larger point that underlies such an investigation and that carries over to our thinking of other genres is that literary history as a whole could be better understood if we considered our cognitive predispositions as an important factor structuring the individual author's attempts to break the mold of what constitutes an acceptable and desirable literary endeavor of their own day.[6]

In what follows, then, I consider four features of the detective story and, in some cases, their respective changes over time. I suggest that these features acquire a new psychological and cultural significance when approached from a cognitive perspective. The first subsection of my argument, "One Liar Is Expensive, Several Liars Are Insupportable," examines the care with which any writer of fiction treats the destabilizing presence of a lying character, the proliferation of potential liars being, of course, a trademark of the detective story. The second, "There Are No Material Clues Independent from Mind-Reading," emphasizes the detective story's ultimate goal of reconstructing the state of multiple minds populating the scene of the crime. The third, "Mind-Reading Is an Equal Opportunity Endeavor," addresses the genre's practice of strategic obfuscation of selected minds. The fourth, "Alone Again, Naturally," offers a cognitive reading of the old rule according to which, in an effective whodunit, the detective should be either celibate or married.

~ 3 ~

METAREPRESENTATIONALITY AND SOME RECURRENT PATTERNS OF THE DETECTIVE STORY

Two points of clarification are in order. First, in the rest of this Part III, I use the term *metarepresentation* interchangeably with the term *metarepresentationally framed information,* meaning, in both cases, "information (or representation) stored under advisement." For example, when in one of my case studies, Maurice Leblanc's "The Red Silk Scarf," the police inspector concludes upon observing the behavior of two suspicious men in the street that they must be "plotting something," I call his interpretation a metarepresentation because it is "good for now," that is, it provides a temporarily useful explanation of the states of mind behind the suspicious behavior, but it can be adjusted, confirmed, or discarded any moment once more information comes in. In other words, I take it as a given (even though I do not say it again and again in every such case) that this explanation is stored with some sort of metarepresentational "tag," such as "the inspector thinks" or "we think," and that it is the implicit functional presence of such tags that makes it possible for us and for the inspector to revise our interpretations as we go along.

Second, I use here more insistently than in the previous sections such expressions as a "strong" and a "weak" metarepresentational framing to indicate that there are different degrees of advisement under which we "store" representations. For example, if I say to you that the rest of this section is divided into four parts, you have no particular reason to distrust me, and so you store this information with a "weak" metarepresentational tag, "Zunshine says that. . . ." If, however, you are reading a detective story, you are encouraged by the laws of the genre to store nearly every attribution of the mental state behind each character's behavior with a very "strong" metarepresentational tag. If, for example, a potential suspect, "Flora," says that she left her room on the night of the murder because she wanted to get some water, the "Flora says" part of the representation—that is, its source tag—ensures that we still take her explanation into account, but we are strongly prepared to find that it is not true.

The concept of variously weighted metarepresentational framings provides us with a useful framework for comparing detective novels with other works of fiction that have at different times been productively likened to them, such as Austen's *Emma.* Austen's novel has been described as "the most fiendishly difficult of detective stories,"[1] and, indeed, its ending requires from us the type of cognitive work associated with the endings of detective novels. In a typical detective narrative, once the murderer is found out and his/her motivation is explained, we have to think back and revise our earlier interpretations of the events of the story, an important metarepresentational readjustment. Similarly, in *Emma,* once we are told the truth about Frank Churchill and Jane Fairfax, we have to reflect back onto the entire novel and modify our earlier interpretations of certain "clues," such as the timing of Frank's first arrival at Hartfield, the gift of the piano, Jane's insistence on getting her mail herself, and so on. Note, however, that when we read *Emma* the first time, we store the interpretations of these "clues," mostly provided by Emma, with relatively weak metarepresentational framing because, although ready to readjust them to some degree, we do not expect that they will have to be revamped so drastically. By contrast, the "real" detective novel alerts its readers early on to the fact that every bit of interpretation provided by characters ought to be distrusted until the end—an example of a very strong metarepresentational framing. Of course, within the same detective story, we can store information provided by different suspects, or even the same suspect on different occasions, under very different degrees of advisement; and, moreover, as we go on reading, we constantly modulate the relative strength of metarepresentational framing used to process the characters' presumed or claimed mental states. Still, the whodunit is associated with a much stronger internal metarepresentational framing than, say, a comedy of manners, such as *Emma*.[2]

(a) One Liar Is Expensive, Several Liars Are Insupportable

The reader of the detective story is supposed to "suspect everybody" (Paretsky, *Bitter Medicine,* 48). This constant readiness to keep under strong advisement any current explanation of any character's mental state comes at a price. To understand why it is so, we can turn again to the argument of the first section, in which I showed that *Mrs. Dalloway* at times pushes our ability to process embedded intentionalities beyond our cognitive zone of comfort (i.e., beyond the fourth level). I think that it is significant that on such occasions Woolf does not try to make us *guess* at her characters' states of mind. Instead, she tells us quite explicitly what they are thinking, feeling, or desiring. In the scene at Lady Bruton's that I discussed earlier, we are told what Lady Bruton feels as she watches Hugh; we are told what Hugh thinks as he unscrews the cap of his pen and begins to write; and we are told what Richard thinks as he watches Hugh and observes Lady Bruton's reaction to Hugh's implicit assertions. The scene is challenging because the reader has to process a string of five- and six-order intentionalities. But at least Woolf does not require us to store the information about Lady Bruton's and Hugh's states of mind *under advisement* by having implied, for example, that Lady Bruton and Hugh *just pretend* to be thinking about the letter to the editor and are really concerned about something else, and so Richard's complex reconstruction of their states of mind could be all wrong, and we have to wait for another ten or ninety pages to find out what Lady Bruton and Hugh were *really* thinking about. That is, within the world of the novel, we are allowed to consider the thoughts of the characters at this particular junction not as tentative guesses to be verified later but as architectural truths that can circulate freely among and affect indiscriminately our cognitive databases concerned with the lives and feelings of *Mrs. Dalloway's* characters.

Now imagine a scene in a novel that embeds five or six levels of intentionality, as in, "A says that B thinks that C wants D to consider E's idea that F believes that X." This is already fairly difficult to follow for any reader. Let us, however, complicate it even further and suggest that this is a scene from a *detective* novel, whose credo is to "suspect everybody." What it would mean is that not only do we have to process five or six embedded levels of intentionality, but we also have to consider *on top of it* that either A, or B, or C, or D, or E, or F; or both A and B; or C, D, and F; or all six of them are lying. I am not saying that is impossible to write such a scene (in fact, it may have been written at some point), but I strongly suspect that at least in the context of the literary history of our present moment, readers may find it rather incomprehensible. An author could play with multiplying the levels of embedded intentionality, as Woolf did, or an author could deliberately mislead us about the thoughts, desires, and intentions of her characters, as Sayers says all detective story writers should do; but it may take a presently unforeseen form of literary experimentation to usher in a work or a series of works of fiction that could successfully do both. At this point in our literary history, an effective whodunit can offer us red herrings again and again, but it tends to stay around or below the fourth level of embedded intentionality, and more reliably so than a non–detective story.

Here is one fairly straightforward observation that follows from such reasoning. Adding strong metarepresentational framing to any information about a character's state of mind (that is, implying that the character might be lying about his intentions or feelings) does not simply add an extra level of intentional embedment to the scene in question, as, say, in, "A says that B thinks that C wants D to consider a certain factor X, but B is in fact misleading A about his thoughts." Rather, it fundamentally upsets the whole setup of this particular scene and often of the whole story. Quite naturally, it raises questions about B's motivations. Furthermore, it prompts us to inquire into A's true knowledge and motivations, and into what C really wants, and into what D really cares about. In other words, liars are a liability, both in real life and in fiction. Introducing just *one* lying character into the plot can have an immediate cascading effect on the rest of the narrative, for we have to reconsider thoughts, feelings, and motivations of other characters who have come in contact with the liar, and such reconsideration can cardinally transform our understanding of the story. Introducing two or more liars multiplies such effects to an alarming degree.

Not surprisingly, then, writers are quite frugal about how many liars they will allow into their stories, and they are very careful about charting out each liar's progress. Each instance of lying, be it the Golden Dustman's pretending that he is mean and avaricious to test Bella, or Bulstrode's concealing his past to conquer Middlemarch, or Wickham's telling Elizabeth about Mr. Darcy's past cruelties, or Humbert Humbert's talking himself and his readers into believing that Lolita has really seduced *him,* is a potentially destabilizing structural event. The author, thus, should be very particular about delineating the liar's sphere of influence by specifying who is liable to be affected by the liar's behavior, at what point in time and in what particular ways. Of course, a story can run away from its creator if the readers think they have a reason to question the author's description of the limits of the liar's sphere of influence. But, if anything, such reading against the author's apparent intentions testifies to the enduring shock value of every act of lying and our need to test the boundaries of truth once the potentially reordering element has been introduced into the narrative.

Let me bring together several points that I have made so far. On the one hand, it is possible that detective stories tease our metarepresentational ability by taking to the extreme our cognitive capacity to, first, store information under advisement and, then, once the truth-value of this information is decided, to think back to the beginning of the story and to readjust our understanding of a whole series of occurrences. On the other hand, storing information under advisement, particularly if the information concerns one character's manipulation of the state of mind of other characters, could be cognitively "expensive" because lying does not simply add an extra level of intentionality to the given situation. Instead, it frequently has a "cascading" effect, demanding from us a readjustment of what we know about other characters' knowledge, the knowledge that they in turn may have used to influence the states of mind of other characters, and so forth. Thus, a story whose premise is that "everybody could be lying" is a narrative minefield, and turning it into an enjoyable reading experience may require a particular set of formal adjustments.

Such adjustments include the drastic narrowing of the focus of the story. A whodunit allows that anybody and everybody can be lying (and, famously, in Christie's *Murder on the Orient Express,* that actually turns out to be the case), but the threateningly expanding universe of information about the characters' mental states that we thus have to store under advisement is mercifully constrained. Everybody's lying tends in the same direction, focusing on his/her relationship with the murdered Roger Ackroyd; or on that string of pearls that went missing from Mrs. Penruddock's household (in Raymond Chandler, "Pearls Are a Nuisance"); or on those hate letters that have been disrupting the quiet life of Shrewsbury College (in Sayers, *Gaudy Night*). If I am correct in considering lying in fiction as potentially cognitively "expensive," then the narrowing of the focus of a story insisting that *any* of its characters may turn out to have been lying to everybody else is not even a matter of choice for the author. It is rather an absolute prerequisite of making this story cognitively manageable. Again, I am speaking here about the kinds of detective narratives that currently dominate the genre; future generations of writers may develop ways of circumventing or reorienting this prerequisite.

(b) There Are No Material Clues Independent from Mind-Reading

Let me restate the key point of my argument. Whereas *any* work of fiction engages our Theory of Mind, detective novels engage our ToM by experimenting in a particularly strenuous fashion with certain aspects of our metarepresentational ability. By creating a narrative framework in which *everybody could be lying,* such novels push to its furthest limits our ability to store information about our own and other people's mental states under advisement.

Given what we know now about our mind-reading capacity, we should thus be quite wary about advancing any interpretive framework that either ignores the "Theory-of-Mind" aspect of a detective narrative or insists on separating the analysis of the "material" clues present in such a narrative from the analysis of the states of mind of its protagonists. Witness a recent work of Ronald R. Thomas, who argues that the emergence of "detective fiction as a form" coincided "with the development of the modern police force and the creation of the modern bureaucratic state." The detective story has thus participated in the "cultural work performed by the societies that were increasingly preoccupied with . . . bringing under control the potentially anarchic forces unleashed by democratic reform, urban growth, national expansion, and imperial management." As the new forensic technology was a crucial means in identifying and controlling the potential deviants, the fledgling genre became particularly apt at reporting the clues that would allow the investigator to "read" and manage the "criminal body."[3] Following this compelling analysis, however, is a startlingly dualistic assertion that "the detective novel is fundamentally preoccupied with physical evidence and with investigating the suspect body rather than with exploring the complexities of the mind."[4]

Here is how Thomas's argument can be qualified using the cognitive perspective: We care about the clues provided by the criminal bodies because other people's bodies are our pathways to their minds (however misleading and limited these clues may turn out to be). Furthermore, it can certainly be argued that the desire to read minds via bodies becomes particularly pronounced at the times of "urban growth, national expansion, and imperial management," when one is constantly thrown in with strangers whose social accountability is virtually unknown. Overwhelmed by the influx of foreigners in their community, people can indeed be particularly hungry for the fictional narratives that assure them that bodies, if read correctly, can offer them some valid information about the states of mind behind them. What Thomas characterizes as the desire to manage the criminal body is in reality a desire to manage the criminal mind.[5]

It seems almost superfluous to quote a passage from a detective story in order to demonstrate that "physical evidence" matters only insofar as it helps the detective to reconstruct the states of mind behind it, for no functional whodunit uses clues in any other fashion. Still, I will turn to one such passage, coming from Leblanc's 1907 story "The Red Silk Scarf" (not least because Leblanc had prefigured some of the later experimentations with combining the detective and the criminal in one figure, which I will discuss in one of the following subsections). At one point in the story, Arsène Lupin, an amateur sleuth, presents Chief Inspector Ganimard of Paris (a stock "dense policeman" character) with a pile of objects presumably relevant for the crime that Ganimard will soon need to solve, and invites him to figure out the meaning of these objects:

> There were, first of all, the torn pieces of newspaper. Next came a large cut-glass inkstand, with a long piece of string fastened to the lid. There was a bit of broken glass and a sort of flexible cardboard, reduced to shreds. Lastly, there was a piece of bright scarlet silk, ending in a tassel of the same material and color. (182)

After ascertaining that the objects don't hold any meaning for the dumbfounded inspector, Lupin tells the story that *he* has deduced from them, still leaving out, however, with small titillating exceptions that I will italicize, the stuff that we really want to know—the history of minds behind the "exhibit" as well as Lupin's own thought processes:

> "I see that we are entirely of one mind," continued Lupin, without appearing to remark the chief inspector's silence. "And I can sum up the matter briefly, as told us by these exhibits. Yesterday evening, between nine and twelve o'clock, a *showily dressed* young woman was wounded

with a knife and then caught round the throat and choked to death by a *well-dressed* gentleman, wearing a single eyeglass and *interested in racing,* with whom the aforesaid showily dressed young lady had been eating three meringues and a coffee éclair. (183)

"Interested in racing" is a pretty straightforward attribution of a state of mind. Thomas may argue, however, that some of the other descriptions that I have highlighted, such as "showily dressed" or "well-dressed," indeed point to the text's "preoccupation with physical evidence and with investigating the suspect body" rather than with "exploring the complexities of the mind" of the young woman and the gentleman in question. However, this would be an untenable distinction. "Showily dressed" catches our attention because it implies a mind concerned with impressing other people in a certain way. "Well-dressed," on the other hand, implies a person who can afford to dress well and has taste. Moreover, contrasted with "showily dressed," "well-dressed" indicates the workings of yet another mind, that of Lupin himself, attuned to the variety of subtle ways in which different people try to manipulate other people's states of mind by their appearance.

Of course, in spite of Lupin's ironic, "I see that we are entirely of one mind," we haven't yet arrived at the actual explanation of the crime. When that comes, the material evidence— specifically, the red scarf—will acquire at least five different meanings, all of them reflecting the workings of scheming human minds attempting to influence other people's thinking.

It turns out that the showily dressed young lady was an aspiring singer who had in her possession a precious stone, a "magnificent sapphire" (187). Foreseeing that one day somebody may try to steal the stone (*one instance of mind-reading, that is, of predicting what somebody else will be thinking in the future*), she has stitched it into the tassel of the red scarf that she wore. When the murderer, who had pretended to be her admirer (*another complex instance of mind-reading and mind-misreading*) stabbed her with a knife, he used the scarf to wipe the blood off the knife, so as to leave no traces for the detectives (*thus foreseeing and attempting to influence the detectives' thinking*). The scarf was torn into two pieces during the scuffle accompanying the murder. The piece with bloody marks was found by Lupin, whereas the piece concealing the sapphire was held as material evidence by police, who did not know, however, what was hidden inside the tassel. When, acting on Lupin's suggestions, Ganimard arrests the murderer, he cannot prove the suspect's guilt to the public because to do so he needs the part of the scarf bearing the bloody marks. Ganimard, thus, cannot make the public share his views about the murder scenario without producing both halves of the scarf (*yet another example of attempting to influence other people's state of mind*).

Lupin knows all along that Ganimard will at some point find himself in this predicament, and he makes an appointment with him requiring him to bring along the piece of scarf found by the police. During the meeting, Lupin unravels the tassel and takes out the sapphire under the astonished gaze of the inspector who then tries to prevent Lupin from getting away with the precious stone only to find out that Lupin has anticipated the inspector's reaction (*massive agglomeration of mind-reading*) and has outfitted the doors of their meeting place with special locks that he but not the inspector can open. The actual act of murder, in other words, and the apparently crucial piece of evidence, the red scarf, are there to lead us to the real business of the detective story: the reconstruction of the plotting minds, whose machinations play off each other in unexpected ways to the delight of the reader.

Let us see how the story "works out" the reader's metarepresentational capacity. The story begins when one morning, Inspector Ganimard notices a "shabbily dressed" man in the street, who stoops "at every thirty or forty yards to fasten his bootlace, or pick up his stick, or for some other reason." Each time he stoops, he takes a "little piece of orange peel from his pocket and [lays] it stealthily on the curb of the pavement." This behavior is naturally puzzling, and here is our first bit of mind-reading that can explain this behavior and that we store as a metarepresentation, that is, as an explanation that is good for now but will very likely get modified as more data come in: "It was probably a mere display of eccentricity, a childish amusement" not deserving anybody's "attention" (178).

Inspector Ganimard, however, is never satisfied "until [he knows] the secret cause of things." He begins to follow the man and soon notices something even stranger. The man seems to exchange mysterious signals with a boy walking on the other side of the street. After each such exchange, the boy draws with a piece of chalk white cross "on the wall of the house next to him." Inspector Ganimard now has good reasons to dismiss the previous interpretation of the situation, for clearly the first man is not just a harmless eccentric. And here we have the second bit of mind-reading that the story prompts us to store as a metarepresentation. Inspector Ganimard is now convinced that those two "merchants" are "plotting" something (179).

At some point, the two "merchants" finally come together and start talking to each other. The hypothetical explanation of their behavior, that is, that they are plotting something, seems to get a strong boost when "quick as thought, the boy [hands] his companion an object which [looks]—at least so the inspector believed—like a revolver. They both [bend] over this object; and the man, standing with his face to the wall, put his hand six times in his pocket and [makes] a movement as though he were loading a weapon" (180). The two are clearly planning a crime— or such is the latest metarepresentation of their minds that the author wants us and Ganimard to consider now.

The suspicious duo enter the "gateway of an old house of which all the shutters [are] closed," and Ganimard, of course, hurries "in after them" (180). Awaiting him on the third landing is Arsène Lupin himself. We now get the real explanation of the situation and thus have to radically revise the information about the man's and the boy's minds that we have been storing as metarepresentations. It turns out that Lupin hired the two in order to attract the inspector's attention in the street and to bring him to this abandoned house. Given Lupin's past brushes with Parisian police and the inspector's dislike and even fear of him, Lupin knows that had he "written or telephoned," the inspector "wouldn't have come . . . or else [he] would have come with a regiment" (181) to arrest Lupin.

Once the first set of metarepresentations is taken away and replaced with the true explanation, we are immediately offered another mind-reading mystery. Why has Lupin gone to all this trouble to see the inspector? Lupin explains that he wanted to present the inspector with a bunch of clues (the above-mentioned pieces of newspaper, cut-glass inkstand, a string, a piece of bright scarlet silk, etc.) connected to the crime which was committed in Paris yesterday and which Lupin wants the inspector to solve. This explanation, however, is maddeningly incomplete, for it leaves open the question, Why does Lupin care about this crime in the first place? Is he driven by the righteous desire to see justice served? Is he in love with the young woman? Is he somehow implicated in the crime? Does he want to ruin the man whom he accuses of the murder? Does he want to humiliate, as he has in the past, the inspector who has to reluctantly rely on his help while being unable to figure anything out himself? The story thus subtly offers us one metarepresentation after another that can explain the workings of the mind behind Lupin's actions, only to surprise us at the very end with the truth, which is that Lupin needed the inspector to bring him the other end of the scarf in which the sapphire was concealed. It is also quite possible that Lupin saw no harm in having justice served and the inspector humiliated, but these were destined to remain his secondary motives.

Whew. This is what I call a workout for our metarepresentational capacity.

(c) Mind-Reading Is an Equal Opportunity Endeavor

Agatha Christie's 1926 novel, *The Murder of Roger Ackroyd,* is considered something of a watershed in the history of the genre. Challenging the established tradition of a clueless narrator/sidekick, Christie made the "Dr. Watson" figure of her story the murderer. This "trick," writes Haycraft, "provoked the most violent debate in detective story history . . . , in which representatives of one school of thought were crying, 'Foul play!'" while other readers and critics "rallied to Mrs. Christie's defense, chanting the dictum: 'It is the reader's business to suspect *every one.*'"[6] And so it is. (And so it has been, we should add, at least since the publication of "The Silk Red Scarf," in which Lupin treads a thin line between being a criminal and a detective.)

There is a good reason why no literary convention specifying immunity of one type of character or another from turning out to be the criminal (or the investigator) remains unchallenged for long. Because we are in the business of mind-reading, one mind is as good a candidate for being concealed, misread, and willfully misrepresented as any other. Looking back at the development of the detective story in the last one hundred fifty years, we see that mind-reading, mind-misreading, and mind-concealing are truly equal opportunity endeavors, even if specific historical epochs have worked hard to ascribe either subhuman or superhuman qualities to criminals and sleuths of specific social and ethnic backgrounds. Yesterday's unspoken injunctions, whether dictated by literary tradition, by racial, social, and gender prejudices, or by current mores of political correctness about who could or could not be caught lying, are tomorrow's extra selling points.

The entire history of the detective genre thus can be viewed as a chronicle of the writers' experimentation with the question of whose minds the readers should be allowed to read and when they should be able to read them. One interesting development here concerns the mind of the detective. Think about Sherlock Holmes, Auguste Dupin, and Hercule Poirot. They rarely divulge their insights until that triumphant final scene, in which the story of the crime—that is, the *éclaircissement* of the minds behind the crime—is presented for the stunned reader. Some later-day writers, however, have experimented with how much of the detective's mind they can lay bare for us while still ensuring that the final revelation arrives as a surprise. Here is a bit of a game that one can play with a contemporary whodunit. Once we realize that many writers today consider it good form to sustain for as long as possible their readers' impression that they know exactly as much as the detective, we can hunt for those moments in the story when the mind of the detective gets decisively closed off from us. Such moments are rare and not particularly conspicuous, unless, that is, we consciously look for them as part of our project of understanding how fiction "works" our Theory of Mind. Then they literally leap up at us from the page.

For example, private investigator Cordelia Gray in P. D. James's *An Unsuitable Job for a Woman* starts off by sharing all of her surmises with us, until we arrive at the following passage describing her reaction to the suicide note containing a quotation from Blake's poem: "It was then that two things about the quotation caught at her breath. The first was not something which she intended to share with Sergeant Maskell but there was no reason why she should not comment on the second" (88). Of course, it is not just Sergeant Maskell, but we, the readers, who get the door into the detective's mind slammed on our hopeful noses. The narrative then continues, having seemingly resumed its earnest intention to divulge all of the investigator's thoughts to the readers. Toward the end of the story, of course, the bit of information that was thus strategically concealed from us develops into a full-blown explanation of the crime as Cordelia addresses one of the criminals: "I wasn't sure if it was you. . . . I first [thought about you] when I visited the police station and was shown the note. It pointed directly to you. That was the strongest evidence I had" (207).

Here is a different novel by the same author. In *Shroud for a Nightingale,* James makes a point of following every intimate movement of Chief Superintendent Adam Dalgliesh's soul for exactly half of the book. Then, nearly two hundred pages into the novel, we encounter a tiny sentence buried in Dalgliesh's exchange with his underling, one Sergeant Masterson. The sergeant wonders at what point the fatal poison was added to the bottle of milk used for training purposes in a hospital, observing that it "couldn't have been in a hurry." Dalgliesh replies:

> "I've no doubt a great deal of care and time were taken. But I think I know how it was done."

He described his theory. Sergeant Masterson, cross with himself for
having missed the obvious, said:

"Of course. It must have been done that way."

"Not must, Sergeant. It was probably done that way." (186; emphasis
added)

We are not to learn, until time is very ripe, what Dalgliesh's "theory" was.
After having thus reminded us who is really in charge of the novel's mind-
reading, James then reverts to generously elucidating Dalgliesh's surmises
for another sixty or so pages. Then she slides in yet another "mind-closing"
sentence. Speaking with one of the novel's multiple suspects, Sister Brum-
fett, Dalgliesh asks a seemingly irrelevant question and immediately
apologizes:

"I'm sorry if I sound presumptuous. This conversation hasn't much to do
with my business here, I know. But I'm curious."

It had a great deal to do with his business there; his curiosity wasn't
irrelevant. *But she wasn't to know that.* (245; emphasis added)

Neither are we to know for many pages what Dalgliesh's question had to
do with the issue at hand and how it fed into the "theory" that James had
casually dangled in front of her readers earlier.

Other writers have made a point of *never* obscuring the mind of the
detective from us, as have, for example, Sue Grafton in her "alphabet" novels and Sarah Paretsky in *Burn Marks* and *Bitter Medicine.* Here is a characteristic passage from a whodunit emphasizing the so-un-Sherlock-
Holmes transparency of the detective's thought processes. Presenting a
rather stark contrast to Raymond Chandler's previous novels, such as *The
Long Good-Bye, The Big Sleep,* and *Playback,* it comes from *Poodle Springs,*
the last "Marlowe" story, revised and finished after Chandler's death by
another author, Robert B. Parker:

I lay back down on the bunk. . . .

I did some deep breathing.

And where was the picture? Lola would have kept a copy. It wasn't in
her house. If the cops had found it, it would have led them somewhere.
They were as stuck as I was, stucker because they didn't know the things
that I was stuck about. Could be in a safe-deposit box. Except where was
the key? And whiskey-voiced old broads like Lola didn't usually keep safe-
deposit boxes. Maybe she stashed the negative with a friend. Except

whiskey-voiced old broads like Lola didn't usually trust friends with valuable property. The simplest answer was Larry again, and the simplest answer on Lippy was Les. And Les was Larry.

I did some more deep breathing. (191)

Approaching the detective narrative from a cognitive perspective helps us to understand why writers can, if they wish, abandon the Sherlock-Holmesian grandstanding and reveal to the reader every or almost every thought of the detective. It turns out that it does not really matter *whose* minds we are reading as long as there *are* some strategically concealed minds to read and as long as the topic of such a reading is highly focused (e.g., on a murder). It appears, then, that the writer's decision of whether or not to leave the thought processes of the detective open throughout the narrative correlates, at least on some level, with the length of the story. The narrative economics of the short story, which necessarily limit the number of minds that could be read and misread, makes it convenient to posit the detective's mind as one of the "mystery" minds, along with that of the main suspect. In a novel, where a larger number of minds can be contemplated, the mind of the detective does not have to be one of them.

Note that this is not some kind of absolute rule. There are plenty of novels in which the mind of the detective is closed off to us along with the minds of the suspects, especially those written early in the twentieth century, during what could be characterized as a cultural transition from the short story to the novel as the main medium of the genre. It seems that by exploring the new mind-reading possibilities of the longer form, writers have gradually discovered that there is nothing sacred about the tendency to keep the detective's thought processes enigmatic. Discoveries of this kind tacitly accompany each individual project of writing, for each whodunit tries something different in its treatment of mind-reading, and the cumulative effect of the most recent attempts will make the detective narrative of the coming decades different from what it is today.

(d) "Alone Again, Naturally"

Here is a peculiarly tenacious, though not for the want of writers who have worked hard to undermine it, "rule" of a detective story: "In his sexual life, the detective must be either celibate or happily married."[7] W. H. Auden formulated it rather succinctly in 1948, although, of course, he was neither the first nor the last to notice it. Already in 1836, the brothers Goncourt asserted on first reading Poe's detective stories that they bear "signs of the literature of the twentieth century—love giving place to deductions . . . the interest of the story moved from the heart to the head . . . from the drama to solution."[8] Haycraft reports that in 1941, Columbia University Press conducted a survey among "several hundred habitual readers" of detective stories, asking them in particular to identify their "pet dislikes." The aficionados of the genre, both male and female, voted "too much love and romance" to the top of the list of the undesirables.[9] Several years later, Frederick Dannay and Manfred B. Lee, the joint creators of Ellery Queen, echoed, perhaps unintentionally, this sentiment of the survey participants. In response to Dashiel Hammett's question, "Mr. Queen, will you be good enough to explain your famous character's sex life, if any?" Dannay and Lee suggested that "a wife, mistress or even physical love affair planted on Ellery after all these years would upset readers."[10] Again, in 1965, Margery Allingham observed that detective fiction is "structurally unsuited to the steady use of romantic love. It can accommodate a brief encounter, or even a series of them, but anything more and the danger of upset becomes an embarrassment" (7).

Writers fought valiantly to loosen up this "strictly puritan"[11] bent of the murder mystery. Allingham herself authored a series of novels featuring her favorite detective Albert Campion that explicitly challenged the rigid construction of that "very tight little box whose four walls consist of a killing, a mystery, an enquiry and a conclusion" with no "room for much else" (11). In *Sweet Danger,* Campion meets and admires the teenage Lady Amanda Fitton, who clearly "fits" his intellectual, emotional, and social class profile. In *The Fashion in Shrouds,* he sees her again after several years, admires her some more, and even agrees to affiance her. In *Traitor's Purse,* he is literally bludgeoned by the author into admitting to himself how ardently he loves and is afraid to lose Amanda to whom he has been engaged for the last eight (!) years. At the end of the novel he finally tells her "let's get married early tomorrow . . . I've only got thirty-six hours leave" (505), to which the ever "real cool" (14) Amanda, who has just gotten over her infatuation with the wrong man, replies "yes, . . . it's time we got married" (505). In all three cases, Allingham attempts to upset and complicate the traditional balance of the detective plot by adding to the main mystery of each novel the mystery of Campion's and Amanda's feelings for each other.

Similarly, Sayers structures her *Gaudy Night* (1936) so that the question of whether or not the professional detective-story writer Harriet Vane will agree to marry the love-struck detective Lord Peter Wimsey is billed as just as important as the question of who has been wreaking havoc in Shrewsbury College by writing hate letters to the faculty and students and destroying their work. By portraying the criminal as driven by a distinctly antifeminist agenda, Sayers connects the straightforward "mystery" part of the novel with Harriet's tortured mulling over of whether a woman can preserve her emotional and professional independence after being married, particularly if the husband is as brilliant and strong-willed as Wimsey.

Sayers has thus anticipated the detective novels of the 1980s and 1990s, in which the question of how much "room" there is in a detective story for "love and romance" was compellingly rearticulated with the introduction of the female private investigator. Though perceived by some of her chauvinist male colleagues as an "alien monster" rather than a "real girl" (Paretsky, *Burn Marks,* 339), such a heroine is routinely depicted as negotiating romantic relationship, as is Kat Colorado (Karen Kijewski, *Alley Kat Blues*), V. I. Warshawski (Paretsky, *Bitter Medicine*), Kinsey Millhone (Sue Grafton, *"P" is for Peril*), Stoner McTavish (Sarah Dreher, *Stoner McTavish; Something Shady*), and Thursday Next (Jasper Fforde, *The Eyre Affair*). Some critics have hailed such plot developments as a sign that the detective novel has indeed escaped the "very tight little box" confining its predecessors. Ian Ousby suggests that the female investigator's "personal involvement" with lovers, friends, and family members "is not just a convenience to get the story going but a signal that its theme will be the detective's own self-discovery and self-definition." A private eye is "not just there to solve a mystery but to learn about herself by understanding women from her family past better, or to see herself more clearly by comparing her life with the fate of women friends,"[12] an observation that seems to be borne out by the material of, say, Paretsky's *Total Recall.*

My response to such claims is cautiously optimistic. When researching this topic, I have read more detective novels than I have ever thought possible, and I came to believe that on some important level the kind of mind-reading expected from the reader of the detective novel is indeed not particularly compatible with the kind of mind-reading expected from the reader of the story focusing on a romantic relationship.[13] At the same time, it seems that benefiting from the years of experimentation and failure, detective writers have certainly learned how to hierarchize various elements of the two kinds of mind-reading and thus how to successfully incorporate some romantic themes into their murder mysteries.

Contemporary cognitive research offers a fascinating (if, at this point, unavoidably rudimentary and tentative) way of modeling some of those

FIGURE 3. Book cover of MANEATER by Gigi Levangie Grazer reproduced with the permission of Simon & Schuster Adult Publishing Group. Book cover, Copyright © 2003 by Simon & Schuster. All rights reserved. Michael Mahovlich / Masterfile (image code 700-075736).

failures and successes. First of all, we have to remember that our Theory of Mind is not an adaptation that enables us to apply a *single universal set of inferences* to any situation that calls for attributing desires, thoughts, and intentions to another living creature. Rather, it could be thought of as a "cluster" of multiple adaptations, many of them functionally geared toward specific social contexts. For example, the kind of mind-reading that we use in the process of selecting and courting a mate is on some important level quite different from the mind-reading we deploy when we try to escape a predator. Trying to guess what that cute person at the adjacent table is thinking every time she provocatively glances up at you from her plate must recruit cognitive adaptations for mind-reading somewhat different from those recruited when you are trying to guess what that tiger is thinking as she leisurely approaches you in the street after having escaped her cage in the zoo. Specifically, the same question aimed at figuring the other's state of mind, for example, "I wonder if she is still hungry?" automatically activates a very different suite of inferences depending on whether it is applied to a potential mate or to a wild animal. (Of course, in certain situations, the two can overlap on select levels: just think of the various fascinating shades of anxiety we may feel when we fall in love with a notorious "lady-killer" or "femme fatale," or consider our emotional response to the cover illustration of Gigi Levangie Grazer's 2003 novel *Maneater* [figure 3]. I will address this topic later in this subsection.)

Second, trying to figure out how the person that you have a crush on feels about you and what you should do based on your far-from-perfect understanding of his/her state of mind requires a complex balancing and adjustment of several metarepresentationally framed interpretations of the situation. For example, you need to try to keep track of the version of that person's thoughts that are based on your own wishful thinking (this would be a metarepresentation with a source tag such as, "I would love it if . . ."); as well as of the version that is based on what your friends think about that person's feelings about you as distinct, for example, from what they thought about it yesterday; as well as of what that person has intimated to you about his/her feelings yesterday as opposed to what he/she is telling you today; and so on. This may sound too involved, but I suspect that the cognitive reality of this process is much more complicated, and it is important for us to get a glimpse of this complexity in order to realize how extremely emotionally/cognitively consuming this endeavor can be. Our Theory of Mind gets fully engaged with this task, "turning on," so to speak, the system of inferences that have evolved to enable us to negotiate the mate-selection process.

But, then, trying to decide which of the ten ostensibly pleasant and law-abiding citizens in our snow-trapped train car is a psychopathic mass murderer could be just as emotionally/cognitively challenging because *this* task also requires us to process numerous interpretations of our fellow-passengers' mental states with various degrees of metarepresentational framing. Only it is likely that in this case our mind-reading processes activate systems of inferences quite distinct from those used in guessing the state of mind of a potential mate. It is possible, for example, that among the mind-reading adaptations activated in this particular context are those particularly geared toward enabling us to negotiate situations involving violations of social contract and situations involving avoidance of predators.

It seems then that the "economics" of the evolved cognitive architecture of our species could explain why one may have a difficult time dwelling on the absent beloved's possible thoughts while being threatened by a homicidal maniac. Detective stories cultivate in their readers a very particular group of emotions, clustering more often than not around fear. And fear, as Patrick Colm Hogan has compellingly argued, drawing on the work of cognitive psychologist Keith Oatley and neuroscientist Antonio Damasio, tends to focus our emotions to the exclusion of irrelevant environmental stimuli. It is just as well that it does, so that upon spotting a lion in the distance, we "do not spend time considering all [our] options, potentially getting 'lost in the byways of . . . calculation.'"[14] The "limitation of procedural schemas"—flee or fight!—and the "narrowing of attentional focus"—THINK LION!—"are both clearly functional here."[15]

And if calculate we must—as, for example, when knowing that one of our pleasant fellow passengers is, in effect, a predator but not knowing which one—we had better have *all* of our attention focused on the problem at hand. Trying to figure out who among our present company is a murderer involves not only attempting to read the minds of everybody around us but also constantly imagining our behavior from their point of view, for we don't want the criminal to guess that we suspect him/her. Imagine walking leisurely round the *really* hungry lion, picking up its tail, and casually patting it on the head, all the while pretending that the lion is not even there. Not an ideal situation for analyzing the feelings of one's beloved.

But, one could say, *reading* about the homicidal maniac is not the same as being actually stalked by him. By the same token, trying to guess together with Austen's Anne Eliot whether Captain Wentworth still loves her is not the same as actually going through such emotional upheavals yourself. It could be very difficult to do both at the same time in real life—to think, that is, of how to outsmart a rapidly approaching murderer while you are figuring out what your beloved *really* meant yesterday when he said that the weather was particularly friendly for outdoor rambles—but what prevents us from combining these two "activities" in our imagination? Why can't we control our emotions and manipulate them into "multitasking" by reminding ourselves that *we* personally are not threatened by the murderer-at-large and *we* personally are not worried about Captain Wentworth's feelings?

This question dovetails a much larger issue: "how is it that we respond emotionally to literature at all?"[16] For a detailed analysis of this issue, I refer the reader to Hogan's two most recent studies.[17] For the purpose of the present argument, I want to focus on his observation that our emotional response to fiction is a "matter of trigger perception, concrete imagination, and emotional memory. The issue of fictionality just does not enter."[18] Note, incidentally, how well this works with my earlier argument that once we have bracketed off the fictional story as a whole as a metarepresentation with a source tag pointing to its author, we proceed to consider its constituent parts as more or less architecturally true. "To know that something is fictional," Hogan continues, "is to make a judgment that it does not exist. But existence judgments are cortical. They have relatively little to do with our emotional responses to anything. The intensity of emotional response is affected by a number of variables . . . [which] include, for example, proximity and speed, vividness, expectedness and so on."[19]

To illustrate Hogan's point about the variables affecting our emotional response to fiction, think of yourself reading the second to last chapter of a murder mystery. You know that a murderer, whose identity is still hidden, is getting closer and closer (the issue of proximity) to the protagonist you have come to associate with. You know how the protagonist feels sitting there trapped in her own creaky house (the issue of vividness) with no phone lines working, and the slightly intoxicated neighbor, who has accidentally wandered in earlier, as her only, and clearly inadequate, protection. Then—boom!—the suddenly sobered-up neighbor turns out to be the murderer (the issue of expectedness), and there seems to be no escape for the heroine now.

And when it comes to all these emotion-triggering variables, we have to remember that after tens of thousands of years of collective cultural experience of storytelling, authors have at their disposal a bag of rather effective tricks aimed at emotionally hooking us on whatever mind-reading scenario they are activating. A compelling love story knows how to push your emotional buttons by making you guess and second-guess the characters' states of mind because it is built on the bones of millions of forgotten love stories that didn't. Detective narratives have not been around for so long, but still, given that fewer than one-half of one percent of such narratives published since the nineteenth century have survived in cultural memory,[20] we may assume that authors have learned a thing or two about how to keep you on the edge of your seat with guesswork concerning the mental processes of their characters.

It could be, then, that the narrative that attempts to be simultaneously a *high-intensity* love story (i.e., a love story that keeps us working hard on figuring out the lovers' state of mind) and a *high-intensity* detective story (i.e., a story that keeps us working hard at figuring the suspected criminal's state of mind) proves "too much" for us, at least in the currently familiar literary format. Just imagine a narrative that skillfully forces you to anxiously keep track of the thoughts of twelve different people (for any of them, or perhaps all of them, as in Christie's novel, could be involved in that deviously arranged murder) *and* that also forces you to hang with bated breath on every sidelong look of the heroine who apparently does not want to show her rival that she cares that her beloved has read the letter that the rival has written to him five years ago about that conversation that the heroine and the hero had as children in that garden at their eccentric aunt's estate because that letter implies that the rival is much more emotionally suited to the hero than the romantic heroine herself is, and so on. Clearly, something's got to give. Hence, we have successful detective stories with some romantic elements, but the metarepresentational framing needed to process those romantic elements is carefully calibrated so as not to compete with the metarepresentational framing required to process the detecting elements of the story. Conversely, we have compelling romances with elements of detection, but the metarepresentational framing of the detecting elements is skillfully subdued so as to add some extra level of mind-reading to the story without making it compete with the *main* type of mind-reading expected from its readers.

Of course, in its present embryonic state, a "cognitive-literary" perspective may not be able to explain why certain combinations of different kinds of mind-reading in the story are more felicitous than others. Still, it points us to the areas of cognitive research to watch. If, at least on some level, the narrative focusing on a romance and the narrative focusing on the detection of the murder may appeal to differently specialized adaptations within our Theory of Mind module (e.g., the one evolved to facilitate mating and the one evolved to facilitate predator avoidance), then the narrative that combines the two by demanding an equally high emotional attendance both to the romance and to the detection of murder overloads some of our attention-focusing and information-processing systems.

Literary history can be thus viewed as a continuous experimentation with recombining metarepresentational units that used to feel overwhelming for our representation-hungry brain-mind but that have come to feel pleasurable in new, hitherto-unexpected, ways. Hybrid genres emerge all the time as a testimony to this experimental endeavor.[21] Who knows?—in five hundred years, we may have a genre of murder mystery/romance/family chronicle that will hit our Theory-of-Mind "spots" in all the right ways and feel as "natural" as a "pure" detective story feels today. In fact, I would say that *because* the combination of the equally emotionally engaging detective plot and romance plot remains so challenging today, we have a "guarantee" of sorts that writers will continue experimenting in the direction of integrating the two. The culturally embedded cognitive "limits" (i.e., the limits that became apparent only because of certain paths taken by literary history) thus present us with creative openings rather than with a promise of stagnation and endless replication of the established forms.

Meanwhile, let us take a closer look at the detective mysteries that have indeed incorporated romance into their main plot of detection. First of all, it seems that many writers have learned to skirt the issue altogether by either having their detectives go through regular and not particularly involving love affairs or by keeping them married. Both casual affairs and marriage require a minimal amount of metarepresentational framing involved in figuring out the romantic partner's state of mind.

Thus the thirty-something female detective has a reasonably clear idea of what a college student who ogles her at a party is thinking (as in James's *Unsuitable Job for a Woman*). Similarly, the newly married, hunky, but unfortunately swamped-with-work Marlowe knows exactly what his rich and idle wife *really* wants (as in Raymond Chandler and Robert B. Parker's *Poodle Springs*). Casual affairs and married states are good for the detective story because they let us focus our mind-reading energies on figuring out the crime and suspecting everybody, while still making us appreciate that all-human aspect of the investigator's personality. It really *is* a neat narrative trick. No modern-day Dashiel Hammett would be able to quiz Sara Paretsky or Sue Grafton on the subject of their heroines' unnatural celibacy, for, look: V. I. Warshawsky and Kinsey Millhone hop in bed with a different man in nearly every novel or else reminisce about their recent affairs.

On the far opposite end of the spectrum are the detective story writers who overinvest in the romance, an instructive sight. Sarah Dreher's novels feature a shy travel agent, Stoner McTavish, whose emotional energies are focused on winning the heart of the enchanting Gwen and who prevents murders as a way of deepening her relationship with Gwen. The compelling romance part of the story leaves very little room for guessing the states of mind of potential criminals: Gwen is a delightful mystery, but we can easily figure out what the baddies are thinking.

Ironically, although I am not sure if there is any causal connection here, the "real," challenging, metarepresentationally framed mind-reading that we expect from the detective story is substituted in one of Dreher's novels by plain old telepathy. I stopped considering *Something Shady* a detective narrative after the heroine, locked in the room by the criminals who were getting ready to kill her, apparently sent a psychic signal to her aunt in a different city, and the aunt started calling the baddies' enclave, thus nearly distracting them for a while from their evil designs. (Like Peter Rabinowitz, I feel "entitled to assume that the supernatural cannot intrude" in the detective narrative.[22])

Dreher's overinvestment in romantic mind-reading at the expense of "detective" mind-reading provides an illuminating contrast to Allingham's *Sweet Danger, The Fashion in Shrouds,* and *Traitor's Purse,* and Sayers's *Gaudy Night.* Those four novels were just as ambitious in their attempt to break the celibate mold of the murder mystery, but they succeeded where the "Stoner McTavish" series fails,[23] and here is why: the "relationship" plots in Allingham and Sayers are engaging enough, but they are skillfully underemotionalized compared to the gripping detective plots of each novel. The mutual attraction of Amanda Fitton and Albert Campion is cute, but, for some reason, we are just as happy to keep their romance unresolved until the next published installment of Campion's adventures, whenever it comes, as are Amanda and Albert themselves. Similarly, in the case of *Gaudy Night,* we understand early on that Harriet Vane either will marry Lord Peter Wimsey after a requisite amount of soul-searching or will not, but we don't particularly care anyway. By contrast, we do care about the identity of the increasingly violent college malefactor, and we dutifully begin to suspect every innocent middle-aged professor whom Sayers grooms for that wicked role.

In other words, both Allingham and Sayers "advertise" their stories as detective narratives with a strong element of romance by increasing, in particular, the amount of time they spend talking about their protagonists' love interests. Because, however, they *do not* build in a strong metarepresentational framing for this aspect of the story, that is, they *do not* make us guess, second-guess, misread, and then head-slappingly correct our misreading of, the characters' romantic feelings, the romance remains a tame "junior partner"[24] to their main business of detection.

Hammett's *The Maltese Falcon* is an important example of yet a different strategy. Brigid O'Shaughnessy, the woman with whom the private

FIGURE 4. "What else is there that I can buy you with?" Sam Spade and Brigid O'Shaughnessy before Sam finds out that she killed Archer.

FIGURE 5. "When one in your organization gets killed, it is a bad business to let the killer get away with it—bad all around, bad for every detective everywhere." Sam and Brigid after he realizes that she killed Archer.

investigator Sam Spade falls in love, is one of the suspects in the case of the murder of his partner, Miles Archer. The criminal and the romantic aspects of the novel are so intertwined that if Brigid is concealing the truth about her role in the killing of Archer, it means she is lying to Sam about her feelings for him, for had she really loved him, she would not have kept him in the dark about the story of the crime (figures 4 and 5). The romantic mind-reading thus nearly completely overlaps with the mind-reading oriented toward the detection of the crime.[25]

Here is what is particularly interesting about this frugal "two-for-one" scenario. On the one hand, I have argued above that because, *at least on some level,* the romance plot and the detection plot "feed" their respective information into different adaptations within our Theory of Mind module (i.e., the mind-reading adaptation geared toward mate selection and the mind-reading adaptation geared toward predator avoidance), writers may generally have a difficult time when they want to combine the two plots so as to give them an equal emotional weight within the story. Hammett, however, seems to have circumvented this difficulty by merging the two plots into one. To understand some of the emotional effects of such a merger, think again of my earlier examples of the cultural images of "maneater" and "ladykiller" that emphasize the danger of falling in love with a predator. The detective story in which the investigator's love interest is also one of the suspects exploits the suggestive cognitive ambiguity of such a situation. Such a story derives titillating emotional mileage from making the readers mix the inferences from the mate-selection aspect of mind-reading with inferences from the predator-avoidance aspect of mind-reading.

Misreading the mind of the predator by approaching him/her with the view of romantic relationship may result in a personal disaster, as so happens in Hammett's *Maltese Falcon,* Paretsky's *Bitter Medicine,* and Hitchcock's *Vertigo.* On the other hand, the love interest may turn out to have been unjustly suspected of predatory tendencies (as is Vivian Sternwood in the Hollywood version of Chandler's *The Big Sleep* or Linda Loring in the original *The Long Goodbye*). In a very mild variation on the two-for-one scenario, Karen Kijewski's *Alley Kat Blues,* the policeman-boyfriend of the female investigator, Kat Colorado, gets entangled with a woman implicated in the crime that Kat is trying to solve. By solving the murder case, Kat thus also gets to figure out the feelings of her boyfriend who has been acting strangely lately. *Alley Kat Blues* is significantly more invested in romance than many of the detective novels discussed above (though it does not approach the level of *Stoner McTavish* or *Something Shady*), and it pulls it off precisely by creating a situation in which the mind-reading oriented toward solving the crime overlaps with the mind-reading oriented toward figuring out the feelings of the romantic partner. In other words, unless used too often and thus rendered predictable, the conveniently economic focusing of the two different kinds of mind-reading on one person can work for writers who are intent on opening up that "very tight little box" of the classic detective story.

Note that by construing a spectrum, on the one end of which there are detective stories with the minimum of romance and, on the other, the stories in which romance overwhelms detection, with a variety of other narratives gravitating toward either end of the spectrum, I do not intend to pronounce on the aesthetic value of any of these books. Nor do I make any sort of prediction about their chances for survival in what Franco Moretti calls the "slaughterhouse" of the long-term literary market. Instead, I suggest that by articulating the difference between the love story and the detective story in terms of the dominant type of mind-reading required from the reader in each case,[26] we can reground and systematize our intuitions about the differences between the two genres. In general, we can now start thinking of our concept of the literary genre as reflecting, at least on some level, our intuitive awareness that even though *all* fictional narratives rely on and tease our Theory of Mind, some narratives engage to a higher degree one cluster of cognitive adaptations associated with our ToM than another cluster of such adaptations.

~4~

A COGNITIVE EVOLUTIONARY PERSPECTIVE:
ALWAYS HISTORICIZE!

S o what have I really been saying by insisting on grounding our enjoyment of detective stories in the workings of our metarepresentational ability and our Theory of Mind? A quarter-century ago, in his influential *Adventure, Mystery, and Romance,* John Cawelti cautioned literary critics about the dangers of assuming that the process of writing and reading fiction is "dependent, contingent, or a mere reflection of other more basic social and psychological processes."[1] Have I recruited research from the currently fashionable field of cognitive science to smuggle in the same old fallacy of explaining away a complex cultural artifact as a mere reflection of a basic psychological process? Have I tumbled headlong into the pit that Cawelti warned us about?

If I have, my response is to dig myself further in. I shall start by quoting more of Cawelti's argument:

> In the present state of our knowledge, it seems more reasonable to treat social and psychological factors not as single determinant causes of literary expression but as elements in a complex process that limits in various ways the complete autonomy of art. In making cultural interpretations of literary patterns, we should consider them not as simple reflections of social ideologies or psychological needs but as instances of a relatively autonomous mode of behavior that is involved in a complex dialectic with other aspects of human life.[2]

My main rejoinder to the quite irreproachable case made by Cawelti is that, although certainly focusing on "psychological factors," a cognitive-evolutionary approach to literature does not subscribe to the traditional notion of psychology that he may have had in mind in his influential study. First of all, as I have argued earlier with my "weightlifting" example, our cognitive predispositions do not enter the "cause-effect" relationship with complex cultural artifacts such as works of fiction. Our Theory of Mind and our metarepresentational ability render the detective stories cognitively possible, but they by no means make their emergence and popularity inevitable. Too many locally contingent historical factors influence the process of the establishment of the new genre for us to suggest otherwise. In fact, it is quite possible that many other genres, currently latent and perhaps *never* to be explicitly culturally articulated, would have engaged our ToM and metarepresentationality equally well or much better, but the myriad of historical contingencies "conspire" to keep them dormant.

Hence my qualification of the second point made by Cawelti. When he observes that "psychological factors" should be considered as "elements in a complex process that limits in various ways the complete autonomy of art," we recognize in his formulation the traditional view of our culture as "limited," via a complex mediation of multiple factors, by our biological (here, cognitive) endowment. Cognitive evolutionary perspective holds the promise of the productive reversal of this model. It seems that, if anything, it is the specific historical contingencies—or "culture"—that limit the concrete expressions of our cognitive endowment, for, as I have pointed out above, nobody knows how many genre variations that could have worked out our ToM in a particularly felicitous way have never been realized because of a given confluence of historic circumstances (and my concept of historic here includes such factors as the life histories of individual authors).

Ellen Spolsky captures this important reversal of the traditional understanding of the relationship between the "cultural" and the "cognitive" when she suggests that the "theoretically infinite number of creative possibilities will in practice always be channeled and restricted by the cultural surround [even if] those restrictions are themselves often negotiable."[3] Thus in spite of our evolved cognitive ability to attribute states of mind to ourselves and other people and to store information metarepresentationally, there is no predicting what cultural forms, literary or otherwise, these cognitive abilities can take. To quote Spolsky again, attention "to the complexity of the interrelationships among cognitive and cultural phenomena and the sheer number of possible local variations of these phenomena suggest why a commitment to the existence of evolved (innate or emergent) cognitive structures could never be a commitment to either philosophical or behavioral determinism—quite the opposite."[4] In other words, by introducing cognitive evolutionary psychology into our study of the genre, we do not, as a matter of fact, give in to the "psychological" determinism of the kind Cawelti justly feared, but rather we develop a conceptual framework that truly commits us to historicizing our data.

It is tempting to seize on Cawelti's opening proviso about the "present state of our knowledge" and suggest that because back in the 1970s, when he was writing his *Adventure, Mystery, and Romance,* literary critics indeed did not have at their disposal conceptual tools made possible by the recent advances in cognitive evolutionary science, he was only too right to be chary about the tendency to reduce "literary expression" to "psychological factors." Although nothing would date my own work more effectively than claiming that we have *now* attained the state of scientific sophistication unavailable to the benighted literary critics of the previous decades, at least a very mild version of this claim has to be ventured forth because even in its rudimentary state, cognitive evolutionary psychology does offer us a principally new way of approaching fictional narratives. By seeing such narratives as endlessly *experimenting* with rather than *automatically executing* given psychological tendencies, this approach opens new venues for literary historians wishing to integrate their knowledge of specific cultural circumstances implicated in the production of literary texts with important new insights into the workings of our brain/mind.

CONCLUSION

WHY DO WE READ (AND WRITE) FICTION?

~ 1 ~

AUTHORS MEET THEIR READERS

I have argued throughout this book that certain fictional texts, such as eighteenth-century epistolary novels (e.g., *Clarissa*), early nineteenth-century comedies of manners (e.g., *Emma*), detective novels, stream-of-consciousness novels (e.g., *Mrs. Dalloway*), and novels featuring unreliable narrators (e.g., *Lolita*) all engage clusters of cognitive adaptations associated with our ToM and metarepresentational ability in a particularly focused way. This is not to say that other novels *do not* (for a characteristically excellent discussion of this issue, see Palmer's *Fictional Minds*) or that all of the above novels do it in the *same* way. Clearly, the novels of Woolf and Chandler affect readers very differently and may indeed appeal to very distinct audiences. Still, most of these narratives seem to demand outright that we process complexly embedded intentionalities of their characters, configuring their minds as represented by other minds, whose representations we may or may not trust.

I have also suggested that at certain junctures of human history (e.g., with the advent of print culture and growing literacy), a combination of new technological developments and socioeconomic conditions may make the cultural transmission of such "ToM-intense" fictional narratives possible. Such texts can then find their readers, that is, the people who like their ToM teased in this particular manner and who, once having gotten a taste of such a cognitive workout, want and can afford more and more of it.

Moreover, when we think of this cultural-historical process of "matching" texts with their readers, perhaps it makes more sense to speak not just in terms of the text that serendipitously finds its audience but also in terms of the writer who finds hers. For it seems to me that working on a story that engages the reader's Theory of Mind in a particularly focused way must hit the author's own mind-reading spot as few other activities do. The process of writing can be excruciatingly difficult and is sometimes described in terms reminiscent of torture, but for a mind constituted the way the writer's mind is constituted, that process must represent something of a cognitive necessity. I am not saying that people who write fiction do it purely to stimulate or express their own peculiarly developed mind-reading ability. I do suspect, however, that other conscious and semiconscious incentives for writing, such as making a living, impressing potential mates, and advancing pet ideological agendas, would hardly suffice to make one offer up so much of her life to constructing elaborate mental worlds of people who never existed.

P. G. Wodehouse insisted that authors conjure up fictional worlds precisely for that kick of creating, controlling, and inhabiting other people's states of mind. He called it "liking to write," but the example that he used to illustrate that elusive "liking" shows that he thought that "what urges a writer to write" is the pleasurable opportunity for a particularly focused mind-reading:

> I should imagine that even the man who compiles a railroad timetable is thinking much more of what fun it all is than of the check he is going to get when he turns in the completed script. Watch his eyes sparkle as he puts a very small (a) against the line
> 4:51 arr. 6:22
> knowing that the reader will not notice it and turn to the bottom of the page, where it says
> (a) On Saturdays only
> but will dash off with his suitcase and golf clubs all merry and bright, arriving in good time at the station on the afternoon of Friday. Money is the last thing such a writer has in mind. (110–11)

In response to Dr. Johnson's categorical "nobody but a blockhead ever wrote except for money," Wodehouse would say that when the author has "written something, he wants to get as much for it as he can, but that is a very different thing from writing for money" (110). What drives the creative process is our hankering for mind-making and mind-reading. Some of us work it by compiling railroad timetables, others by writing scholarly books, still others by sailing the empyrean with the likes of Galahad Treepwood, Jeeves, and Ukridge.

Note how this view of writing fiction complicates an influential postulate of reader-response theory that "a text can only come to life when it is read, and if it is to be examined, it must therefore be studied through the eyes of the reader."[1] By now we are accustomed to thinking of a fictional narrative in terms of what it does to us (e.g., Booth is convinced that "it is good for [him] to be required to go through" *The Wings of the Dove*[2]) and what we do to it (e.g., we bring it to life; we "participate in the production of [its] meaning"[3]). Deeply congenial as these two views are to the perspective espoused by this study, we need to add the third component to them: the mind-reading mind of the writer. To poach on Booth's formulation, "[I]t is good" for the author to engage in the cognitive workout of constructing fictional minds. To poach on Iser's, a text "comes to life" in the mind of the author just as richly as—if not more richly than, in some aspects—it does in the mind of her readers because it engages her ToM in a unique and pleasurable (if at times torturous) manner.

The novel, then, is truly a meeting of the minds—of the particularly inclined minds in a particular historical moment that has made the encounter serendipitously possible. Samuel Richardson could indulge the quirks of his ToM (boy, was he one interesting London businessman!) and write the 1,500-page *Clarissa* focusing obsessively on mind-reading and misreading because he had first tried it first on a lesser scale in *Pamela*. He must have liked how it felt, and, moreover, he must have come to believe that his second novel would be able to reach a group of readers who love just this kind of cognitive stimulation. Or, to put it slightly differently, some of the people (by no means all) who read *Pamela* when it first came out discovered that they like this kind of story, wished for more, and could afford more (what with reasonable book prices and increasing leisure time for readers of a certain social standing), thus ensuring that what we call today a "psychological" or "sentimental" novel would survive and give birth to several related genres.

I speak of the "ensured" survival of the psychological novel guardedly. It did not have to happen like this. As I argued in Part III, there is nothing really ensured or determined about how genres arise, metamorphose into other genres, or die out, even if they do "get at" our ToM in a particularly felicitous way. For all that we know, there might have been a man or a woman in the eighteenth century who wrote an experimental novel that could have started a new literary tradition stimulating our ToM in a wonderfully unpredictable fashion. That novel did not find a publisher; or it was lost in the mail; or its author changed his/her mind and never revisited this particular style of writing in his/her subsequent publications. Literary history reflects only a tiny subset of realized cognitive possibilities constrained by the myriad of local contingencies, and those contingencies include personal inclinations and histories of individual writers and readers.

~2~

IS THIS WHY WE READ FICTION?
SURELY, THERE IS MORE TO IT!

*T*his emphasis on local contingencies carries over to another claim that I think you think I have been making throughout this book (yes, that's the third level of embedment—we handle it easily). Theory of Mind is a cluster of cognitive adaptations that allows us to navigate our social world and also structures that world. Intensely social species that we are, we thus read fiction because it engages, in a variety of particularly focused ways, our Theory of Mind.

That's my general claim, and here are the promised qualifications. First of all, some texts experiment with our ToM more intensely than others, and some readers appreciate that experimentation more than others, or appreciate some forms of that experimentation more than others. (Again, neither preference is a meaningful indicator of the reader's emotional intelligence or any other personal characteristic. For example, people who love Woolf's prose at times apply to graduate programs in English, and that's as much as I can say about their overall personal profiles.)

Second, the reader's predilection for a certain form of novelistic experimentation with ToM does not mean that she is guaranteed to enjoy every well-written novel adhering to that form. For example, among the people who like the cognitive thrill offered by the figure of the unreliable narrator, somebody could be turned off by *Lolita's* theme of pedophilia. By the same token, an aficionado of a detective novel could find too depressing certain aspects of P. D. James's *The Black Tower.* Conversely, a person could find intolerable James's depiction of corruption in the house of assisted living but still be deeply touched by her portrayal of the novel's murdered protagonist, Father Baddeley. This is to say that factors other than the form of the novel's engagement with ToM enter into the assessment of our personal liking of the novel or our assessment of its relative aesthetic value.

Third—but here I ought to be interrupted by my long-suffering reader who feels badly misrepresented by the argument of this book, in spite of all my qualifications. Let me play the role of that impatient reader myself and voice her main objection, which would sound (in case she happens to like Henry James) something like this:

> There is more to my reading of fiction than simply having my ToM tickled! The argument of your book does not even begin to explain what I feel when I learn that the dearest wish of incurably ill Ralph Touchett of James's *The Portrait of a Lady* has always been to die at the same time with his father, and that Ralph is "steeped in melancholy" (84) when he realizes that this wish will not be granted, and, ill as he is, he will still outlive his father. As James puts it, "The father and the son had been close companions, and the idea of being left alone with the remnants of a tasteless life on his hands was not gratifying to the young man, who had always and tacitly counted upon his elder's help in making the best of a poor business" (85). Why I relate to this sentiment so strongly is my own business, but isn't it obvious that your book's theorizing on ToM and fiction does not capture or explain the instant recognition and heartache that is such an important part of my interaction with the novel? (A hypothetical reader, who insists, quite rightly, on the complexity and unpredictability of her feelings)

I expect that by now you have also thought of episodes like this and concluded that there must be more to our response to our favorite fictional stories than just having our ToM stimulated by them. Except that if you have, you are mistaken, and your mistake stems from our use of that little word "just." It is fair to say that my book has dealt with just a few aspects of the relationship between our ToM and fiction—with a tiny subset of that relationship, in fact. It does not make sense, however, to say that our interaction with fiction entails much more than just having our ToM stimulated. When it comes to our everyday social functioning (which includes making sense of the social world of the novel), ToM is always much more than whatever cluster of cognitive adaptations we have isolated to make the discussion of it manageable.

For instance, in practical terms, how do you separate our ToM and emotions? If, using my source-monitoring ability, I remember that it was my enemy who wanted my boss to promote me into a certain department, my emotions concerning that impending promotion might be quite different from what they were had I known that he hated the idea of my transfer. I might feel anxiety and anger instead of happy anticipation, and

I might imagine unknown dangers and difficulties lurking behind my new appointment. ToM gives meaning to our emotions and is in turn given meaning by them. As Palmer observes, "[T]he interconnections between cognition and emotion . . . are difficult if not impossible to disentangle. Cognitions tend to have a strong emotional element and vice versa. They also relate closely in causal terms: a character's anger might be caused by a cognition of some sort that in turn results in further emotions and then other cognitions."[1]

By the same token, my imagined reader's argument about *The Portrait of a Lady* is a complex amalgamation of dynamically interacting emotions and cognitions. Her personal feelings about some elder relative that she herself feels very close to are made more poignant, first, because she is able to attribute a particular sentiment to a literary character; second, because she can keep track of the complex source of the sentiment, seeing it issuing from James via "Ralph" and not from herself; and third, because she is titillated by the similarity between something that she has quietly felt for a long time and something that a highly sympathetic personage, such as Ralph, is experiencing. She realizes that she is not alone in the wish that she used to consider odd, and her new awareness of this fragile but comforting community is not reducible to the sum of cognitions and emotions that went into it.

In other words, we do read novels because they engage our ToM, but we are at present a long way off from grasping fully the levels of complexity that this engagement entails. Fiction helps us to pattern in newly nuanced ways our emotions and perceptions;[2] it bestows "new knowledge or increased understanding" and gives "the chance for a sharpened ethical sense";[3] and it creates new forms of meaning for our everyday existence. All of this exploratory work is inextricably bound up with ToM, and the overall effect of it on the reader is not reducible to the sum of this narrative's engagements with our various cognitive adaptations. Some day we may have a conceptual framework that will allow us to speak about this overall effect—that "emergent meaning"[4] of the literary narrative. In preparation for that sophisticated future, here is a very specific, modest, take-home claim from my book. I can say that I personally read fiction because it offers a pleasurable and intensive workout for my Theory of Mind. And, if you have indeed read this study of mine from cover to cover and followed attentively its arguments about Clarissa, Lolita, Arsène Lupin, and Mrs. Dalloway, I suspect that this is why *you* read fiction, too.

Notes

I: 1

1. Like Hermione Lee, we could ground it in Woolf's position as a "pioneer of reader-response theory." Woolf, she writes, "was extremely interested in the two-way dialogue between readers and writers. Books change their readers; they teach you how to read them. But readers also change books. 'Undoubtedly,' Woolf herself had written, 'all writers are immensely influenced by the people who read them'" ("Virginia Woolf's Essays," 91).

2. On the possibility of connecting "cognition and culture, to question the boundaries which keep apart . . . psychology and history," see Sutton, 30–31.

3. For a suggestive discussion of such, see Meir Sternberg, "Universals of Narrative," I and II.

4. For an overview of the work of literary critics who call for an abandonment of the traditional criticism in favor of that grounded in cognitive sciences, see Richardson, "Studies in Literature and Cognition," 12–14.

5. Compare to Spolsky's hope that the work in cognitive literary criticism will "supplement rather than supplant current work in literary and cultural studies" ("Preface," *The Work of Fiction,* viii).

6. See Spolsky for a critique of the "common mistake of interdisciplinary studies" which consists in adapting a theory from a field outside of one's professional expertise as "(somehow) more reliable than the more familiar, but embattled assertions" in one's own field (*Gaps in Nature,* 2). Also, on the production of original readings of literary texts while using the cognitive framework, see Tabbi, 169.

7. Sperber, "In Defense of Massive Modularity," 49.

I: 2

1. For a useful introductory overview of the term, see Gopnik, "Theory of Mind," in *The MIT Encyclopedia.*

2. Brook and Ross, 81.

3. On the social intelligence of nonhuman primates, see Byrne and Whiten, *Machiavellian Intelligence* and "The Emergence of Metarepresentation"; Gomez, "Visual Behavior"; and Premack and Dasser, "Perceptual Origins."

4. Baron-Cohen, 21. For a discussion of alternatives to the Theory of Mind approach, see Dennett, *The Intentional Stance.*

5. For a useful related discussion of how we begin to articulate our thought processes when explicitly asked to explain the observed action, see Palmer, *Fictional Minds,* 105–6.

6. Baron-Cohen, 60.

7. Origgi and Sperber, 163.

8. Baron-Cohen, 60.

9. Autism was first described in 1943 by Leo Kanner, 217–50. For more than twenty years after that, autism was "mistakenly thought to be caused by a cold family environment." In 1977, however, "a landmark twin study showed that the incidence of autism is strongly influenced by genetic factors," and, since then, "numerous other investigations have since confirmed that autism is a highly heritable disorder" (Hughes and Plomin, 48). For the "pre-history" of the term *autism,* particularly as introduced by Eugen Bleuler in 1911 and developed by Piaget in 1923, see Harris, 3.

10. Baron-Cohen, 60.

11. For a discussion of the comparative mind-reading prowess of fifteen- and eighteen-month-olds, see Paul Bloom, 18–19.

12. See Clark H. Barrett, "Adaptations to Predators and Prey," and Lawrence Hirschfeld, "Who Needs a Theory of Mind."

13. As Robin Dunbar points out, "Children develop ToM at about the age of four years, following a period in which they engage in what has come to be known as 'Belief-Desire Psychology.' During this early stage, children are able to express their own feelings quite cogently, and this appears to act as a kind of scaffolding for the development of the true ToM (at which point they can ascribe the same kinds of beliefs and desires to others)" ("On the Origin of the Human Mind," 239).

14. Baron-Cohen, 71.

15. Sacks, *An Anthropologist on Mars,* 272.

16. Ibid., 259–60.

17. Ibid., 259.

18. An important tenet of a cognitive approach to literature is that, as Paul Hernadi puts it, "there is no clear division between literary and nonliterary signification. . . . Literary experience is not triggered in a cognitive or emotive vacuum: modern readers, listeners, and spectators mentally process the virtual comings and goings of imagined characters as if they were analogous to remembered actual events" (60, 62). For a related discussion, see Mark Turner, *The Literary Mind.* When it comes to the construction of literary characters, see Hogan's argument that we build up the "intentional" (that is, as imagined by [us]) characters "just the same way that [we] build up intentional versions of real people, imputing motives and broad character traits on the basis of the per-

son's/character's actions, statements, and so on." We may know that Hamlet "is not real, but the process of constituting an intentional version of Hamlet is automatic or spontaneous. [We] do not plan it out. It is just part of the way our minds work. Once an intentional person is constituted, then he/she is open to the same sort of emotive response as anyone else" (*The Mind and Its Stories,* 70). For further discussion, see Boyd, *Heads and Tales,* forthcoming.

19. By using the word *mechanism,* I am not trying to smuggle the outdated "body as a machine" metaphor into literary studies. Tainted as this word is by its previous history, it can still function as a convenient shorthand designation for extremely complex cognitive processes.

20. The scale of such investment emerges as truly staggering if we attempt to spell out the host of unspoken assumptions that make it possible. This realization lends new support to what theorists of narrative view as the essential underdetermination or "undertelling" of fiction, its "interior nonrepresentation" (Sternberg, "How Narrativity Makes a Difference," 119). See also Herman's argument that "narrative comprehension *requires* situating participants within networks of beliefs, desires, and intentions" ("Stories as a Tool for Thinking," 169).

21. Compare my argument here to that developed in Steven Pinker's *How the Mind Works,* 524–26.

22. The question of just how we manage to keep track of the "unreality" of literary characters is very complicated. I address some aspects of it in later sections when I speak of source monitoring. For a further discussion, see the debates by cognitive scientists and cognitive literary critics of what cognitive mechanisms or processes make pretence (and imagination as such) possible: Leslie, 120–25; Carruthers, "Autism as Mind-Blindness," 262–63; and Spolsky, "Why and How."

23. Compare to Palmer's argument that "the constructions of the minds of fictional characters by narrators and readers are central to our understanding of how novels work because, in essence, narrative is the description of mental functioning" (*Fictional Minds,* 12). Palmer further observes (an observation with which I strongly agree) that this claim applies not just to "the consciousness novels of Henry James or the stream of consciousness or interior monologue novels," but to "the novel as a whole, because all novels include a balance of behavior description and internal analysis of characters' minds" (25).

24. I am borrowing the term from Andy Clark, 167. For a discussion of Clark's theory of representational hunger and its application to literary criticism, see Spolsky, "Women's Work."

I: 3

1. Fred Volkmar, quoted in "Uncovering Autism's Mysteries." Online at http://www.cnn.com /2003/HEALTH/conditions/03/02/autism.ap/ (March 2, 2003).

2. For further information about Asperger syndrome, see Uta Frith's edited volume, *Autism and Asperger Syndrome.* Particularly relevant for the present discussion are the essays by Frith, Dewey, and Happe.

3. For a discussion, see Frith, 12.

4. Ibid., 31.

5. Another reason is their tendency to use metaphors (Haddon, 15).

6. For a discussion of autobiographies written by adults with Asperger syndrome, see Happe.

I: 4

1. Baron-Cohen, 29; emphasis added.

2. Dennet, 48.

3. See Sacks, *An Anthropologist on Mars,* 269.

4. Easterlin, "Making Knowledge," 137. For a qualification of the term *inborn* in relation to the processing of incoming data, see Spolsky, *Satisfying Skepticism,* 164.

5. Hayles, 145. For a discussion of "constraints," see Spolsky, "Cognitive Literary Historicism."

6. For a discussion of individual readers' reactions, see Hogan, *Cognitive Science,* 130, 160, and 162–65.

7. Fish, "How to Recognize a Poem," 110–11.

8. Ibid., 110.

9. Brook and Ross, 81.

10. Ibid., 112; emphasis in original.

11. For a discussion, see Fish, *Is There a Text in this Class?,* 197–267.

I: 5

1. For a discussion, see Leslie, 120–25; Carruthers, "Autism as Mind-Blindness," 262–63; Hernadi, 58; and Spolsky, "Why and How."

2. Carruthers also sees decoupling as an unnecessarily complicated attempt to strengthen the mind-blindness theory of autism in the face of alternative explanation posited by such scholars as Alison Gopnik, Andrew Meltzoff, and Uta Frith, who argue that "mind-blindness of autistic people is a consequence of some other basic deficit" (Carruthers, 258). See Gopnik and Meltzoff, "The Role of Imitation," and Uta Frith, *Autism: Explaining the Enigma.* For Gopnik and Meltzoff's suggestive alternative to the Theory of Mind theory—their "child as scientist" paradigm—see Gopnik and Meltzoff, *Words, Thoughts, and Theories.* For a response to the "child as scientist" paradigm, see Carruthers, "Simulation and Self-Knowledge."

3. Carruthers, "Autism as Mind-Blindness," 265. Emphasis in original. For the most recent revision of this argument, see Carruthers, *The Architecture of the Mind.*

4. Carruthers, "Autism," 264. Though the terms of this comparison may be too broad, still compare Carruthers's observation that autistic children do less pretending because they do not enjoy it to David Miall and Don Kuiken's observation that the "less experienced readers seem less committed to the act of reading" (335). Enjoyment of mind-imagining, both in real life and in reading fiction, seems to come with practice.

5. Carruthers, "Autism," 267. For an interesting complication of the idea of enjoyment predicated upon nonautistic mind-reading, see Stuart Murray, "Bartleby, Preference, Pleasure and Autistic Presence."

6. Tsur, "Horror Jokes," 243. Compare to Dorrit Cohn's argument that "in narra-

tology, 'as elsewhere, norms have a way of remaining uninteresting, often even invisible, until and unless we find that they have been broken—or want to show that that they have been broken'" (*The Distinction of Fiction,* 43; quoted in Palmer, *Fictional Minds,* 6). Compare, also, to Margolin: "The fictional presentation of cognitive mechanisms in action, especially of their breakdown or failure[,] is itself a powerful cognitive tool which may make us aware of actual cognitive mechanisms and, more specifically, of our own mental functioning" ("Cognitive Science," 278).

7. Tsur, 248–49; emphasis in original. For a more detailed treatment of the topic, see Tsur, *Toward a Theory of Cognitive Poetics.*

8. Phelan, *Living to Tell about It,* 28.

9. Ibid., 20.

10. Marvin Mudrick, 211.

11. The colleague shall remain anonymous. His students' debate was apparently prompted by the interview between Colin Firth and Bridget Jones in Helen Fielding's *Bridget Jones: The Edge of Reason.*

12. For very different and suggestive discussions of this point, see Peter Rabinowitz, *Before Reading,* 94, 96, and Paul Bloom, 218–19.

13. Henry Fielding, *Tom Jones,* 599.

14. Palmer, *Fictional Minds,* 10.

15. Ibid., 35.

16. Auerbach, *Mimesis,* 549.

17. Note that I am drastically simplifying Booth's argument in order to keep my own argument easy to follow. In the quoted passage, Booth writes not about Henry James—the "real" James, "capable in his 'declining' years" of "daily pettiness," but of the "great implied author" of *The Wings of the Dove*—the "James" who was "superior" to his maker, "purged of whatever [that maker] took to be [his] living faults" ("The Ethics of Forms," 114), an entity characterized by Booth on a different occasion as our "intuitive apprehension of a completed artistic whole" (*The Rhetoric of Fiction,* 73). For further discussion, see Part II, Section 9, "Source-Monitoring and the Implied Author," in this book.

18. Again, here Booth contrasts the "real" James with the "implied" James of the novel.

19. Booth, "The Ethics of Forms," 114–15, 120. Emphasis in original.

I: 6

1. For an important related discussion, see Palmer, *Fictional Minds,* chapter 6.

2. Compare to Palmer's argument that a "good deal of twentieth-century narration is characterized by a reluctance to make the decoding of action too explicit and a disinclination to use too much indicative description or contextual thought report." Palmer further points out that in the "behaviorist narratives of Ernest Hemingway, Raymond Chandler, and Dashiell Hammett, in which very little direct access to minds is given, the behavior of the characters only makes sense when it is read as the manifestation of an underlying mental reality" (*Fictional Minds,* 140). For a related discussion, see Fludernik on "neutral narratives" (*Toward a 'Natural' Narratology,* 172–75), and Cohn and Genette on a form of narration that "yells for interpretation" (263).

3. Anton Chekhov, *Three Sisters* [*Tri Sestry*], 120. Translation mine.

4. Chekhov, *Seagull* [*Chaika*], 22.

5. Ibid., 27.

6. Compare to the important discussion of misreadings in Rabinowitz, *Before Reading*, 173–208.

7. Phelan, e-mail communication, May 23, 2005.

8. For an important related discussion of animism, see Blakey Vermeule, *Making Sense of Fictional People: A Cognitive and Literary Project,* in press.

9. As Marie-Laure Ryan puts it, "How many of us can honestly say that we never skip descriptions?" ("Cognitive Maps," 219).

10. Compare to Ryan's elaboration of Ralf Schneider's observation that "readers focus their interest in the fictional world on the characters, rather than, for instance, fictional time or space or narrative situations." As Ryan demonstrates, in constructing mental models of the fictional narrative's topography, readers start with the characters and remember most effortlessly the landmarks associated with the dramatic turns in the careers of the characters: "Mental models of narrative space are centered on the characters, and they grow out of them" ("Cognitive Maps," 236).

I: 7

1. Dunbar, "On the Origin of the Human Mind," 241.

2. For the more recent version of this study, which sets the bar at the fifth level by factoring in the mind of the author (which does not change the present results if we do not factor in the author), see Stiller and Dunbar.

3. For a discussion, see Carey and Spelke, and Cosmides and Tooby, on domain specificity; and Dunbar, *Grooming*. For a recent application of the theory of domain specificity to the study of literature, see Zunshine, "Rhetoric, Cognition, and Ideology."

4. To which Uri Margolin may add: and *how* it is being represented. As he puts it, the "reason for the difference is that the first [sequence] is linear or sequential, unfolding step by step with all members being on the same level, while the second is hierarchical and simultaneous and needs to be grasped in its totality or unpacked in reverse order of presentation" ("Reader's Report," 3). One may thus speculate that the linear processing might be supported by cognitive adaptations somewhat different from ones supporting the simultaneous processing, the emergence of the latter correlated with our evolutionary history as an intensely social species.

5. For a discussion, see Part III, Section 4, "A Cognitive Evolutionary Perspective: Always Historicize!," of this book.

6. Now, of course, it does not seem that random anymore, since it has served my purposes so well. Perhaps I should consider it a "randomly selected serendipitous" passage.

7. Dunbar, "On the Origin of the Human Mind," 240.

8. Thus, bringing the findings of cognitive scientists to bear upon the literary text does not diminish its aesthetic value. As Scarry has argued in response to the fear that science would "unweave the rainbow" of artistic creation, "[T]he fact of the matter is that when we actually look at the nature of artistic creation and composition, understanding it does not mean doing it less well. To become a dancer, for example, one must

do the small steps again and again and understand them, if one is to achieve virtuosity. Right now we need virtuosity, not only within each discipline, but across the disciplines as well" ("Panel Discussion," 253).

I: 8

1. For a discussion, see Easterlin, "Voyages in the Verbal Universe."

2. As Blakey Vermeule observes, "[L]iterature-fiction-writing is so powerful because it eats theories for breakfast, including cognitive/evolutionary approaches" (personal communication, November 20, 2002).

3. For a useful most recent review of the field of cognitive approaches to literature, see Richardson, "Studies in Literature and Cognition."

4. Hogan, "Literary Universals," 226. For a discussion of embodied cognition, see also Hart, "Epistemology."

5. Herman, "Regrouping Narratology."

6. Butte, 237.

7. For a related discussion, see Spolsky, "Preface," ix.

8. Benjamin, 97.

9. For a related discussion, see Hogan, "Literary Universals," 242–43.

10. Hernadi argues that "literature, whether encountered in live performance or in textual and electronic recording, can challenge and thus enhance our brains' vital capacities for expression, communication, representation, and signification." He further connects the fictional text's capacity for developing our minds to the evolutionary history of the literary endeavor. He points out that "the protoliterary experiences of some early humans could, other things being equal, enable them to outdo their less imaginative rivals in the biological competition for becoming the ancestors of later men and women" (56).

11. Richardson and Steen, 3.

12. Michael Whitworth, 150.

13. Susan Dick, 51, 52.

14. Auerbach, 531. Strictly speaking, Auerbach's question refers to *To the Lighthouse*, but it is equally pertinent for our discussion of *Mrs. Dalloway.*

15. A valuable new study by George Butte, *I Know That You Know That I Know: Narrating Subjects from* Moll Flanders *to* Marnie, offers a fascinating perspective on a writer's interest in constructing a "present moment" as a delicate "connection" among the characters' subjectivities. Applying Merleau-Ponty's analysis of interlocking consciousnesses (*Phenomenology of Perception*) to a broad selection of eighteenth- and nineteenth-century novels, as well as to the films of Hitchcock, Hawks, and Woody Allen, Butte argues compellingly that something had changed in the narrative representation of consciousness at the time of Jane Austen: writers became able to represent the "deep intersubjectivity" (39) of their characters, portraying them as aware of each other's perceptions of themselves and responding to such perceptions with body language observable by their interlocutors and generating a further series of mutual perceptions and reactions. Although Butte does not refer in his work to cognitive science or the Theory of Mind, his argument is in many respects compatible with the literary criticism that does.

16. On Woolf's definition of narrative ventriloquism, see Maria DiBattista, 132.
17. Phelan, e-mail communication, May 23, 2005.

I: 9

1. Pinker, *The Blank Slate,* 413.
2. Ibid., 404, 409–10.
3. Anonymous reader for *PMLA.*
4. For a related discussion of cognitive scientists' interest in literature and the arts, see Hogan, *Cognitive Science,* 3.
5. For a discussion of Heliodorus's influence, see Doody, *The True Story of the Novel.*
6. Compare to my argument in the last chapter about a compelling love story that knows how to push our emotional buttons because it is built on the bones of millions of forgotten love stores that didn't. Note that even the most difficult experimental modernist or postmodernist text would still have to engage the reader emotionally, and, in doing so, it does *not* depend on preserving "omniscient narration, structured plots, the orderly introduction of characters, and general readability."
7. Palmer, *Fictional Minds,* 53.
8. Fludernik, *Towards a 'Natural' Narratology,* 170.
9. Compare to Richardson's programmatic assertion that cognitive literary criticism "rejects naïve realism. It refuses to dismiss (for example) important twentieth-century avant-garde traditions as unnatural or misguided, but rather seeks to understand their appeal to serious artists and informed audiences. Nor does it typically designate certain forms of literary activity . . . as 'natural' or normative in order to devalue others" ("Studies in Literature and Cognition," 24).
10. James Phelan, personal communication, April 17, 2003.

NOTES TO PART II

II: 1

1. For a useful introductory discussion of the term, see Sperber, "Metarepresentation," in *The MIT Encyclopedia.*
2. Cosmides and Tooby, "Consider the Source," 60–61.
3. Compare to David Herman's discussion of Jerome Bruner's argument that when "an interlocutor tells me a story incriminating a mutual acquaintance, I am likely to construe specific details in the light of what I know about the storyteller's past history with the person who is the focus of the story" ("Stories as a Tool for Thinking," 164).
4. For a further discussion of our ability to carry our inferences on information that we know to be false or that we do not (fully) understand, see Sperber, "The Modularity of Thought." Also, compare to Wittgenstein's observation that one "can *draw inferences* from a false proposition" (41; emphasis in original).
5. Cosmides and Tooby, "Consider the Source," 69.
6. For a discussion of episodic and semantic memories, see Tulving.
7. Klein et al., "Is There Something Special about the Self?," 491.

8. Ibid.

9. Cosmides and Tooby, "Consider the Source," 53, 57.

10. Ibid., 54.

11. Ibid., 58.

12. Ibid., 60.

13. Ibid., 105.

14. Ibid., 104. See also Sperber, *Explaining Culture,* 146–50.

15. Cosmides and Tooby, "Consider the Source," 77.

16. Ibid., 104.

17. Sacks, "The Mind's Eye," 52.

18. Ibid., 55.

19. Compare to a discussion of metarepresentationality by Antonio Damasio, who sees "constructing metarepresentations of our own mental process" as "a high-level operation in which a part of the mind represents another part of the mind. This allows us to register the fact that our thoughts slow down or speed up as more or less attention is devoted to them; or the fact that thoughts depict objects at close range or at a distance" (*Looking for Spinoza,* 86).

II: 2

1. Cosmides and Tooby, "Consider the Source," 101.

2. Klein et al., "A Social-Cognitive Neuroscience," 111.

3. Ibid., 127.

4. Frith, *The Cognitive Neuropsychology of Schizophrenia,* 116, 133–34.

5. Ibid., 115.

6. Ibid, 127, table 7.1.

7. Ibid., 126.

8. Ibid., 122.

II: 3

1. Compare to Mitchell's argument in "The Psychology of Human Deception," 837.

2. Spolsky, "Iconotropism"; *Satisfying Skepticism,* 7; "Darwin and Derrida," 52.

3. See Tooby and Cosmides, "The Psychological Foundations of Culture," 53–55; "Origins of Domain Specificity," 87; "From Evolution to Behavior," 293.

II: 4

1. For a suggestive related analysis of Darcy and Elizabeth's conversation, see Nicholas Dames, 26.

2. For a useful background discussion of the literary phenomenon of "idiom of the group," see Brian McHale, 270.

3. Of course, as Hilary Schor reminds us, the story's outcome bears out the truth of the former belief—"there are no wealthy bachelors at the end of *Pride and Prejudice*"—"but that does not mean that no experimentation went on in between" (97).

4. Belton, "Mystery without Murder," 55–56; emphasis added.

5. Cosmides and Tooby, "Consider the Source," 61.

6. Ibid., 58.

II: 5

1. Cosmides and Tooby, "Consider the Source," 91–92.

2. Cuddon, *Dictionary of Literary Terms,* 67.

3. Barthes, "The Death of the Author," 148.

4. Cosmides and Tooby, 92.

5. Ibid., 90.

6. Quoted in Mayer, 2, 224.

7. Compare to Lanser's discussion of "the readers' outrage" in the cases of *Famous All Over Town, The Education of Little Tree,* and Alan Socal/*Social Text* Affair ("The 'I' of the Beholder").

8. For further discussion, see Zunshine, "Eighteenth-Century Print Culture."

9. Lloyd, 6.

10. Ibid., 16.

11. Cosmides and Tooby, 58.

12. Compare to the discussion of progressive modalization in Bruno Latour's *Science in Action* and Latour and Steve Woolgar's *Laboratory Life,* especially as adapted by Derek Edwards and Jonathan Potter, 104–7.

13. Compare to Lanser's discussion of "the rather flimsy and accidental form of a narrative's placement within categorical space . . . [such as] the 'fiction' or 'nonfiction' shelves in a bookstore" ("The 'I' of the Beholder").

14. Lloyd, 17.

II: 6

1. Compare to Tabbi's assertion that the "cognitive framework," while including "the main features of modernist reflexivity," also introduces "a more supple materialism, one that preserves literature's capacity for achieving common understanding in terms that remain specific to each text and true to the moment by moment operations of the reading mind" (168).

2. Compare to Hogan's development of Chomsky's point that "the normal use of language is constantly innovative" (*Cognitive Science,* 62).

II: 7

1. For a suggestive related discussion, see Francis Steen.

2. Another such character is Ian McEwan's Briony (*Atonement*). Briony, incidentally,

writes a play, *The Trials of Arabella,* in which she intends to star herself as the "sponta-neous . . . but inexperienced" title heroine (15–16)—McEwan's nod, perhaps, to the "troublesome adventures" (Lennox, 87–88) of that other eighteenth-century Arabella, whose source-monitoring has gone seriously awry. For a discussion of McEwan's con-struction of Briony's unreliability, see Phelan, "Narrative Judgments."

II: 8

1. Culler, *Structuralist Poetics,* 157. Quoted in Nunning, 59–60.
2. Fludernik, *The Fictions of Language,* 349. Quoted in Nunning, 66.
3. Margolin, "Cognitive Science," 284.
4. Phelan, *Living to Tell about It,* 219.
5. Ibid., 52.
6. For discussion, see ibid., 34–35, 51–52.
7. Ibid., 51.
8. Ibid.
9. Ibid.
10. Ibid., 219.
11. Ibid., 53.

II: 9

1. Prince, 42; quoted in Palmer, *Fictional Minds,* 17.
2. Booth, *The Rhetoric of Fiction,* 73.
3. Nunning, 55–57.
4. Palmer, *Fictional Minds,* 17.
5. The stricter source-monitoring here, as Phelan points out, would be, "Austen has her narrator claim that Lydia ran away with Wickham" (personal communication, May 23, 2005). I am tempted here, however, to stretch Lanser's argument that "readers have very little incentive to distinguish the narrator of *Northanger Abbey* from Austen" ("The 'I' of the Beholder") to make it apply to *Pride and Prejudice* as well.
6. Lanser, *The Narrative Act,* 49–50.
7. Ibid., 46. For Lanser's most recent discussion of the term *implied author,* see "The 'I' of the Beholder."

II: 10

1. As Fludernik observes, the "rise of the consciousness novel would be unthinkable without *Clarissa*" (*Towards a 'Natural' Narratology,* 171). For a suggestive discussion of Richardson (but also Fielding!—a claim that Butte may disagree with [see *I Know That You Know,* 74–79]) as representing the beginnings of what she calls "'the high theory of mind tradition' in the English novel," see Vermeule, "God Novels," 148.
2. This interpretation is owed to Warner's *Reading Clarissa,* especially chapter 4.
3. Blythe, xiv.

4. Compare to Mitchell's argument that "by introducing safeguards against deception, victims influence deceivers to introduce further deceptions to quash the skepticism and satisfy the new evidence requirements, and, thus, deception escalates" (853).

5. Christopher Frith, 122.

6. Mitchell, 832; emphasis in original.

II: 11

1. See Eaves and Kimpel, "The Composition of *Clarissa.*" But also see Sabor on Richardson's occasional "startling defense of certain aspects of his hero" (36) and Barchas on Richardson's confession that he liked playing "'the Rogue' with his readers, 'intending them to think now one way, now another of the very same Characters'" (Richardson, *Selected Letters,* 248; quoted in Barchas, 121).

2. A new modern edition of *Clarissa* is currently being prepared by John Richetti and Toni Bowers, based on the 1751 revision. It will be interesting to see if a back cover of that edition will reflect a darker view of Lovelace.

3. Boyd, *Vladimir Nabokov,* 230.

4. Ibid., 232.

5. Rabinowitz, "Lolita: Solipsized or Sodomized?" 326, 327.

6. Compare to Rabinowitz's argument in "Lolita: Solipsized or Sodomized?," especially on p. 327.

7. The concept of distributed social cognition in fictional narrative has been compellingly explored by Alan Palmer and by David Herman. In his discussion of Eliot's *Middlemarch,* Palmer points out that Tertius Lydgate's "identity is socially distributed before we meet him, and there are a number of discussions of him throughout the novel that continue the town's exploration of his identity. It is striking that the early part of the novel contains far more information on the 'Lydgates' that exist in the minds of other characters than it does the 'Lydgate' that emerges from direct access to his own mind" ("The Lydgate Storyworld," in press). See also chapter 5 (part 5.5: "The Mind beyond the Skin") of Palmer's *Fictional Minds.* Similarly, Herman argues that cognition "should be viewed as a supra- or transindividual activity distributed across groups functioning in specific contexts, rather than as a wholly internal process unfolding within the minds of solitary, autonomous, and de-situated cognizers," and he demonstrates compellingly the workings of this "distributed social cognition" in Edith Wharton's 1934 story "Roman Fever" ("Regrounding Narratology," in press).

8. Of course, this is not an altogether *unpleasant* mental vertigo. Compare to Fludernik's argument about the "delight" experienced by readers faced with unreliable narrators ("Natural Narratology and Cognitive Parameters," 257).

9. For a useful discussion, see Rabinowitz, *Before Reading,* 96. Although Rabinowitz does not deal with *Lolita* in his study, his analysis of "narrative audience" and "authorial audience" is highly pertinent to the present argument about Humbert's construction of his reader.

10. Though, as Rabinowitz reminds us, the scene might be "quite funny even from a non-pedophilic perspective." As he points out, "[A]fter all, anyone who's ever attempted a tryst at a hotel—or imagined attempting a tryst at a hotel—has experienced the same 'trouble'; and even those who haven't can certainly imagine themselves in Humbert's

position" (Reader's Report). I agree with Rabinowitz and, in fact, see his point as illuminating certain limitations of my "metarepresentational" reading of *Lolita.* Once you start applying the missing source tags to *Lolita,* it is very easy to lose sight of the comic side of the text.

11. Same as note 10 above.

12. Compare to Crane's useful discussion of how "claims to knowledge based on embodied feelings can [be] easily be falsified, simplified, and used as a rhetorical tool" ("'Fair Is Foul,'" 120).

13. Sterne, *Sentimental Journey,* 96.

14. Sterne, *Tristam Shandy,* 1–2.

15. Phelan, *Living to Tell about It,* 51.

16. Ibid., 121.

17. Ibid., 129.

18. Ibid., 120.

19. Ibid., 119.

20. Ibid., 120.

21. Ibid., 121.

22. Ibid., 121–22.

23. Ibid., 129.

24. Ibid., 127.

25. Cohn, "Discordant Narration," 312.

26. See Patricia Merivale and Susan Elizabeth Sweeney, *Detecting Texts.*

NOTES TO PART III

III: 1

1. Sayers, "Aristotle on Detective Fiction," 31.

2. Belton, 50.

3. Routley, 176.

4. For example, we can consider a bildüngsroman a safe-setting exploration of the real fears and anxieties of both adolescent children and their parents.

III: 2

1. Compare my argument here to Palmer's discussion of what narrative theorist Menakhem Perry calls the "primacy effect." As Palmer points out, when we begin to read a fictional story, "the initial reading frames that are set up at the beginning of a text have long-lasting effects, and they tend to persist until the reader is compelled by the accumulating weight of contrary evidence to abandon them and set up new frames" ("The Lydgate Storyworld"). For a related discussion, see Shlomith Rimmon-Kenan, who builds on the work of Perry and Jonathan Culler to observe that the "dynamics of reading can thus be seen not only as a formation, development, modification, and replacement of hypothesis . . . , but also—simultaneously—as the construction of

frames, their transformation, and dismantling" (123–24).

2. However, as Phelan correctly observes, weightlifting is not really "decoupled from reality" for "competitive athletes and people who lift to rehabilitate injuries." For them, weightlifting is crucial part of their reality. Similarly, "people who write detective stories or who write about and teach them find them integral to their reality" ("Reader's Report," 6).

3. The argument about the instructive value of a detective novel or the pointed lack thereof can be expanded to doubt the instructive value of any fictional narrative. I thus strongly agree with Hogan's critique of Pinker's argument that "fictional narratives supply us with a mental catalogue of the fatal conundrums we might face someday and the outcomes of strategies we could deploy in them." Using as an example Shakespeare's *Hamlet,* Pinker suggests that we consider the following question: "What are the options if I were to suspect that my uncle killed my father, took his position, and married my mother?" (*How the Mind Works,* 543; quoted in Hogan, *Cognitive Science,* 211). As Hogan observes, "*Hamlet* does not actually teach us how to respond in that situation . . . The very best it could be said to do is to teach us to check someone's identity before killing him (due to the Polonius accident)" (211). Along the same lines, Hogan points out in *The Mind and Its Stories* that although literature "humanizes us in the sense that it tends to develop certain sorts of compassionate identification, [it is] not at all clear that this sort of identification extends beyond the literary work to the real world" (206). See Spolsky ("Purposes Mistook") for a related response to Hernadi's argument that "the creation and consumption of fictional narratives provide evolutionary advantages to a group that prepares them to anticipate challenges they may some day face by familiarizing its young with a range of hypothetical scenarios." Finally, see David Lodge for the discussion of the ambiguous feeling that we have after reading a novel that we have "'learned' something" (30–32).

4. Womack, 266.

5. Two of these examples are taken from Charney, 101; Oedipus has been suggested by James Phelan.

6. The issue of genre has been a topic of a productive inquiry by several literary critics interested in cognitive approaches. See Spolsky, *Gaps in Nature* and "Darwin and Derrida," and Hart, "Embodied Literature."

III: 3

1. The phrase comes from Ronald Blythe's Introduction to the 1966 Penguin edition of the novel and is quoted in Catherine Kenney, "The Mystery of *Emma* . . . ," 138. See also P. D. James, "*Emma* Considered as a Detective Story," an appendix to *A Time to Be in Earnest: A Fragment of an Autobiography,* 243–59. For an analysis of mind-reading in *Emma,* see Alan Richardson, "Reading Minds and Bodies in *Emma.*"

2. I use the word *internal* to emphasize again that, apart from what is going on *inside* the fictional story, we store the story as a whole as a large metarepresentation with an implicit source tag, such as, "Austen says" or "Conan Doyle says."

3. Ronald R. Thomas, 4.

4. Ibid., 9.

5. Similarly, we can tweak the terms of Cawelti's observation that when we are read-

ing a detective story, "in addition to the attempt to figure out the crime, we are also confronted with the puzzle of the detective's [mental] activity" (190). The puzzle of another person's (here, the detective's) mental activity is not something we figure out "also," or "in addition to," the main puzzle of the crime. Instead, the puzzle of crime is a handy pretext to let us fall to our favorite activity of mind-reading. For a related discussion, see Vermeule, "Theory of Mind," in which she offers a valuable analysis of mind-reading behind clues-reading as a correction to Franco Moretti's recent groundbreaking work on detective fiction ("Slaughterhouse of Literature"). For a broader discussion of mind-reading and fiction, see also Vermeule, "Satirical Mind Blindness" and "God Novels"

6. Howard Haycraft, 130.

7. W. H. Auden, "The Guilty Vicarage," 21.

8. Quoted in John T. Irwin, 28.

9. Haycraft, 239.

10. Symons, 138.

11. Routley, 177.

12. Ousby, 187.

13. One could say that it is this intuitive acknowledgment that a detective story focuses on one particular kind of mind-reading and is not amenable to others that has fueled the traditional criticism of the genre as "wasteful of time and degrading to intellect" (Robin W. Winks, 1). For a famous articulation of this view, see Edmund Wilson's essay, "Who Cares Who Killed Roger Ackroyd?"

14. Damasio, *Descartes Error;* quoted in Hogan, *Cognitive Science,* 170.

15. Hogan, *Cognitive Science,* 170.

16. Ibid., 185.

17. See Hogan's *The Mind and Its Stories* and *Cognitive Science, Literature, and the Arts: A Guide for Humanists.*

18. Compare Hogan's argument here to that of Uri Margolin, who points out that "folk psychology itself *is* a part of psychological reality! On occasion, upon reading a literary representation of some aspect of cognitive mental functioning, a reader also feels something akin to Buhler's Aha-Erlebnis ('Aha! experience') . . . , realizing all of a sudden that this is how she herself perceives, categorizes, or recalls, that the fictional representation has made her aware of the very nature of mental activity in which she constantly engages, but of which she had not been aware ever before, or which she had not been unable to describe so effectively. This point is reinforced by the claim of cognitive science that many of our cognitive processing activities are indeed 'unconscious,' not accompanied by any self-awareness of self-consciousness. The reading of literary representations of mental functioning is also a major source of another undeniable common psychological fact, namely, readerly engagement with fictional figures, caring for their fortunes, and sometimes empathizing with their mental states and episodes" ("Cognitive Science," 285).

19. Hogan, *Cognitive Science,* 185.

20. For a discussion of this "slaughterhouse of literature," see Moretti, 207–10.

21. See, for example, the discussion of various hybrid forms of the detective story in the volume edited by Merivale and Sweeney.

22. Rabinowitz, *Before Reading,* 211.

23. Of course, my evaluation of "success" and "failure" is open to debate. Sayers's experimentation with romance in *Gaudy Night* has led one critic to pronounce that

novel "less than successful" (Haycraft, 138) and another to assert that Sayers "has now almost ceased to be a first-rate detective writer and has become an exceedingly snobbish popular novelist" (John Strachey; quoted in Haycraft, 138).

24. Jacques Barzun, 150.

25. Compare to Rabinowitz's excellent discussion of detective-story readers' "presumption that diverse strand of action will in some way be linked" (*Before Reading*, 132).

26. Compare to Rabinowitz's view of the genre "as preformed bundles of operations performed by readers in order to recover the meanings texts" (ibid., 177).

III: 4

1. Cawelti, 134.
2. Ibid., 135.
3. Spolsky, *Satisfying Skepticism,* 4.
4. Ibid., 10.

NOTES TO CONCLUSION

Conclusion: 1

1. Iser, 2–3.
2. Booth, "The Ethics of Forms," 120.
3. Rimmon-Kenan, 117.

Conclusion: 2

1. Palmer, *Fictional Minds,* 19. Compare to Margolin's argument in "Cognitive Science," 272.

2. For a related analysis of the "environment of information" created by cultural representations, see Tabbi, 174.

3. Phelan, *Living,* 143.

4. For a useful discussion of emergent meaning and cognition, see Mark Turner, *Cognitive Dimensions,* 9, 138–43

Bibliography

Anonymous. Beowulf. Translated by Seamus Heaney. *The Norton Anthology of English Literature*. Seventh Edition, Volume I. Eds. M. H. Abrams and Stephen Greenblatt. New York: Norton, 2000. 32–99.

Abbott, Porter. "Humanists, Scientists and Cultural Surplus." *Substance* 94/95: 30 (2001): 203–17.

Aldama, Frederick Luis. "Cultural Studies in Today's Chicano/Latino Scholarship: Wishful Thinking, *Flatus Voci*, or Scientific Endeavor?" *Aztlan* 29:1 (Spring 2004): 191–216.

———. "Race, Cognition, and Emotion: Shakespeare on Film." *Humanities Retooled*. Online at http://www.humanitiesretooled.org/index.php?sm=hrt_articles.php &modCMS_cidd=111.

Allingham, Margery. *Mr. Campion's Lady: An Allingham Omnibus*. London: Chatto and Windus, 1965.

Atran, Scott. *In Gods We Trust: The Evolutionary Landscape of Religion*. Oxford: Oxford University Press, 2002.

Auden, W. H. "The Guilty Vicarage." *Detective Fiction: A Collection of Critical Essays*. Ed. Robin W. Winks. Woodstock, VT: The Countryman Press, 1988. 15–24.

Auerbach, Erich. *Mimesis*. Princeton: Princeton University Press, 1991.

Austen, Jane. *Emma*. New York: Bantam Books, 1969.

———. *Northanger Abbey*. London: Penguin, 1995.

———. *Pride and Prejudice*. New York: Dover Publications, 1995.

Bakhtin, Michail. *The Dialogic Imagination: Four Essays by M. M. Bakhtin*. Edited by Michael Holquist; translated by Caryl Emerson and Michael Holquist. Austin: University of Texas Press, 1981.

Barchas, Janine. "The Antipodean Pleasures of Teaching *Clarissa* in 'Real Time.'" *Approaches to Teaching the Novels of Samuel Richardson*. Eds. Lisa Zunshine and Jocelyn Harris. New York: Modern Language Association, 2005. 120–27.

Baron-Cohen, Simon. *Mindblindness: An Essay on Autism and Theory of Mind.* Cambridge: The MIT Press, 1995.

Barrett, Clark H. "Adaptations to Predators and Prey." *The Evolutionary Psychology Handbook.* Ed. David Buss. New York: Wiley. Forthcoming.

Bathes, Roland. "The Death of the Author." *Image—Music—Text.* Trans. Stephen Heath. London: Fontana, 1977. 142–48.

Barzun, Jacques. "Detection and the Literary Art." *Detective Fiction: A Collection of Critical Essays.* Ed. Robin W. Winks. Woodstock, VT: The Countryman Press, 1988. 144–53.

Belton, Ellen R. "Mystery without Murder: The Detective Plots of Jane Austen." *Nineteenth-Century Literature* 43.1 (June 1988): 42–59.

Benjamin, Walter. *Illuminations.* New York: Harcourt, Brace & World, 1955.

Bloom, Paul. *Descartes's Baby: How the Science of Child Development Explains What Makes Us Human.* New York: Basic Books, 2004.

Blythe, Ronald. "Introduction." Henry James, *The Awkward Age.* London: Penguin, 1987. vii–xix.

Booth, Wayne C. "The Ethics of Forms: Taking Flight with *The Wings of the Dove.*" *Understanding Narrative.* Eds. James Phelan and Peter J. Rabinowitz. Columbus: The Ohio State University Press, 1994. 99–135.

———. *The Rhetoric of Fiction* [1961]. Harmondsworth, England: Penguin, 1987.

Boyd, Brian. *Heads and Tales: On the Origins of Stories.* Forthcoming.

———. *Vladimir Nabokov: The American Years.* Princeton: Princeton University Press, 1991.

Boyer, Pascal. *Religion Explained: The Evolutionary Origins of Religious Thought.* New York: Basic Books, 2001.

Brook, Andrew and Don Ross. *Daniel Dennett.* Cambridge: Cambridge University Press, 2002.

Butte, George. *I Know That You Know That I Know: Narrating Subjects from* Moll Flanders *to* Marnie. Columbus: The Ohio State University Press, 2004.

Byrne, Richard W. and Andrew Whiten. "The Emergence of Metarepresentation in Human Ontogeny and Primate Phylogeny." *Natural Theories of Mind: Evolution, Development, and Simulation of Everyday Mindreading.* Ed. Andrew Whiten. Basil Blackwell, 1991. 267–82.

———. *Machiavellian Intelligence: Social Expertise and the Evolution of Intellect in Monkeys, Apes, and Humans.* Oxford: Oxford University Press, 1988.

Carey, Susan and Elizabeth Spelke. "Domain-Specific Knowledge and Conceptual Change." *Mapping the Mind: Domain Specificity in Cognition and Culture.* Eds. Lawrence A. Hirschfeld and Susan A. Gelman. Cambridge: Cambridge University Press, 1994. 169–200.

Carroll, Lewis. "'Alice' on the Stage." *Theatre* 1881.

Carruthers, Peter. *The Architecture of the Mind: Massive Modularity and Flexibility of Thought.* Forthcoming.

———. "Autism as Mind-Blindness: An Elaboration and Partial Defense." *Theories of Theories of Mind.* Eds. Peter Carruthers and Peter K. Smith. Cambridge: Cambridge University Press, 1996. 257–73.

———. "Simulation and Self-Knowledge: *A Defense of the Theory-Theory.*" *Theories of Theories of Mind.* Eds. Peter Carruthers and Peter K. Smith. Cambridge: Cambridge University Press, 1996. 22–38.

Carruthers, Peter and Andrew Chamberlain, eds. *Evolution and the Human Mind: Modularity, Language, and Meta-Cognition.* Cambridge: Cambridge University Press, 2000. 140–69.

Cawelti, John. "The Study of Literary Formulas." *Detective Fiction: A Collection of Critical Essays.* Ed. Robin W. Winks. Woodstock, VT: The Countryman Press, 1988. 121–43.

Chandler, Raymond. *The Big Sleep.* New York: Vintage Crime/Black Lizard Vintage Books, 1992.

———. *The Long Good-Bye.* Middlesex, England: Penguin, in Association with Hamish Hamilton, 1959.

———. "Pearls Are a Nuisance." *The Simple Art of Murder.* New York: Vintage Books, 1988. 139–86.

———. *Playback.* New York: Vintage Crime/Black Lizard Vintage Books, 1988.

———. "The Simple Act of Murder, an Essay." *The Simple Art of Murder.* New York: Vintage Books, 1988.1–18.

Chandler, Raymond and Robert B. Parker. *Poodle Springs.* New York: G. P. Putnam's Sons, 1989.

Charney, Hannah. *The Detective Novel of Manners.* Teaneck: Farleigh Dickinson University Press, 1981.

Chekhov, Anton. *Chaika* [1896], in A. P. Chekhov, *Sochinenia, Tom Trinadzatyi. P'esy, 1895–1904.* Moscow, 1978. 3–60.

———. *Tri Sestry* [1900], in A. P. Chekhov, *Sochinenia, Tom Trinadzatyi. P'esy, 1895–1904.* Moscow, 1978. 117–88.

Clark, Andy. *Being There: Putting Brain, Body, and World Together Again.* Cambridge: The MIT Press, 2001.

Cohn, Dorrit. "Discordant Narration." *Style* 34.2 (Summer 2000): 307–16.

———. *The Distinction of Fiction.* Baltimore: Johns Hopkins University Press, 1999.

Cohn, Dorrit and Gerard Genette. "A Narratological Exchange." *Neverending Stories. Toward a Critical Narratology.* Eds. Ann Fenn, Ingeborg Hoesterey, and Maria Tatar. Princeton: Princeton University Press, 1992. 258–66.

Colley, Linda. *Britons: Forging the Nation 1707–1837.* New Haven: Yale University Press, 1992.

Cosmides, Leda and John Tooby. "Consider the Source: The Evolution of Adaptations for Decoupling and Metarepresentations." *Metarepresentations: A Multidisciplinary Perspective.* Ed. Dan Sperber. New York: Oxford University Press, 2000. 53–116.

———. "From Evolution to Behavior: Evolutionary Psychology as the Missing Link." The Latest and the Best Essays on Evolution and Optimality. Ed. John Dupre. Cambridge: The MIT Press, 1987. 277–306.

———. "Origins of Domain Specificity: The Evolution of Functional Organization." *Mapping the Mind: Domain Specificity in Cognition and Culture.* Eds. Lawrence A. Hirschfeld and Susan A. Gelman. New York: Cambridge University Press, 1994. 85–116.

Christie, Agatha. *The Murder of Roger Ackroyd.* New York: Bantam Books, 1983.

Crane, Mary Thomas. "'Fair Is Foul': *Macbeth* and Binary Logic. *The Work of Fiction: Cognition, Culture, and Complexity.* Eds. Alan Richardson and Ellen Spolsky. Aldershot, UK: Ashgate, 2004. 107–26.

————. *Shakespeare's Brain: Reading with Cognitive Theory.* Princeton: Princeton University Press, 2001.

Cuddon, J. A. *The Penguin Dictionary of Literary Terms and Literary Theory.* London: Penguin, 1992.

Culler, Jonathan. *Structuralist Poetics. Structuralism, Linguistics and the Study of Literature.* Ithaca: Cornell University Press, 1975.

Damasio, Antonio. *Looking for Spinoza: Joy, Sorrow, and the Feeling Brain.* New York: Harcourt, 2003.

Dames, Nicholas. *Amnesiac Selves: Nostalgia, Forgetting, and British Fiction, 1810–1870.* Cambridge: Oxford University Press, 2001.

Dennett, Daniel. *The Intentional Stance.* Cambridge: The MIT Press, 1987.

Dewey, Margaret. "Living with Asperger's Syndrome." *Autism and Asperger Syndrome.* Ed. Uta Frith. New York: Cambridge University Press, 1991. 184–206.

DiBattista, Maria. "Virginia Woolf and the Language of Authorship." *The Cambridge Companion to Virginia Woolf.* Eds. Sue Roe and Susan Sellers. Cambridge: Cambridge University Press, 2000. 127–45.

Dick, Susan. "Literary Realism in *Mrs. Dalloway, To the Lighthouse, Orlando* and *The Waves.*" *The Cambridge Companion to Virginia Woolf.* Eds. Sue Roe and Susan Sellers. Cambridge: Cambridge University Press, 2000. 50–71.

Dole el, Lubomír. *Heterocosmica: Fiction and Possible Worlds.* Baltimore: Johns Hopkins University Press, 1998.

Doody, Margaret Anne. *The True Story of the Novel.* New Brunswick: Rutgers University Press, 1996.

Dostoyevski, Fedor Mikhailovich. *Sobranie Sochineni. Tom Piatyi. Prestuplenie i Nakazanie.* Moskva: Gosudarstvennoye Izdatelstvo Khudozhestvennoi Literatury, 1957.

Dreher, Sarah. *Something Shady.* Norwich, VT: New Victoria Publishers, 1986.

————. *Stoner McTavish.* Norwich, VT: New Victoria Publishers, 1994.

Dunbar, R. I. M., N. Duncan, and D. Nettle. "Size and Structure of Freely-Forming Conversational Groups." *Human Nature* 6 (1994): 67–78.

Dunbar, Robin. "Coevolution of Neocortical Size, Group Size and Language in Humans." *Behavioural and Brain Sciences* 16 (1993): 681–735.

————. *Grooming, Gossip, and the Evolution of Language.* Cambridge: Harvard University Press, 1996.

————. "On the Origin of the Human Mind." *Evolution and the Human Mind: Modularity, Language, and Meta-Cognition.* Eds. Peter Carruthers and Andrew Chamberlain. Cambridge: Cambridge University Press, 2000. 238–53.

Easterlin, Nancy. "Making Knowledge: Bioepistemology and the Foundations of Literary Theory." *Mosaic* 32.1 (1999): 131–47.

————. "Voyages in the Verbal Universe: The Role of Speculation in Darwinian Literary Criticism." *Interdisciplinary Literary Studies: A Journal of Criticism and Theory* 2.2 (Spring 2001): 59–73.

Eaves, T. C. Duncan and Ben D. Kimpel. "The Composition of *Clarissa* and Its Revision before Publication." *PMLA* 83 (May 1968): 416–28.

Edwards, Derek and Jonathan Potter. *Discursive Psychology.* London: Sage Publications, 1992.

Fauconnier, Gilles and Mark Turner. *The Way We Think: Conceptual Blending and the Mind's Hidden Compexities.* New York: Basic Books, 2002.

Fforde, Jasper. *The Eyre Affair.* New York: Penguin, 2001.

Fielding, Henry. *Tom Jones.* Eds. John Bender and Simon Stern. Oxford, England: Oxford University Press, 1996.

Fish, Stanley. "How to Recognize a Poem When You See One." *American Criticism in the Poststructuralist Age.* Ed. Ira Konigsberg. Ann Arbor: University of Michigan Press, 1981. 102–15.

———. *Is There a Text in This Class?* Cambridge, MA: Cambridge University Press, 1980. 197–267.

Fludernik, Monika. *The Fictions of Language and the Languages of Fiction. The Linguistic Representations of Speech and Consciousness.* London: Routledge, 1993.

———. "Natural Narratology and Cognitive Parameters." *Narrative Theory and the Cognitive Sciences.* Ed. David Herman. Stanford, CA: Center for the Study of Language and Information, 2003. 243–67.

———. *Toward a 'Natural' Narratology.* London and New York: Routledge, 1996.

Foucalt, Michel. "What Is an Author?" *Language, Counter-Memory, Practice: Selected Essays and Interviews.* Ed. Donald R. Bouchard, trans. Donald F. Bouchard and Sherry Simon. Oxford: Blackwell, 1977. 113–38.

Friends. Episode 5.14, "The One Where Everybody Finds Out." Written by Alexa Junge, directed by Michael Lembeck. Aired 2/11/99, 5/18/99, 6/17/99, 3/18/04.

Frith, Christopher D. *The Cognitive Neuropsychology of Schizophrenia.* Hove, UK: Lawrence Erlbaum Associates, Publishers, 1992.

Frith, Uta. "Asperger and His Syndrome." *Autism and Asperger Syndrome.* Ed. Uta Frith. New York: Cambridge University Press, 1991. 1–36.

———. *Autism: Explaining the Enigma.* Oxford: Blackwell, 1989.

Gomez, Juan C. "Visual Behavior as a Window for Reading the Mind of Others in Primates." *Natural Theories of Mind: Evolution, Development, and Simulation of Everyday Mindreading.* Ed. Andrew Whiten. Basil Blackwell, 1991. 195–208.

Gopnik, Alison. "Theory of Mind." *The MIT Encyclopedia of the Cognitive Sciences.* Eds. Robert A. Wilson and Frank C. Keil. Cambridge: The MIT Press, 1999. 838–41.

Gopnik, Alison and Andrew M. Melzoff. "The Role of Imitation in Understanding Persons and Developing a Theory of Mind." *Understanding Other Minds: Perspective from Autism.* Eds. Simon Baron-Cohen, M. Tager-Flushberg, and D. J. Cohen. Oxford: Oxford University Press, 1993.

———. *Words, Thoughts, and Theories.* Cambridge: MIT Press, 1996.

Grandin, Temple. *Thinking in Pictures: and Other Reports from My Life with Autism.* New York: Vintage, 1996.

Grosz, Elizabeth. "Feminist Futures?" *Tulsa Studies in Women's Literature* 21.1 (Spring 2002): 13–20.

Haddon, Mark. *The Curious Incident of the Dog in the Night-Time.* New York: Vintage, 2004.

Happe, Francesca G. E. "The Autobiographical Writings of Three Asperger Syndrome Adults: Problems of Interpretation and Implications for Theory." *Autism and Asperger Syndrome.* Ed. Uta Frith. New York: Cambridge University Press, 1991. 207–42.

Harris, Paul L. *The Work of Imagination.* Oxford: Blackwell Publishers, 2001.

Hart, F. Elizabeth. "Embodied Literature: A Cognitive-Poststructuralist Approach to Genre." *The Work of Fiction: Cognition, Culture, and Complexity.* Eds. Alan

Richardson and Ellen Spolsky. Aldershot, UK: Ashgate, 2004. 85–106.

———. "The Epistemology of Cognitive Literary Studies," *Philosophy and Literature* 25 (2002): 314–34.

Haycraft, Howard. *Murder for Pleasure: The Life and Times of the Detective Story.* New York: D. Appleton-Century, 1941.

Hayles, N. Katherine. "Desiring Agency: Limiting Metaphors and Enabling Constraints in Dawkins and Deleuze/Guattari." *Substance* 94/95: 30 (2001): 144–59.

Hemingway, Ernest. *A Farewell to Arms.* New York: Charles Scribner's Sons, 1929.

Herman, David. "Introduction." *Narrative Theory and the Cognitive Sciences.* Ed. David Herman. Stanford, CA: Center for the Study of Language and Information, 2003. 1–30.

———. "Regrounding Narratology: The Study of Narratively Organized Systems for Thinking." *What Is Narratology?* Eds. Jan-Christoph Meister, Tom Kindt, and Hans-Harald Müller. Berlin: de Gruyter, 2003. 303–32.

———. "Scripts, Sequences, and Stories: Elements of a Postclassical Narratology." *PMLA* 112 (1997): 1046–59.

———. "Stories as a Tool for Thinking." *Narrative Theory and the Cognitive Sciences.* Ed. David Herman. Stanford, CA: Center for the Study of Language and Information, 2003. 163–92.

Hernadi, Paul. "Literature and Evolution." *Substance* 94/95: 30 (2001): 55–71.

Hirschfeld, Lawrence A. "Who Needs a Theory of Mind." *Biological and Cultural Biases of Human Inference.* Eds. R. Viale, D. Andler, and L. Hirschfeld. Mahwah, NJ: Lawrence Erlbaum. Forthcoming.

Hirschfeld, Lawrence and Susan Gelman, eds. *Mapping the Mind: Domain Specificity in Cognition and Culture.* New York: Cambridge University Press, 1994. 119–48.

Hogan, Patrick Colm. *Cognitive Science, Literature, and the Arts: A Guide for Humanists.* New York and London: Routledge, 2003.

———. "Literary Universals." *Poetics Today* 18:2 (Summer 1997): 223–49.

———. *The Mind and Its Stories: Narrative Universals and Human Emotion.* Cambridge: Cambridge University Press, 2003.

Hughes, Claire and Robert Plomin. "Individual Differences in Early Understanding of Mind: Genes, Non-Shared Environment and Modularity." *Evolution and the Human Mind: Modularity, Language, and Meta-Cognition.* Eds. Peter Carruthers and Andrew Chamberlain. Cambridge: Cambridge University Press, 2000. 47–61.

Hunter, J. Paul. *Before Novels: The Cultural Contexts of Eighteenth-Century English Fiction.* New York: Norton, 1990.

Irwin, John T. "Mysteries We Reread, Mysteries of Rereading: Poe, Borges and the Analytical Detective Story." *Detecting Texts: The Metaphysical Detective Story from Poe to Postmodernism.* Eds. Patricia Merrivale and Susan Elizabeth Sweeney. Philadelphia: University of Pennsylvania Press, 1999. 27–54.

Iser, Wolfgang. "Indeterminacy and the Reader's Response to Prose Fiction." *Aspects of Narrative.* Ed. J. Hillis Miller. New York: Columbia University Press, 1971. 1–45.

Jackson, Tony E. "Issues and Problems in the Blending of Cognitive Science, Evolutionary Psychology, and Literary Study." *Poetics Today* 23.1 (Spring 2002): 161–79.

James, Henry. *The Awkward Age.* London: Penguin, 1987.

———. *The Portrait of a Lady.* New York: The Modern Library, 1909.

James, P. D. *The Black Tower.* New York: Scribner, 1975.

———. *Shroud for a Nightingale.* New York: Scribner, 1971.

——— *Time to Be in Earnest: A Fragment of Autobiography.* New York, Knopf, 2000.

———. *An Unsuitable Job for a Woman.* New York: Scribner, 1977.

Kanner, Leo. "Autistic Disturbances of Affective Contact." *Nervous Children* 2 (1943): 217–50.

Kaplan, Bruce Eric. "Of course I care about how you imagined I thought you perceived I wanted you to feel." *The New Yorker,* October 26, 1998.

Kenney, Catherine. "The Mystery of Emma . . . or the Consummate Case of the Least Likely Heroine." *Persuasions* 13 (December 1991): 138–45.

Klein, Stanley B., Keith Rozendal, and Leda Cosmides. "A Social-Cognitive Neuroscience Analysis of the Self." *Social Cognition* 20.2 (2002): 105–35.

Klein, Stanley B. et al. "Decisions and the Evolution of Memory: Multiple Systems, Multiple Functions." *Psychological Review* 109.2 (2002): 306–29.

———. "Is There Something Special about the Self? A Neuropsychological Case Study." *Journal of Research in Personality* 36 (2002): 490–506.

———. "Priming Exceptions: A Test of the Scope Hypothesis in Naturalistic Trait Judgments." *Social Cognition* 19.4 (2001): 443–68.

Lanser, Susan S. "The 'I' of the Beholder: Equivocal Attachments and the Limits of Structuralist Narratology." *The Blackwell Companion to Narrative Theory.* Eds. James Phelan and Peter Rabinowitz. Malden: Blackwell, 2005.

———. *The Narrative Act: Points of View Prose Fiction.* Princeton: Princeton University Press, 1981.

Latour, Bruno. *Science in Action.* Milton Keynes: Open University Press, 1987.

Latour, Bruno and Steve Woolgar. *Laboratory Life: The Social Construction of Scientific Facts.* Princeton: Princeton University Press, 1986.

Leblanc, Maurice. "The Red Silk Scarf." *101 Years' Entertainment: The Great Detective Stories, 1841–1941.* Ed. Ellery Queen. Boston: Little, Brown and Company, 1941. 178–200.

Lee, Hermione. *Virginia Woolf.* New York: Alfred A. Knopf, 1997.

———. "Virginia Woolf's Essays." *The Cambridge Companion to Virginia Woolf.* Eds. Sue Roe and Susan Sellers. Cambridge: Cambridge University Press, 2000. 91–108.

Leslie, Alan "ToMM, ToBY, and Agency: Core Architecture and Domain Specificity." *The Ambitions of Curiosity: Understanding the World in Ancient Greece and China.* Ed. G. E. R. Lloyd. New York: Cambridge University Press, 2002. 2.

Lodge, David. *Consciousness and the Novel: Connected Essays.* Cambridge: Harvard University Press, 2002.

Margolin, Uri. "Cognitive Science, the Thinking Mind, and Literary Narrative." *Narrative Theory and the Cognitive Sciences.* Ed. David Herman. Stanford, CA: Center for the Study of Language and Information, 2003. 271–94.

———. "Reader's Report on Lisa Zunshine's *Why We Read Fiction.*" Prepared for The Ohio State University Press, October 29, 2004.

Mayer, Robert. *History and the Early English Novel: Matter of Fact from Bacon to Defoe.* Cambridge: Cambridge University Press, 1997.

McEwan, Ian. *Atonement.* New York: Anchor Books, 2003.

McHale, Brian. "Free Indirect Discourse: A Survey of Recent Accounts." *PTL: Journal for Descriptive Poetics and the Theory of Literature* 3 (1978): 249–87.

McLuhan, Marshall. *The Gutenberg Galaxy: The Making of Typographic Man.* Toronto:

University of Toronto Press, 1965.

Merivale, Patricia and Susan Elizabeth Sweeney, eds. *Detecting Texts: The Metaphysical Detective Story from Poe to Postmodernism*. Philadelphia: University of Pennsylvania Press, 1999.

Miall, David S. and Don Kuiken. "The Form of Reading: Empirical Studies of Literariness." *Poetics* 25 (1998): 275–98.

Milton, John. *Paradise Lost*. Ed. Scott Elledge. New York: Norton, 1993.

Mitchell, Robert W. "The Psychology of Human Deception." *Social Research* 63.3 (Fall 1996): 819–61.

Moretti, Franco. "The Slaughterhouse of Literature." *Modern Language Quarterly* 61:1 (March 2000): 207–28.

Mudrick, Marvin. "Character and Event in Fiction." *Yale Review* 50 (1961): 202–18.

Murray, Stuart. "Bartleby, Preference, Pleasure and Autistic Presence." Presented as part of the session on "Cognitive Disability and Textuality: Autism and Fiction," 2004 MLA Convention. Philadelphia, PA. Online at http://www.cwru.edu/affil/sce/Texts_2004/murray.htm.

Nabokov, Vladimir. *Lolita*. New York: Vintage International, 1997.

———. *Strong Opinions*. New York: McGraw-Hill, 1973.

Nunning, Ansgar. "Unreliable, Compared to What? Towards a Cognitive Theory of *Unreliable* Narration: Prolegomena and Hypothesis." In *Grenzuberschreitungen: Narratologie im Kontext*. Eds. Walter Grunzweig and Andreas Solbach. Tubingen: Gunter Narr Verlag, 1999. 53–73.

Origgi, Gloria and Dan Sperber. "Evolution, Communication and the Proper Function of Language." *Evolution and the Human Mind: Modularity, Language, and Metacognition*. Eds. Peter Carruthers and Andrew Chamberlain. Cambridge: Cambridge University Press, 2000. 140–69.

Ousby, Ian, ed. *The Crime and Mystery Book: A Reader's Companion*. Hong Kong: Thames and Hudson, 1997.

Palmer, Alan. *Fictional Minds*. Lincoln: University of Nebraska Press, 2004.

———. "The Lydgate Storyworld." *Narratology beyond Literary Criticism*. Ed. Jan Christoph Meister, in cooperation with Tom Kindt, Wilhelm Schernus, and Malte Stein. Berlin, New York: Walter De Gruyter, 2005. 151–72.

Paretsky, Sara. *Bitter Medicine*. New York: Dell Publishing, 1987.

———. *Burn Marks*. New York: Delacorte Press, 1990.

———. *Total Recall*. New York: Delacorte Press, 2001.

Perry, Menakhem. "Literary Dynamics: How the Order of a Text Creates Its Meanings." *Poetics Today* 1. 1–2 (1979): 35–64, 311–61.

Phelan, James. *Living to Tell about It: A Rhetoric and Ethics of Character Narration*. Ithaca: Cornell University Press, 2004.

———. "Narrative Judgments and the Rhetorical Theory of Narrative: Ian McEwan's *Atonement*. In *A Companion to Narrative Theory*. Eds. James Phelan and Peter J. Rabinowitz. Malden: Blackwell, 2005. 322–36.

———. "Reader's Report on Lisa Zunshine's *Why We Read Fiction*." Prepared for The Ohio State University Press, October 29, 2004.

Pinker, Steven. *The Blank Slate: The Modern Denial of Human Nature*. New York: Viking, 2002.

———. *How the Mind Works*. New York: Norton, 1997.

Plemmons, Robyn Elizabeth. "Austen Wasn't Kidding. A Serious Look at Some Silly Women." A term paper written for English 395, University of Kentucky, Lexington, May 2003.

Poe, Edgar Allan. "The Purloined Letter." *101 Years' Entertainment: The Great Detective Stories, 1841–1941*. Ed. Ellery Queen. Boston: Little, Brown and Company, 1941. 3–21.

Premack David and Verena Dasser. "Perceptual Origins and Conceptual Evidence for Theory of Mind in Apes and Children." *Natural Theories of Mind: Evolution, Development, and Simulation of Everyday Mindreading*. Ed. Andrew Whiten. Basil Blackwell, 1991. 253–66.

Prince, Gerald. *A Dictionary of Narratology*. London: Scolar, 1987.

Rabinowitz, Peter J. *Before Reading: Narrative Conventions and the Politics of Interpretation*. Columbus: The Ohio State University Press, 1998.

———. "Lolita: Solipsized or Sodomized?; or, Against Abstraction—in General." *A Companion to Rhetoric and Rhetorical Criticism*. Eds. Walter Jost and Wendy Olmsted. Molden, MA: Blackwell, 2004. 325–39.

———. "Reader's Report on Lisa Zunshine's *Why We Read Fiction*." Prepared for The Ohio State University Press, October 29, 2004.

Richardson, Alan. *British Romanticism and the Science of Mind*. Cambridge: Cambridge University Press, 2001.

———. "Reading Minds and Bodies in *Emma*." Talk delivered at the panel on "Cognitive Approaches to Narrative" at the annual meeting of the Society for the Study of Narrative, Burlington, VT, 2004.

———. "Studies in Literature and Cognition: A Field Map." *The Work of Fiction: Cognition, Culture, and Complexity*. Eds. Alan Richardson and Ellen Spolsky. Aldershot, UK: Ashgate, 2004. 1–30.

Richardson, Alan and Ellen Spolsky, eds. *The Work of Fiction: Cognition, Culture, and Complexity*. Aldershot, UK: Ashgate, 2004.

Richardson, Alan and Francis Steen. "Literature and the Cognitive Revolution: An Introduction." *Poetics Today* 23:1 (Spring 2002): 1–8.

Richardson, Samuel. *Clarissa or The History of a Young Lady*. Ed. Angus Ross. London: Penguin, 1986.

———. *Selected Letters of Samuel Richardson*. Ed. John Carroll. Oxford: Clarendon, 1964.

Rimmon-Kenan, Shlomith. *Narrative Fiction: Contemporary Poetics*. Methuen: London and New York, 1983.

Rousseau, Jean-Jacques. *Emile or On Education*. Introduction, Translation, and Notes by Allan Bloom. New York: Basic Books, 1979.

Routley, Erik. "The Case against the Detective Story." *Detective Fiction: A Collection of Critical Essays*. Ed. Robin W. Winks. Woodstock, VT: The Countryman Press, 1988. 161–78.

Ryan, Marie-Laure. "Cognitive Maps and the Construction of Narrative Space." *Narrative Theory and the Cognitive Sciences*. Ed. David Herman. Stanford, CA: Center for the Study of Language and Information, 2003. 214–42.

———. *Possible Worlds, Artificial Intelligence, and Narrative Theory*. Bloomington: Indiana University Press, 1991.

Sabor, Peter. "Teaching *Pamela* and *Clarissa* through Richardson's Correspondence."

Approaches to Teaching the Novels of Samuel Richardson. Eds. Lisa Zunshine and Jocelyn Harris. New York: Modern Language Association, 2005. 32–38.

Sacks, Oliver. *An Anthropologist on Mars.* New York: Alfred A. Knopf, 1995.

———. "The Mind's Eye." *The New Yorker* (July 28, 2003): 48–59.

Sayers, Dorothy. "Aristotle on Detective Fiction." *Detective Fiction: A Collection of Critical Essays.* Ed. Robin W. Winks. Woodstock, VT: The Countryman Press, 1988. 25–34.

———. *Gaudy Night.* New York: Harcourt, Brace and Company, 1936.

Scarry, Elaine. *Dreaming by the Book.* New York: Farrar, Straus, Giroux, 1999.

———. "Panel Discussion: Science, Culture, Meaning Values." *Unity of Knowledge: The Convergence of Natural and Human Science.* New York: The New York Academy of Sciences, 2001. 233–57.

Schor, Hilary M. *Dickens and the Daughter of the House.* Cambridge: Cambridge University Press, 1999.

Sperber, Dan. *Explaining Culture: A Naturalistic Approach.* Oxford: Blackwell, 1996.

———. "In Defense of Massive Modularity." *Language, Brain, and Cognitive Development: Essays in Honor of Jacques Mehler.* Ed. Emmanuel Dupoux. Cambridge: The MIT Press, 2001. 47–58.

———. "Introduction." *Metarepresentations: A Multidisciplinary Perspective.* Ed. Dan Sperber. New York: Oxford University Press, 2000. 3–13.

———. "Metarepresentation." *The MIT Encyclopedia of the Cognitive Sciences.* Eds. Robert A. Wilson and Frank C. Keil. Cambridge, MA: The MIT Press, 1999. 541–43.

———. "The Modularity of Thought and the Epidemiology of Representations." *Mapping the Mind: Domain Specificity in Cognition and Culture.* Eds. Lawrence A. Hirschfeld and Susan A. Gelman. New York: Cambridge University Press, 1994. 39–67.

Spolsky, Ellen. "Cognitive Literary Historicism: A Response to Adler and Gross." *Poetics Today* 24:2 (2003): 161–83.

———. "Darwin and Derrida: Cognitive Literary Theory as a Species of Poststructuralism." *Poetics Today* 23.1 (2002): 43–62.

———. *Gaps in Nature: Literary Interpretation and the Modular Mind.* Albany: State University of New York Press, 1993.

———. "Iconotropism, or Representational Hunger: Raphael and Titian." *Iconotropism, or Turning toward Pictures.* Ed. Ellen Spolsky. Lewisburg, PA: Bucknell University Press, 2004.

———. "Preface." *The Work of Fiction: Cognition, Culture, and Complexity.* Eds. Alan Richardson and Ellen Spolsky. Aldershot, UK: Ashgate, 2004. vii–xiii.

———. "Purposes Mistook: Failures Are More Tellable." Talk delivered at the panel on "Cognitive Approaches to Narrative" at the annual meeting of the Society for the Study of Narrative, Burlington, VT, 2004.

———. *Satisfying Skepticism: Embodied Knowledge in the Early Modern World.* Aldershot, UK: Ashgate, 2001.

———. "Why and How to Take the Wheat and Leave the Chaff." *SubStance* 94/95 30.1&2 (2001): 178–98.

———. "Women's Work Is Chastity: Lucretia, Cymbeline, and Cognitive Impenetrability." *The Work of Fiction: Cognition, Culture, and Complexity.* Eds. Alan Richardson and Ellen Spolsky. Aldershot, UK: Ashgate, 2004. 51–84.

Starr, Gabrielle G. "Ethics, Meaning, and the Work of Beauty." *Eighteenth-Century Studies* 35:3 (2002): 361–78.

Steen, Francis. "The Moral Impact of Fictional Language: Lennox vs. Johnson." Presentation. Tenth Annual Conference on Linguistics and Literature, University of North Texas, Denton, January, 1998.

Sternberg, Meir. "How Narrativity Makes a Difference." *Narrative* 9.2 (January 2001): 115–22.

———. "Universals of Narrative and Their Cognitivist Fortunes (I)." *Poetics Today* 24.2 (2003), 297–395.

———. "Universals of Narrative and Their Cognitivist Fortunes (II)." *Poetics Today* 24.3 (2003), 517–638.

Sterne, Lawrence. *The Life and Opinions of Tristam Shandy, Gentleman.* London: Penguin, 1997.

———. *A Sentimental Journey.* London: Penguin, 1986.

Stiller, James and Robin Dunbar. "Perspective-Taking and Social Network Size in Humans." Under consideration.

Sutton, John. *Philosophy and Memory Traces: Descartes to Connectionism.* Cambridge: Cambridge University Press, 1998.

Symons, Julian. *Bloody Murder: From the Detective Story to the Crime Novel.* New York: Faber and Faber, 1972.

Tabbi, Joseph. "Matter into Imagination: The Cognitive Realism of Gilbert Sorrentino's *Imaginative Qualities of Actual Things.*" *The Work of Fiction: Cognition, Culture, and Complexity.* Eds. Alan Richardson and Ellen Spolsky. Aldershot, UK: Ashgate, 2004. 167–86.

Thomas, Ronald R. *Detective Fiction and the Rise of Forensic Science.* New York: Cambridge University Press, 1999.

Toobin, Jeffrey. "A Bad Thing" *The New Yorker,* March 22 (2004). 60–72.

Tooby, John and Leda Cosmides. "The Psychological Foundations of Culture." *The Adapted Mind: Evolutionary Psychology and the Generation of Culture.* Eds. Jerome H. Barkow, Leda Cosmides, and John Tooby. New York: Oxford University Press, 1992. 19–136.

Tsur, Reuven. "Horror Jokes, Black Humor and Cognitive Poetics." *Humor* 2–3 (1989): 243–55.

———. *Toward a Theory of Cognitive Poetics.* Amsterdam: North-Holland, 1992.

Tulving, Endel. "Episodic and Semantic Memory." *Organization of Memory.* Eds. E. Tulving and W. Donaldson. New York: Academic Press, 1972.

Turgenev, Ivan. *Nakanune* [1860]. In I. S. Turgenev, Romany. Moskva: Detskaya Literature, 1975. 285–416.

Turner, Mark. *Cognitive Dimensions of Social Science.* New York: Oxford University Press, 2001.

———. *The Literary Mind.* New York: Oxford University Press, 1996.

Vermeule, Blakey. "God Novels." *The Work of Fiction: Cognition, Culture, and Complexity.* Eds. Alan Richardson and Ellen Spolsky. Aldershot, UK: Ashgate, 2004. 147–66.

———. *Making Sense of Fictional People: A Cognitive and Literary Project.* Forthcoming.

———. *The Party of Humanity: Writing Moral Psychology in Eighteenth-Century Britain.*

Baltimore: The Johns Hopkins University Press, 2000.

―――. "Satirical Mind Blindness." *Classical and Modern Literature* 22.2 (2002): 85–101.

―――. "Theory of Mind." Presented as part of the panel, "Who Cares about Literary Formalism." New York: MLA, 2002.

Warner, William Beatty. *Reading* Clarissa: *The Struggles of Interpretation.* New Haven: Yale University Press, 1979.

Whitworth, Michael. "Virginia Woolf and Modernism." *The Cambridge Companion to Virginia Woolf.* Eds. Sue Roe and Susan Sellers. Cambridge: Cambridge University Press, 2000. 146–63.

Wilson, Edmund. "Who Cares Who Killed Roger Ackroyd?" *Detective Fiction: A Collection of Critical Essays.* Ed. Robin W. Winks. Woodstock, VT: The Countryman Press, 1988. 35–40.

Winks, Robert. "Introduction." *Detective Fiction: A Collection of Critical Essays.* Ed. Robin W. Winks. Woodstock, Vermont: The Countryman Press, 1988. 1–14.

Wittgenstein, Ludwig. *Tractatus Logico-Philosophicus.* London: Routledge & Kegan Paul, 1971.

Wodehouse, P. G. *Author! Author!* New York: Simon and Schuster, 1962.

Womack, Jack. "Some Dark Holler." Afterword to William Gibson, *Neuromancer.* New York: Ace Books, 2000.

Woolf, Virginia. *The Diary of Virginia Woolf.* Ed. Anne Olivier Bell. London: Penguin, 1977–84. Five volumes.

―――. *Jacob's Room.* London: Hogarth, 1976.

―――. *The Letters of Virginia Woolf.* Ed. Nigel Nicholson. London: Hogarth Press, 1975–80. Volume Two.

―――. *Mrs. Dalloway.* San Diego: Harcourt Brace, 1981.

Zunshine, Lisa. "Eighteenth-Century Print Culture and the 'Truth' of Fictional Narrative." *Philosophy and Literature* 25.2 (Fall 2001): 215–32.

―――. "Rhetoric, Cognition, and Ideology in Anna Laetitia Barbauld's 1781 *Hymns in Prose for Children.*" *Poetics Today* 23.1 (2001): 231–59.

―――. "Richardson's *Clarissa* and a Theory of Mind." *The Work of Fiction: Cognition, Culture, and Complexity.* Eds. Alan Richardson and Ellen Spolsky. Aldershot, UK: Ashgate, 2004. 127–46.

―――. "Theory of Mind and Experimental Representations of Fictional Consciousness." *Narrative* 11.3 (2003): 270–91.

~Index~

Theory and Interpretation of Narrative

JAMES PHELAN AND PETER J. RABINOWITZ, Series Editors

Because the series editors believe that the most significant work in narrative studies today contributes both to our knowledge of specific narratives and to our understanding of narrative in general, studies in the series typically offer interpretations of individual narratives and address significant theoretical issues underlying those interpretations. The series does not privilege one critical perspective but is open to work from any strong theoretical position.